Read this book online today:

With SAP PRESS BooksOnline we offer you online access to knowledge from the leading SAP experts. Whether you use it as a beneficial supplement or as an alternative to the printed book, with SAP PRESS BooksOnline you can:

- Access your book anywhere, at any time. All you need is an Internet connection.
- Perform full text searches on your book and on the entire SAP PRESS library.
- Build your own personalized SAP library.

The SAP PRESS customer advantage:

Register this book today at *www.sap-press.com* and obtain exclusive free trial access to its online version. If you like it (and we think you will), you can choose to purchase permanent, unrestricted access to the online edition at a very special price!

Here's how to get started:

1. Visit *www.sap-press.com*.
2. Click on the link for SAP PRESS BooksOnline and login (or create an account).
3. Enter your free trial license key, shown below in the corner of the page.
4. Try out your online book with full, unrestricted access for a limited time!

Your personal free trial **license key** for this online book is:

5zie-4bkg-n7f9-sxwq

Talent Management with SAP® ERP HCM

SAP PRESS is a joint initiative of SAP and Galileo Press. The know-how offered by SAP specialists combined with the expertise of the Galileo Press publishing house offers the reader expert books in the field. SAP PRESS features first-hand information and expert advice, and provides useful skills for professional decision-making.

SAP PRESS offers a variety of books on technical and business related topics for the SAP user. For further information, please visit our website: www.sap-press.com.

Masters, Kotsakis, and Krishnamoorthy
E-Recruiting with SAP ERP HCM
2010, 358 pp., hardcover
ISBN 978-1-59229-243-1

Jeremy Masters
SAP ERP HCM Performance Management
2008, 302 pp., hardcover
ISBN 978-1-59229-124-3

Prashanth Padmanabhan et al.
SAP Enterprise Learning
2009, 347 pp., hardcover
ISBN 978-1-59229-269-1

Jeremy Masters and Christos Kotsakis
Enterprise Compensation Management with SAP ERP HCM
2010, 405 pp., hardcover
ISBN 978-1-59229-207-3

Joe Lee and Tim Simmons

Talent Management with SAP® ERP HCM

Bonn • Boston

Galileo Press is named after the Italian physicist, mathematician and philosopher Galileo Galilei (1564–1642). He is known as one of the founders of modern science and an advocate of our contemporary, heliocentric worldview. His words *Eppur si muove* (And yet it moves) have become legendary. The Galileo Press logo depicts Jupiter orbited by the four Galilean moons, which were discovered by Galileo in 1610.

Editor Emily Nicholls
Copyeditor Julie McNamee
Cover Design Graham Geary
Photo Credit iStockPhoto.com/eyewave
Layout Design Vera Brauner
Production Graham Geary
Typesetting Publishers' Design and Production Services, Inc.
Printed and bound in the United States of America, on paper from sustainable sources

ISBN 978-1-59229-413-8

© 2012 by Galileo Press Inc., Boston (MA)
1st edition 2012

Library of Congress Cataloging-in-Publication Data
Talent management with SAP ERP HCM / Joe Lee ... [et al.]. — 1st ed.
  p. cm.
ISBN 978-1-59229-413-8 — ISBN 1-59229-413-8
 1. SAP ERP. 2. Personnel management—Computer programs. 3. Manpower planning—Computer programs. I. Lee, Joe.
 HF5549.5.D37T35 2013
 658.300285'53—dc23
                                                            2012020672

All rights reserved. Neither this publication nor any part of it may be copied or reproduced in any form or by any means or translated into another language, without the prior consent of Galileo Press GmbH, Rheinwerkallee 4, 53227 Bonn, Germany.

Galileo Press makes no warranties or representations with respect to the content hereof and specifically disclaims any implied warranties of merchantability or fitness for any particular purpose. Galileo Press assumes no responsibility for any errors that may appear in this publication.

"Galileo Press" and the Galileo Press logo are registered trademarks of Galileo Press GmbH, Bonn, Germany. SAP PRESS is an imprint of Galileo Press.

All of the screenshots and graphics reproduced in this book are subject to copyright © SAP AG, Dietmar-Hopp-Allee 16, 69190 Walldorf, Germany.

SAP, the SAP-Logo, mySAP, mySAP.com, mySAP Business Suite, SAP NetWeaver, SAP R/3, SAP R/2, SAP B2B, SAPtronic, SAPscript, SAP BW, SAP CRM, SAP Early Watch, SAP ArchiveLink, SAP GUI, SAP Business Workflow, SAP Business Engineer, SAP Business Navigator, SAP Business Framework, SAP Business Information Warehouse, SAP inter-enterprise solutions, SAP APO, AcceleratedSAP, InterSAP, SAPoffice, SAPfind, SAPfile, SAPtime, SAPmail, SAPaccess, SAP-EDI, R/3 Retail, Accelerated HR, Accelerated HiTech, Accelerated Consumer Products, ABAP, ABAP/4, ALE/WEB, Alloy, BAPI, Business Framework, BW Explorer, Duet, EnjoySAP, mySAP.com e-business platform, mySAP Enterprise Portals, RIVA, SAPPHIRE, TeamSAP, Webflow and SAP PRESS are registered or unregistered trademarks of SAP AG, Walldorf, Germany.

All other products mentioned in this book are registered or unregistered trademarks of their respective companies.

Contents at a Glance

1	Introduction	15
2	Talent Management Overview	25
3	Foundations of Talent Management	39
4	How SAP Defines Talent Management	103
5	Induction Phase	181
6	Assessment Phase	227
7	Competency Phase	249
8	Progression Phase	273
9	Technical Considerations	325
10	Best Practices and Lessons Learned	349
11	Talent Management Resources	359

Dear Reader,

Once in a while, projects land on your desktop that you can tell will be enjoyable to work on from start to finish. From their first stabs at a sample chapter to the final page proof checks, Joe Lee and Tim Simmons brought an eagerness and unavailing sense of humor to their project that left me feeling spoiled.

Joined by dedicated contributors Jon Jenkins and Luke Marson, Tim and Joe overcame every editorial and production obstacle the publishing process could deliver. They outmaneuvered domestic and international business requirements, industry-shaping SAP announcements, and onerous image quality specifications, and successfully melded four unique voices to share valuable industry expertise. The result is a refreshing, energized guide to SAP ERP HCM Talent Management that both humanizes business decisions and computerizes human capital management.

I feel confident you'll benefit from the hard work and good nature this Talent Management team invested in this project. As always, we appreciate your business, and welcome your feedback. Your comments and suggestions are the most useful tools to help us improve our books for you, the reader. We encourage you to visit our website at *www.sap-press.com* and share your feedback about *Talent Management with SAP ERP HCM*.

Thank you for purchasing a book from SAP PRESS!

Emily Nicholls
Editor, SAP PRESS

Galileo Press
Boston, MA

emily.nicholls@galileo-press.com
www.sap-press.com

Contents

Acknowledgments 13

1 Introduction 15

    1.1   Target Audience 16
            1.1.1   HR Managers 16
            1.1.2   HR Administrators 17
            1.1.3   IT Managers 19
            1.1.4   Talent Personnel 19
            1.1.5   Implementation Leaders 20
    1.2   Book Layout 20
    1.3   Summary 23

2 Talent Management Overview 25

    2.1   Background 25
            2.1.1   Key to Success 27
            2.1.2   Ownership of Talent Management 28
            2.1.3   Talent Management Maturity Model 30
            2.1.4   Employee Engagement and Its Relationship to Talent Management 31
    2.2   Trends 32
            2.2.1   Organizational Trends 32
            2.2.2   Technological Trends 34
    2.3   Drivers 35
            2.3.1   Labor Force Demographics 35
            2.3.2   Skills Gap 35
            2.3.3   Global/Mobile Talent Market 36
            2.3.4   Employees' Expectation Shift 36
    2.4   Summary 37

3 Foundations of Talent Management 39

    3.1   Organizational Management 39
            3.1.1   Object-Oriented Design 41

	3.1.2	Organizational Plan	41
	3.1.3	Staff Assignments	42
	3.1.4	Organizational Units	43
	3.1.5	Creating Organizational Units	46
	3.1.6	Positions	48
	3.1.7	Chief Positions	53
	3.1.8	Person	53
	3.1.9	Organizational Management Summary	55
3.2	Personnel Administration		57
	3.2.1	Company Code	58
	3.2.2	Personnel Area	58
	3.2.3	Personnel Subarea	59
	3.2.4	Employee Group	60
	3.2.5	Employee Subgroup	61
3.3	SAP Job Architecture		63
	3.3.1	Functional Area	64
	3.3.2	Job Family	67
	3.3.3	Jobs	73
	3.3.4	Position	80
	3.3.5	The Importance of SAP Job Architecture	80
3.4	Qualifications Catalog		81
	3.4.1	Organizational Competencies	82
	3.4.2	Individual Competencies	82
	3.4.3	SAP ERP HCM Qualifications Catalog	82
3.5	Summary		101

4 How SAP Defines Talent Management ... 103

4.1	SAP E-Recruiting		104
	4.1.1	E-Recruiting Process	105
	4.1.2	Integration Points	115
4.2	SAP ERP HCM Performance Management		117
	4.2.1	Predefined versus Flexible Solutions	118
	4.2.2	Performance Management Process	123
	4.2.3	Integration Points	131
4.3	SAP ERP HCM Learning Solution		133
	4.3.1	Learning Solution Process	136
	4.3.2	Integration Points	151
4.4	SAP ERP HCM Enterprise Compensation Management		152

		4.4.1	Enterprise Compensation Process	154
		4.4.2	Integration Points	166
	4.5	SAP ERP HCM Talent Development and Succession Planning		167
		4.5.1	Talent Development Process	168
		4.5.2	Integration Points	176
	4.6	Summary		177
		4.6.1	E-Recruiting	177
		4.6.2	Performance Management	178
		4.6.3	Learning Solution	178
		4.6.4	Enterprise Compensation Management	179
		4.6.5	Talent Development and Succession Planning	179

5 Induction Phase 181

	5.1	Workforce Planning		182
	5.2	Position Management		184
		5.2.1	Position Management Tools	185
		5.2.2	Why Is Position Management Important?	186
		5.2.3	The Cost of Unfilled Positions	186
		5.2.4	Position Management in SAP	187
	5.3	E-Recruiting		193
		5.3.1	Requisition	194
		5.3.2	Source	203
		5.3.3	Screen	208
		5.3.4	Interview	211
		5.3.5	Hire	213
	5.4	Talent Profile		216
		5.4.1	Talent Profile for Employees	217
		5.4.2	Talent Profile for Managers and Talent Management Specialists	221
	5.5	Summary		225

6 Assessment Phase 227

	6.1	SAP ERP HCM Performance Management: Objective Setting		228
		6.1.1	Prepare	228
		6.1.2	Planning	228
	6.2	Talent Assessment		235
		6.2.1	Potential	237

9

	6.2.2	Risks	238
	6.2.3	Competencies	238
	6.2.4	Derailers	239
	6.2.5	Talent Groups	240
6.3	SAP ERP HCM Performance Management: Mid-Year Review		241
	6.3.1	Manager	241
	6.3.2	Employee	244
6.4	Summary		247

7 Competency Phase 249

7.1	SAP ERP HCM Learning Solution		249
	7.1.1	Content	249
	7.1.2	Catalog	253
	7.1.3	Profile	254
	7.1.4	Schedule	258
	7.1.5	Participation	261
	7.1.6	Close-Out	265
7.2	Summary		270

8 Progression Phase 273

8.1	SAP ERP HCM Performance Management: Year-End Review		273
	8.1.1	Complete Self-Assessment	275
	8.1.2	Complete Year-End Assessment	278
8.2	SAP ERP HCM Enterprise Compensation Management		281
	8.2.1	Budgeting Process	281
	8.2.2	Review Process	284
	8.2.3	Controlling Process	287
	8.2.4	Approval Process	289
8.3	Talent Review Meeting		290
	8.3.1	Creating, Planning, and Preparing the Talent Review Meeting	291
	8.3.2	Conducting the Talent Review Meeting	296
	8.3.3	Talent Groups	299
8.4	Succession Planning		300
	8.4.1	STVN SuccessionPlanning	300

	8.4.2	Comparing STVN SuccessionPlanning and SAP Functionality	303
	8.4.3	Status Handling	304
	8.4.4	Successor Pools	304
	8.4.5	Bench Strength	305
	8.4.6	Talent Identification	306
	8.4.7	Assigning Successors	307
	8.4.8	Wizards and Comparison	314
	8.4.9	Reporting and Analytics	315
8.5	Talent Development		319
	8.5.1	Creating the Development Plan	319
	8.5.2	Tracking and Maintaining the Development Plan	322
8.6	Summary		323

9 Technical Considerations ... 325

9.1	Technical Architecture		325
	9.1.1	SAP E-Recruiting	326
	9.1.2	Performance Management	327
	9.1.3	Learning Solution	328
	9.1.4	Enterprise Compensation Management	328
	9.1.5	Talent Development	329
	9.1.6	Succession Management	329
9.2	User Interfaces		329
	9.2.1	SAP NetWeaver Portal	331
	9.2.2	SAP NetWeaver Business Client	331
9.3	Web Dynpro for ABAP		332
	9.3.1	Architecture	333
	9.3.2	Configuration	337
	9.3.3	Developing with Web Dynpro for ABAP	339
9.4	Business Add-Ins		342
9.5	STVN Technical Requirements		346
9.6	Summary		348

10 Best Practices and Lessons Learned ... 349

10.1	Implementation Considerations	350
10.2	Staffing	351

10.3	Change Management		352
	10.3.1	Change Management on Closer Inspection	353
	10.3.2	Change Management Strategy	354
10.4	Summary		357

11 Talent Management Resources 359

11.1	On-Premise and Cloud-Based Talent Management Solutions from SAP		359
	11.1.1	SAP Roadmap	360
	11.1.2	Advantages and Disadvantages	361
	11.1.3	The Future	363
11.2	Mobile Solutions		363
11.3	SAP Resources		365
	11.3.1	SAP Service Marketplace	365
	11.3.2	SAP Community Network	367
11.4	HR Expert		368
11.5	Conferences		369
	11.5.1	SAP HR Conference	370
	11.5.2	SAPPHIRE	370
11.6	SAP User Groups		370
11.7	Social Media		371
	11.7.1	LinkedIn	371
	11.7.2	XING	372
	11.7.3	Facebook, Google+, and Twitter	372
11.8	Summary		373

Appendices 375

A	Bibliography	375
B	The Authors	377
Index		379

Acknowledgments

We would first like to thank Emily Nicholls and Katy Spencer from Galileo Press for their insight, direction, and professionalism through this entire process. Without their help, we would have never completed this project.

We also very much want to thank our families for their love and support throughout this process. Tim's wife, Jennifer Simmons, and their two children, Zack and Ryan, and Joe's wife, Elizabeth Lee, were critical in their ongoing support during the long nights and weekends spent researching and writing.

Special thanks are due to EPI-USE America, and to Verdun Boshoff, Subbu Padmanaaban, and Markus Lamers for their expertise and support.

SAP is known for its solid, reliable enterprise systems. Within the past few years, the talent management area as a whole has become very popular. SAP has acknowledged this by developing talent management solutions based on a solid foundation and state-of-the-art technology.

1   Introduction

Welcome to *Talent Management with SAP ERP HCM*! Talent management is a complex collection of connected HR processes that delivers a fundamental benefit for any organization. From an employer's perspective, finding the right employees, helping employees manage their careers, planning potential succession paths within a company, managing employee learning, fostering employee performance, and effectively managing employee compensation are all parts of the talent management process. This wide-ranging function of HR enables companies to deliver solid solutions to manage some of the most complex HR processes.

Anyone who works in HR will recognize the many challenges a company faces when developing effective programs around recruitment, motivation, learning, career management, and employee compensation. To optimize talent management, companies must embrace a technology that gives them a framework in which to develop and manage their individual processes.

The Talent Management suite in SAP ERP Human Capital Management (SAP HCM) offers solutions for companies looking to improve their talent organization. The many different functions and seamless integration points of the Talent Management modules provide companies with the solutions they need to successfully run a talented organization.

With this book, we aim to give you a solid understanding of the modules, processes, and technology used in SAP ERP HCM Talent Management. (Throughout this book, we will refer to SAP's specific Talent Management suite as Talent Management, and to the generic idea of talent management as simply talent management.)

Let's begin by examining who can benefit from the content presented in this book.

1.1 Target Audience

This book is intended for a variety of professionals. Whether you are new to SAP ERP HCM entirely, or you have already implemented one or many Talent Management solutions in SAP, this book will help you understand key concepts to prepare for, use, and support a successful talent management system.

This book is intended for the following key groups of professionals:

- HR managers
- HR administrators
- IT managers
- Talent personnel
- Implementation leads

Despite the seemingly broad target audience, you'll find relevant information to help you achieve your individual Talent Management implementation goals.

1.1.1 HR Managers

To run a successful organization, it's important to properly manage your personnel. This includes not only hiring qualified job-seekers, but also making sure that the individuals in those jobs can successfully perform their duties. HR managers usually have direct input as to which talent management techniques and processes will be used to ensure that employees remain a successful part of the company. Using the right tool to manage the company's talent is equally as important as having the right person for the right job.

Managers are often directly responsible for their own personnel. This responsibility requires managers to align themselves and their employees with company, team, and individual goals. To accomplish this, managers must provide their personnel with the support and communication they need to reach these goals and encourage individual employee development.

Managers are also responsible for employee compensation and planning. By observing and managing budgets, HR managers' duties extend far beyond solely managing employees. We'll look at how the Talent Management suite in SAP ERP HCM can help an HR professional navigate these tasks.

Let's look at some of the key responsibilities of an HR manager:

- Access and maintain general employee information
  - Contact details
  - Job and position information
  - Organizational information
  - Compensation information
- Manage and invest in personnel development
  - Set, communicate, and manage personnel objectives
  - Execute employee performance reviews
  - Oversee and monitor employee training
  - Manage employee qualifications
- Handle talent acquisition
  - Create requisitions
  - Evaluate and organize candidates
  - Monitor requests for requisitions

HR managers will greatly benefit from the information in this book. We'll discuss how Talent Management can provide all of the functions to hire, develop, evaluate, and compensate employees throughout their organization. This book not only contains information about the tools that SAP offers but also how these tools can fit into various business processes. By understanding both the tool *and* the business process, HR managers can capitalize on Talent Management.

We'll also look at the core of the Talent Management modules; by understanding the way that SAP ERP integrates with these tools, an HR professional can better grasp the benefits of having a well-run talent management system.

1.1.2 HR Administrators

HR administrators know the importance of having one such well-run talent management system. They are responsible for updating and maintaining most of the master data found in the entire talent management system. This information keeps personnel on track with careers and personal development. A talent management system can be a significant asset when companies maintain and administer HR data properly.

The following are some of the administrative functions that we'll discuss in this book:

- Employee data administration
    - Administering contact and personal data changes
    - Making salary adjustments
    - Performing organizational transfers
- New hire administration
- Organizational structure changes
- Job and position creation
- Qualifications maintenance
- Course creation and maintenance
- Performance appraisal administration
    - Maintaining company goals and objectives in the system
    - Cascading goals to the appropriate organizations
    - Creating and maintaining appraisal templates
    - Administering appraisal documents
- Succession planning activities
- Training administration
    - Processing booking activities for personnel
    - Providing attendee maintenance and support
    - Performing instructor support activities

HR administrators have many important responsibilities. The Talent Management modules from SAP, as well as the Organizational Management (OM) and Personnel Administration (PA) modules, give these administrators the tools they need to properly support all of the necessary functions for monitoring, maintaining, and improving company personnel. Within this book, we'll explore these Talent Management functions and cover the important and necessary steps to administer each of the applications, including creating and maintaining the required data to get these applications up and running.

1.1.3　IT Managers

Every member of an IT organization should be familiar with the software the company uses. As Talent Management is implemented in more and more companies, it's critical that IT managers understand the systems. In this book, we'll teach IT managers and personnel about the business need for these systems, as well as provide important technical information concerning how Talent Management applications work.

We'll also show IT managers how streamlining the talent management technology used in Talent Management can greatly reduce the need for specialized skill sets. This will greatly benefit the entire organization in the long run because IT managers are usually responsible for supporting these systems. By exploring the various technologies used in Talent Management, IT managers can staff the appropriate resources and skill sets required to support end users. We'll examine these streamlined technologies in Chapter 9.

1.1.4　Talent Personnel

Talent personnel include a wide variety of employees who fill many different roles, such as recruiters, managers, talent management specialists, and training personnel. Each role is important in talent management as a whole. This book is intended to help these people understand how Talent Management from SAP can greatly benefit their work. We'll explore both the functions of Talent Management tools and the processes that accompany them.

The following are some of the topics that we'll cover in this book relating to the responsibilities of recruiters and hiring managers:

- How SAP defines the recruiting process
- Recruiting process templates
- Requisition to publication processes
- Requisition and candidate approval processes
- Candidate ranking
- Candidate activities and disposition

Managers that are responsible for any employee will need the best tools available to properly grow and manage their personnel. SAP understands the many functions needed to properly manage personnel and consequently delivers multiple tools containing substantial integration that can help managers better grow their employees' talent. The following are just some of the manager functions that will be covered:

- Employee appraisal processes
- Employee compensation processes
- Talent development plans
- Training and qualifications processes
- Succession processes

1.1.5 Implementation Leaders

For those implementing Talent Management in SAP ERP HCM, this book can be a great help in the implementation process. By exploring the core processes and functions of each of the Talent Management tools, implementation team leaders can align these tools as close to the business processes as possible, maximizing usability in an organization.

We'll take a look at the core functionality of each of the modules, as well as the integration points. This can help implementation leads understand where strategic points for seamless data flow can occur, providing the utmost functionality.

We'll also cover the key technologies used in Talent Management to help implementation leads properly staff their projects with the necessary skill sets to get their systems working properly.

1.2 Book Layout

Our objective is to help you learn as much as you can about these topics within the confines of this book. The following list will help you pinpoint specific areas of this book where you can find more information regarding any topic. Figure 1.1 shows the core components that we'll be discussing in the first few chapters, along with the individual modules that make up Talent Management.

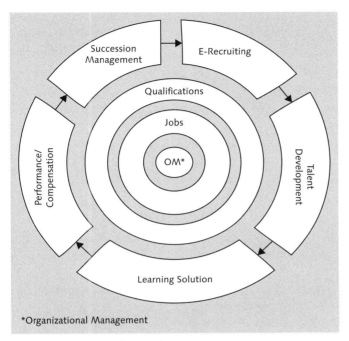

Figure 1.1 Structure of SAP Talent Management

- **Chapter 2: Talent Management Overview**
  This chapter will discuss how you can integrate the talent management processes into your business processes. You'll learn the general business trends and benefits of talent management, how Talent Management with SAP ERP HCM increases communication between management and employees, and how it can be used throughout an employee's career.

- **Chapter 3: Foundation of Talent Management**
  After considering the generic idea of talent management, we will explore the foundations of getting a talent management system up and running. This chapter provides an overview of the core components you need to get your Talent Management suite functioning effectively. Each section also features important data models, flowcharts, and accompanying information about how it all ties together.

- **Chapter 4: How SAP Defines Talent Management**
  If you've read the first three chapters, you will now have a full understanding of the core functions and architecture of Talent Management. This chapter will

provide an overview of how SAP defines and uses Talent Management. It will cover the processes of each module and can be used as a quick reference guide to the different functions of Talent Management. Each core area will have its own subsections respective of the component. Talent Management is tightly integrated both within the module itself and with other SAP modules.

At this point, we'll look at the general talent and engagement lifecycle, which includes four distinct phases; each contains a set of business processes and functions within it. Specific Talent Management modules within SAP ERP HCM are included in each phase. Each module serves a unique purpose and plays an important role in the next subsequent module and phase.

The next group of chapters will explore the integration of the Talent Management modules in further detail as we walk through a year in the life of an employee from an SAP system perspective in these four phases.

- **Chapter 5: Induction Phase**
  The Induction Phase starts with creating a new position, performing the budget planning, and assigning qualification requirements. The candidate will apply for this position through the SAP E-Recruiting module, be screened by a recruiter through various activities, be interviewed, and be hired. The employee's journey in the company starts by maintaining his talent profile of current and previous education, experience, and goals. His manager will assign required qualifications to the profile so that the employee can develop to the point where he will be prepared for his next position.

- **Chapter 6: Assessment Phase**
  In the Assessment Phase, the new employee's company is committed to assessing and developing its personnel. The Assessment Phase kicks off with the Performance Management application, in which the new manager identifies several objectives for the new employee. Next, the potential of each employee is assessed. Finally, the manager provides support and coaching, and specifies a mid-year rating as part of the performance management process.

- **Chapter 7: Competency Phase**
  In the Competency Phase, the new employee can view his required qualifications and mandated training in the Learner Portal. This chapter will discuss the SAP Learning Solution and its processes. We'll explore how employees can either take and complete web-based training or register for instructor-led courses and other live events such as virtual classes via the Learner Portal. We'll also cover

instructor processes, such as closing out all of the completed instructor-led training in the Instructor Portal, thereby giving the new employee the qualifications and completions required.

- **Chapter 8: Progression Phase**
  In the Progression Phase (at the end of an employee's first year of employment with the company), his manager does the final performance appraisal, which produces a performance rating. The employee is reviewed as part of a talent pool in a talent review meeting hosted by the Talent Management specialist. The manager uses the final rating to determine the employee's annual bonus and merit increases. Within one year, the new employee is assigned as a successor to a key position. We'll examine SAP's tools to accomplish these tasks.

- **Chapter 9: Technical Considerations**
  After you understand how Talent Management works as a whole, including the core concepts and data models, the book will explore the technical information needed to successfully implement Talent Management. This chapter will serve as a reference guide for readers who want to know more about the underlying technologies and frameworks used by the Talent Management applications.

- **Chapter 10: Best Practices and Lessons Learned**
  This chapter will focus on best practices and lessons learned for successfully implementing a great talent management application based on key takeaways from our experience with implementations.

- **Chapter 11: Talent Management Resources**
  This important chapter highlights the Talent Management offerings from SAP, as well as upcoming technologies and mobile solutions. This chapter will also provide helpful additional online resources for Talent Management that you can access right away.

1.3 Summary

Talent management is an important part of any organization. In this introductory chapter, we covered the intended audience of this book, as well as the groups and roles that can benefit the most from the information presented here. We looked at the different tasks that each of the important talent management roles performs in SAP, and how they will be described in detail in upcoming chapters. We also explored the layout of this book, and the four phases that will be described in the talent and engagement lifecycle.

By fully using the functions of the Talent Management suite, you can enjoy a successful, stable, and sustainable talent organization.

So let's get started. In the next chapter, we'll cover what it means in today's world to implement talent management as a whole.

Conceptualizing how talent management processes can integrate into your business processes—and understanding the general business trends and benefits of Talent Management—will help you see the big talent management picture.

2   Talent Management Overview

Talent management is a professional term that started gaining popularity in the late 1990s, although it seems like it's been circulating for much longer. Talent management means different things to different organizations. For some, it refers to the process of attracting highly skilled workers from other companies and then crossing their fingers in hopes that those individuals stick around for a while. However, talent management in this philosophical context doesn't do justice to an approach that should be considered to be strategic in nature. Rather than focusing just on recruiting and retaining talent, talent-savvy organizations support their employees on issues they care about the most, such as doing work that engages them and encountering fresh challenges in the process. Leading companies make attracting, engaging, and retaining employees a strategic business priority. Senior leadership focuses on clearly communicating the business strategy to the workforce, as well as defining the roles people play to execute that strategy.

2.1   Background

In a competitive marketplace, talent management is a primary driver for organizational success. Broadly defined, talent management is the implementation of integrated strategies and systems that are designed to increase workplace productivity. To this end, these strategies and systems develop improved processes for attracting, developing, retaining, and utilizing people with the required skills and aptitudes to meet current and future business needs. A structured talent management process will methodically close the gap between the human capital an organization currently has and the leadership talent it will eventually need to respond to tomorrow's business challenges. Simply put, an organization that can effectively manage its talent will provide itself with a critical point of strategic leverage.

Though talent management is complex and continually evolving, it offers tremendous business value to those companies that invest in it. Influenced by external factors (e.g., the economy, global expansion, and mergers and acquisitions), critical success factors for effective talent management include alignment with strategic goals, active CEO participation, and HR management. Recurring themes for successful talent-driven organizations include CEO involvement, culture, management, processes, and accountability. One noteworthy trend is the increased role of line-level managers in the development of talent. For example, in some of the leading organizations, managers are held accountable for employee retention and creating opportunities for high-potential employees.

But moving forward with talent management initiatives requires the entire organization to be in agreement about the significance of talent management strategies. When the CEO and board of directors are involved, talent management becomes noticeable and has high visibility. Yet to be successful, the value it adds must be understood throughout the organization. In high-performing companies, for example, senior management is also very much responsible for the success of the talent management strategies. For talent management initiatives to be effective, organizations need formal processes, with many people involved and where strong links between leadership and talent translate into specific organizational value-based behaviors. A 2011 study conducted by the New Talent Management Network illustrates this point (see Table 2.1 and Table 2.2).

Rank	Factor Responsible For Success
1st	Executive team support
2nd	Manager accountability for completing the process
3rd	CEO support
4th	Design of process/program
5th	Availability of resources
6th	Head of HR support
7th	HR team support
8th	HR technology

Table 2.1 Factors That Contribute to Successful Talent Management

Rank	Factor Responsible For Failure
1st	Lack of manager accountability for completing the process
2nd	Lack of executive team support
3rd	Design of process/program
4th	Lack of resources
5th	Lack of CEO support
6th	Lack of HR team support
7th	HR technology
8th	Lack of head of HR support

Table 2.2 Factors That Impede Successful Talent Management

The New Talent Management Network study indicates that the presence or absence of executive support and clear accountability for results were the key drivers in the success or failure of talent management processes. There were also two noteworthy outcomes from the study: that people with job experience outside of HR were more likely to consider talent process design a key to success, and that HR technology still isn't seen as relevant to talent practice success, and only slightly related to failure.

Remember that companies define talent in different ways, but the belief in talent and its impact on the bottom line is at the heart of talent management. Going beyond succession planning for top leadership positions, companies that value talent have a deep appreciation for the contribution of individuals at all levels, both now and for the future. Talent management decisions are often driven by a set of organizational core competencies as well as position-specific competencies. On a fundamental level, talent is the vehicle that moves the organization where it wants to go.

2.1.1 Key to Success

To be effective, a talent management mindset must be embedded throughout the organization, starting with the CEO.

2.1.2 Ownership of Talent Management

Even though talent management is supported by the CEO and the board of directors, it's headed by the HR department (typically by the vice president of HR or chief HR officer). Responsibility for talent management is shared throughout the organization (from the CEO to the line manager), but the role of HR is to identify and deploy optimal strategies to engage employees by driving satisfaction, loyalty, and retention. Commitment to talent management requires that HR be a strategic business partner.

To fully appreciate the role of today's HR departments, let's first look at the evolution of HR as it relates to talent management, which is shown in Figure 2.1. In the 1970s and 1980s, the role of HR was that of a pure personnel department, which served the business function of hiring employees, paying employees, and distributing their benefits. Later in the 1980s and through the 1990s, HR assumed a more strategic function, becoming a business partner that supported line managers in recruiting, training, and communicating with employees. Even during this time frame, the mindset about employees was very different than it is today. There was a vague notion that people were the most important asset and that HR was responsible for all people management. Today's HR functions are becoming fully integrated with the business and focus on management processes.

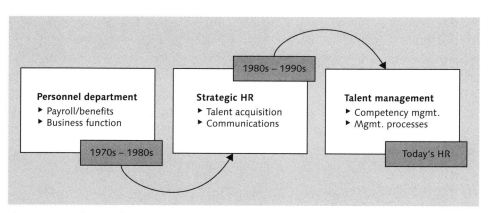

Figure 2.1 Evolution of HR

There has also been a significant shift in the mindset. In the new talent mindset, there is a deep conviction that better talent leads to better corporate performance and that all managers are responsible for strengthening their talent pool.

As the primary owner of talent management, today's HR department wears many hats. One of the most important roles (if not *the* most important) is that of a catalyst of the talent approach. HR leads the way for the company to own the role of talent management for organizational success. HR plays the role of business partner and works closely with the board, the CEO, and senior management to ensure that the company is committed to talent management. As the facilitator of talent management, HR also influences how the company culture supports the talent management strategy. Generally speaking, its role encompasses communicating the talent management philosophy throughout the organization and knowing the industry competitors. In addition, HR should take a proactive lead in developing the integrated strategic approach to talent management. This includes envisioning the "big picture" as well as managing critical metrics such as tracking turnover and understanding what factors contribute to retaining key employees.

To integrate talent management into all areas of the company, HR also plays a key role as change agent. To that end, the department addresses four diverse talent management activities: recruitment, performance management, leadership development, and organizational strategy. In this role, HR manages four major risks to the business: vacancy risk (to safeguard key business capabilities and focus on scarce skills), readiness risk (to accelerate leadership development and provide full business exposure to rising stars), transition risk (to avoid loss of key talent, select successors with leadership ability, and hire for organization capability), and portfolio risk (to maximize strategic talent leverage and focus on senior management's commitment to development and performance standards).

Finally, proactive HR leaders take a holistic approach to talent management. It's important for HR leaders to establish clear expectations and communicate openly about the talent management process. When the HR department explains to management and employees why talent management is important, how it works, and what the benefits are to the organization and participants, these target audience are more likely to see talent management strategies as fair processes and adopt them throughout the entire organization.

2.1.3　Talent Management Maturity Model

Mature, effective talent management doesn't happen overnight. It typically takes several years to construct, optimize, and integrate talent processes. This progression typically occurs through a series of stages.

In its 2010 Talent Management Factbook, Bersin & Associates surveyed a cross-section of small, mid-sized, and large companies about their "Talent Management Maturity." The resulting research findings identified four levels that can help your business gauge where it stands in the process of becoming an employer of choice, and illustrated that as companies move up the maturity ladder, they have lower turnover, greater employee engagement, and more success in nearly every talent area. We recommend that you consult the Bersin & Associates study for more information.

Let's focus on each level individually:

- **Level 1**
  Separate business units develop and manage talent processes within "silos" that have little harmonization. These organizations may have automated systems implemented to undertake various talent initiatives, but the systems can't share data.

- **Level 2**
  The organization has a set of consistent talent processes and begins to understand how those processes might connect even if done manually. HR still owns the talent management initiatives.

- **Level 3**
  The organization shows strong attention to integrated systems and processes, with a talent management executive or team in place. That team shares accountability for meeting talent management objectives.

- **Level 4**
  In the most sophisticated maturity stage, the systems and processes are fully integrated, and a team of professionals is specifically dedicated to and accountable for talent management under an executive leader.

2.1.4 Employee Engagement and Its Relationship to Talent Management

Organizations that are committed to their human capital and can implement talent management practices and policies enjoy lower employee turnover and higher employee engagement. This carries over to the bottom line of the organization: According to the Society of Human Resource Management in a 2006 study, employees who are the most engaged perform 20% better and are 87% less likely to resign. The basis for an engaged workforce is established by two things:

- Quality and accuracy of HR communications to the workforce
- Quality of the supervision

In effect, the manager is the most important enabler of employee commitment and engagement. Finally, when done correctly, policies that support talent management also support employee engagement programs such as flex time, telecommuting, and compressed workweeks.

Rewards and recognition also help both to retain talent and to improve employee performance. Companies are increasingly putting formal and informal reward programs in place. To be most effective, however, information about these rewards programs must be readily and regularly communicated to employees. Discussing reward programs as early as during the interview process and during regularly scheduled performance reviews demonstrates that the organization values its employees.

Hiring for the proper fit between the organization and the employee is crucial to attracting and retaining talent. Some examples of considerations that contribute to a proper fit include (but are not limited to) the following:

- Qualifications of both the position and the candidate
- The corporate culture of an organization relative to the work habits and personal values of the candidate
- Behavior and characteristics of the employee that fit the culture of the team and organization
- Ambitions and motivation that align the employee's aspirations with the goals of the organization

Also, companies with outstanding reputations and strong brands are well positioned to attract top talent. Google exemplifies an organization that effectively links organizational culture and company values in its recruiting strategies to determine the best candidates. This process, however, does take a significant amount of time, and companies need to be steadfast in their efforts to ensure repeated positive outcomes.

Another effective recruiting strategy is tapping into specific labor pools. By assessing the organization's areas of strength in its workplace planning programs and guidelines, HR can identify possible segments of the labor force to target. For example, an organization may consider using a higher percentage of contract labor within the HR Information Services department based on the strategic goals of the company. By carefully assessing the organization's current and future talent needs, HR can develop recruiting and retention strategies that align with the company's strategic goals, thus promoting organizational growth and sustainability.

2.2 Trends

There has been a progressive movement to transform the HR function and establish a human capital management (HCM) environment that truly leverages the workforce as a competitive weapon. To that end, organizations leading the way in the HR transformation are now focused on strategic issues rather than administrative elements. As a result, talent management is rising to the top of the list as a strategy that can drastically improve workforce productivity to drive value for the organization.

The talent management market has changed greatly over the past 10 to 15 years. Companies used to wonder how the idea of computerizing annual appraisal interviews would be received. Today, they are looking to leverage social networks in their HR software solutions. The major changes to the market over the past several years have been both organizational and technological in nature.

2.2.1 Organizational Trends

HR managers no longer want to manage talent processes such as recruitment, training, or compensation within "silos" that have little harmonization. Instead, they want to take all of the processes into consideration in an integrated manner and work with a team of professionals specifically dedicated to and accountable for talent management.

The practice of harmonizing HR practices across the entire organization has been at the heart of many problems for global organizations for several years. In the majority of cases, each division or business unit performed its own appraisals, established its own training plan, managed its pool of candidates in its own way, and so on. Also, the HR manager for a specific division or business unit may not have had access to the record of an employee from another division or business unit, which provided unfavorable mobility opportunities.

As a result, these same organizations are now implementing integrated processes and systems to provide information on all employees within the company in the same way (approaching performance appraisals and establishing training plans consistently, providing access to a shared candidate pool, making use of single job and competency frameworks, etc.). With so much cost-cutting in recent years, HR has had to shift its focus from running day-to-day operations to creating value. It will be interesting to see whether HR will take advantage of its unique opportunity to help drive share price with improved workforce planning, which should include alignment and optimization. In addition, strategic thinking and execution should be at the top of the list of modernizing HR solutions in today's competitive environment.

Another trend is that employee engagement is at an all-time low. In fact, according to the HCM blog "Working Girl," few top performers consider themselves highly engaged and as many as one in five are actively looking for new opportunities. Unfortunately, talent management has not caught up with the cognitive shift that the workforce has gone through in recent years. Given that engaged employees are more productive, profitable, customer-focused, safer, and more likely to withstand temptations to leave, companies will most likely start adopting best practices such as increasing and improving communications between managers and employees, creating meaningful talent pools, increasing management visibility to employees, shifting to a corporate culture that is more work-life balance friendly, improving employee recognition programs, and offering differentiated pay.

Employee engagement is also affected by the current "going global" trend. The offshoring trend—in which business processes are internationally relocated to reduce costs—is generating controversy as more and more high-paying, white-collar jobs are moved overseas. Although arguments can be made that offshoring saves on personnel-related expenses, it can often add to a culture of anxiety among employees who feel their jobs are in jeopardy. This can lead to significantly lower employee morale because job security is a critical factor that contributes to employee engagement. As a result, HR will continue to be at the center of the offshore debate, and the role that the function plays in dealing with the ramifications of offshoring on employee satisfaction, recruitment, and retention will prove to be its biggest challenge.

2.2.2 Technological Trends

Technology is becoming a more integral part of talent management strategies. Modern talent management solution capabilities include online employee portals, side-by-side talent profiles, global talent pools, goal alignment, and collaboration tools. These solutions enable organizations to better assess workforce costs, improve productivity, increase efficiency, and manage a highly diverse workforce.

Employees are also looking to take a more active role in the direction of their career. This is a result of two recent developments: Generation Y's eagerness to find meaning in what it does and to have ever-greater responsibilities, and the rising potential of social networks such as Facebook, LinkedIn, and Twitter. In case anyone still thinks this is just a passing craze, recall that *TIME Magazine* named the founder and president of Facebook, Mark Zuckerberg, as its Person of the Year in 2010. In addition, LinkedIn went public in 2011. For example, organizations are now integrating Facebook, Twitter, and LinkedIn into their recruiting systems. The use of social networking by corporations to further their goals will undoubtedly continue to increase.

The need for career control is also being supported by mobile technologies such as smartphones and touch-screen tablets. These technologies enable employees to remain in real-time contact with their company. For example, they can receive job alerts about new positions within the organization, approve training requests, schedule interviews, or prepare annual reviews. However, confidentiality and security issues must also be taken into consideration. (Recall the issues that surfaced in 2008 and 2009 regarding data privacy and confidentiality with Facebook.)

In the current economic environment, it's essential to keep a watch on all of these trends, whether organizational or technological, in order to make talent management a daily reality—for HR, for managers, and for all employees—with the objective of benefitting both individuals and the organization.

2.3 Drivers

Since talent management is the primary driver for organizational success, top-tier leadership organizations focus on retaining and developing talent instead of simplying attracting talented candidates using pay and benefits as lures. These organizations use their understanding of the key drivers of successful talent management programs to outpace their competitors.

The following are some of the many challenging workforce issues that confront HR:

- Labor force demographics
- Skills gap
- Global/mobile talent market
- Employees expectations shift

We'll now take a look at these issues in greater detail.

2.3.1 Labor Force Demographics

Despite projected growth in the global population, the working-age population is expected to decline in many countries. In Japan and much of Europe, for example, fewer workers are entering the workforce than are exiting. Ernst & Young estimates that other large economies such as Russia, Canada, South Korea, and China will have more workers at retirement age than are entering the workforce within the next 10-15 years.

Other countries stand to profit from those trends. Emerging market economies with younger labor forces such as Brazil, Mexico, and Indonesia may benefit from these demographic disparities if they can provide the younger generation with adequate opportunities to hone their skills.

2.3.2 Skills Gap

According to Ernst & Young, over 80% of companies in fast-growth economic sectors are experiencing difficulty attracting employees with the skills required.

One reason for this is that global skill set requirements are changing, and not enough students are graduating with the skills required to meet the demand of global organizations, despite increased access to education worldwide.

People are the value drivers in today's economy, but certain types of skills are still in short supply. As a result, companies are increasingly pursuing creative tactics to find, acquire, and retain top talent by engaging alternative labor pools such as contractors, remote workers, retirees, and part-time workers. For example, AARP believes that 80% of baby boomers will continue working past their current retirement age.

2.3.3 Global/Mobile Talent Market

More talented workers than ever are searching for career opportunities abroad due to cross-market integration and economic development in emerging market countries. Ernst & Young reports that cross-border migration has grown 42% in the past decade, with most of the traffic directed toward Organization for Economic Co-operation and Development (OECD) countries. In addition, the spread of English as a second language in many European, Middle Eastern, and North African (MENA), and Asia-Pacific (APAC) countries is making it much easier for non-native people with English skills to work in these locations. Recently, however, higher unemployment, local hostility toward migrant workers, and legal restrictions have discouraged many workers from pursuing opportunities abroad.

Even so, labor demand will eventually increase, and when it does, so will global migration. In addition, some countries have changed course on restrictive policies made during the recession years to attract these migrant workers. Migration patterns are also changing as a result of the dramatic growth of these emerging market countries. The World Economic Forum cites reverse migration of highly skilled workers to their home countries as a growing trend that will heavily impact emerging countries' economies.

2.3.4 Employees' Expectation Shift

Employees today are increasingly interested in having challenging and meaningful work, being more loyal to their profession than to the organization, being less accommodating of traditional structures and authority, becoming more concerned about work-life balance, and preparing to take ownership of their careers and development.

This new employee mindset is the result of the significantly weakened relationship between employer and employee over the past three decades. Cost-cutting measures and scheduled personnel reductions signal to employees that their tenure at an organization may be short lived.

At the time this book is being written, unemployment is very high. This current environment empowers the employer to dictate the rules of the workplace. However, the market will turn eventually, and when it does, employees will most certainly be the beneficiary. They will want better and more diverse employment options and a greater say in how work is assigned to them, as well as to understand how they are being assessed and rewarded based on their performance. This will force organizations to place more emphasis on talent management strategies and practices.

2.4 Summary

Leading companies make attracting, engaging, and retaining employees a strategic business priority, and in a competitive marketplace, talent management is a primary driver for organizational success. CEO and board of director involvement is a must, but for organizations to be successful, an understanding of the value of talent management must be shared throughout the organization.

In addition, HR should take a proactive lead in developing the integrated strategic approach to talent management, including (but not limited to) outlining the benefits to both the organization and participants. Organizations that can implement talent management practices and policies generally experience lower turnover and benefit from employees that are more engaged, which positively impacts the bottom line of the organization.

The talent management market has changed immensely over the past few years. The major changes to the market have been both organizational and technological in nature. Organizational changes include implementing integrated processes and systems, offshoring, and the move of HR from administration to business partner. Technological changes include employee portals, side-by-side talent profiles, global talent pools, goal alignment, collaboration tools, integrated and harmonized enterprise resource planning (ERP) systems, and smartphones and tablets.

In the next chapter, we'll take a look at which puzzle pieces you'll need to put together to revitalize your talent management strategy with Talent Management from SAP.

A solid foundation within your talent management system provides additional functionality and enables growth, making it ready for future SAP modules.

3   Foundations of Talent Management

Before any Talent Management module implementation or upgrade, your organization should ensure that the core of your HR system is strong. To do this, core areas of your system need to be set up and maintained correctly. When you properly maintain these systems, your organization is easier to manage, and you open your Talent Management modules up to more functionality, ease of use, and interoperability.

With a strong understanding of these core components, you can fully realize how the Talent Management modules operate within an HR organization. This also allows you to leverage and understand how the Talent Management modules work together as a team to successfully manage your talent from end to end.

In this chapter, we'll first look at the following areas of core HR:

- Organizational Management (OM)
- Personnel Administration (PA)
- SAP Job Architecture
- Qualifications Catalog

Looking into these core areas in detail will set the stage for the rest of this book. Each of the subsequent chapters will touch on some area of these foundational concepts and how they work within Talent Management. If you want a strong and strategic talent management system, start with a solid foundation.

3.1   Organizational Management

Having a strong talent organization starts with having a strong HR system foundation. To start this process of implementing a strategic talent management system, you need to begin by mapping the entire business into a logical hierarchy structure. This systemic structure should match the company structure. The SAP Organization Management (OM) module accomplishes the task of putting your enterprise structure into your SAP ERP system. It defines a "who-reports-to-whom" chain of command for your company, which is an easy way to map departments within your organization to positions and tasks. The OM module puts these departments and positions into a graphical, manageable format that can be used across many modules, including the Talent Management modules.

The following are some of the many benefits of implementing the OM module within your company:

- Keeps your business areas structured and organized
- Defines employee reporting structure
- Enables position-to-position workflow throughout the system
- Creates planning scenarios to simulate new structures within your business process
- Analyzes your current organizational plan

In the context of Talent Management, you can see how OM can be a powerful tool to keep your business areas maintained and organized. By creating a solid organizational structure within the system, you can leverage additional functionality from SAP Talent Management and also maintain a clean, official way of referencing your business reporting structure.

This section is devoted to OM, and will include an overview of the critical OM objects, diagrams of how the object is related to other OM objects, short walkthroughs of how to create the object and screenshots of how the object looks in the system, and important transactions used to create and edit OM objects.

> **Additional Resources**
>
> Much of the information in the subsequent sections is basic, but you can learn more about the OM module from *Mastering SAP ERP HCM Organizational Management* by Sylvia Chaudoir (SAP PRESS, 2009).

3.1.1 Object-Oriented Design

Before we begin talking about how to initiate your own organizational plan, let's talk about its structure. The OM module is based on object-oriented design. This means that an "object," or a single system entity, represents nearly everything within your company that needs to be reflected in your SAP ERP HCM system. An object can represent anything—an entire department, a person, a set of responsibilities, or something in between.

Table 3.1 shows the four main object types that we'll be discussing in this chapter. Each object has its own unique properties and purposes within the system. We'll discuss the purpose and function of each of these main objects, as well as the steps to create these in your own system.

Icon	Name	Description	Object Type
	Organizational unit	The core object within your organizational plan	O
	Job	Classifications of functions within your business	C
	Position	Of direct relation to organizational units and jobs; links functions and responsibilities to an overall organizational unit	S
	Person	Represents an employee within your company	P

Table 3.1 The Main SAP Talent Management Object Types within Organizational Management

In the next few sections, we'll discuss the crucial objects needed to set up a successful organizational plan. The goal is to have a solid foundation so that your Talent Management modules can be used to their full potential.

3.1.2 Organizational Plan

To fully use the OM module, start by placing your departments and divisions into an organizational plan, which will represent all of the organizational units, positions, and chief positions that are present in your system.

After you have successfully mapped all of your divisions and departments into the OM module, as well as placing the positions accordingly, you'll have a completed organizational plan. An organizational plan isn't an object itself, but it refers to the complete map of your company in the system.

The subsequent sections of this chapter will outline each individual aspect of an organizational plan.

3.1.3 Staff Assignments

By creating an organizational plan, you can effectively map out your entire enterprise based on all of the important entities that make up your company. To do this, you'll assign the important objects to your organizational plan. *Staff assignment* is the terminology SAP uses to describe the process of populating an organizational plan. A staff assignment represents all persons and employees that belong to an organizational unit, which we'll discuss in the next section. Note that staff assignments aren't objects within themselves, but instead refer to the assignment of a person to a position, and of positions to an organizational unit.

As they relate to SAP, staff assignments and organizational plans have not changed very much over the course of its lifecycle. Because these are the building blocks and core foundational components to not only Talent Management but to many other SAP modules as well, they are especially important.

As shown in Figure 3.1, you can use many SAP transactions to effectively create your own organizational plan. In this particular example, Transaction PPOME can be used to create, edit, and change a staff assignment for your organizational plan.

As we progress in this chapter, you'll see the many areas of Transaction PPOME because it has a lot of valuable tools to create an effective organizational plan that will be used across all of the Talent Management modules.

The next few sections will discuss the objects that are used in Transaction PPOME for staff assignments. By assigning positions and persons to an organizational unit, you can have a complete staff assignment within your organizational plan.

Organizational Management | **3.1**

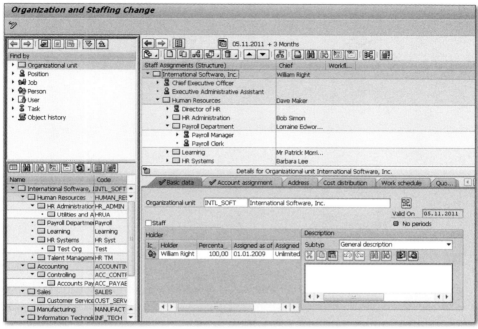

Figure 3.1 Transaction PPOME—Organization and Staff Change

3.1.4 Organizational Units

In the OM module, a single object—an organizational unit—represents each area, division, department, or business unit in your company. Each one of the business areas that you designate has its own organizational unit. Within the SAP system, this organizational unit is designated to the object type O.

In Figure 3.2, the IT department and the HR department are represented in the SAP system by individual organizational units. So whenever you see the type O in the system, you know that this object refers to some type of business area in your organization. You can maintain an efficient and accurate reading of the layout of your business by assigning your business units to organizational units in the system.

However, most businesses don't consist of single over-arching units with employees reporting to them. There are many different groups within each department or division of the company. For example, the HR department contains many different divisions, including Payroll and Benefits. There could be, and probably are, many

43

other divisions within departments. How can you show this within your organizational plan? How is this depicted within the structure?

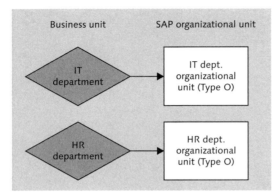

Figure 3.2 Example Departments Represented by Organizational Units

The answer is simple. Each division also has its own organizational unit. Just like the HR department, the Payroll division would also get its own organizational unit in the system. These suborganizational units would also be assigned to object type O; in this way, they are exactly the same as the parent organization.

The only difference is that this division belongs to the greater organizational unit, the HR department. As shown in Figure 3.3, the structure of many divisions or departments reporting to a greater division or department can be many layers deep.

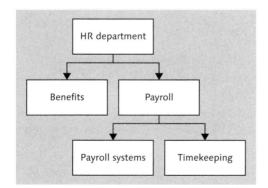

Figure 3.3 Multi-Tiered Organizational Units

Keeping track of a multi-tiered organizational plan via organizational units is a simple and straightforward way to manage your organizational structure. Because businesses are complex, mapping out how your business units report to each other can help clarify the reporting structure.

SAP uses "relationships" to connect multiple entities. For example, the HR department contains the Payroll division, so a relationship exists between these two organizational units: the HR department "is the line supervisor of" the Payroll division, and the Payroll division "reports to" the HR department, as shown in Figure 3.4.

Figure 3.4 SAP-Defined Relationship between Two Organizational Units

By naming the relationship, you can easily distinguish the relativity of one object to another. In relationships between organizational units, SAP uses this terminology. To find which organizational unit the Payroll department reports to, you look for the HR department. Likewise, to locate a subordinate organizational unit of the HR department, you find that the Payroll department falls under this category.

The same goes for all other objects associated with organizational units, positions, jobs, and persons within your entire HR system. Each relationship has its own unique naming convention to describe its relation to another object.

In Figure 3.5, you can see a sample view of an organizational plan and the relationships between many organizational units. In this example, a single organizational unit can contain many other organizational units.

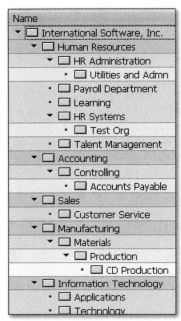

Figure 3.5 Sample Organizational Structure in Transaction PP01

If your enterprise contains many different departments and divisions, you can easily map this structure within the system with the tools provided by SAP.

3.1.5 Creating Organizational Units

You can create your own organizational unit within SAP in several ways. For the purposes of this example, we'll use Transaction PPOME because it lets you create your own organizational unit that can house all of the new relationships to the rest of the OM objects.

In the walkthrough that follows, we'll use an organization that already exists in the system. We'll add a new organizational unit—the Payroll department—to the HR department. Transaction PPOME is used to edit details about this organizational unit in the system, as shown in Figure 3.6.

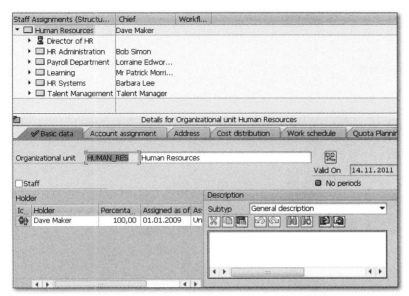

Figure 3.6 Human Resources Department in Transaction PPOME

To add the organizational unit, follow these steps:

1. Go to Transaction PPOME, and choose the organizational unit that you want to create a child organization for, as shown in Figure 3.6. In this case, choose the HUMAN RESOURCES department, and create the Payroll department, which will be reporting to the Human Resources department.

2. Click the CREATE ( ) button, which will send you to the Choose Relationship screen. This screen shows the two relationships that can be created (see Figure 3.7).

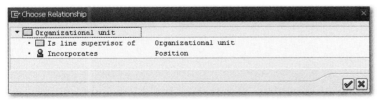

Figure 3.7 Creating an Organizational Unit in Transaction PPOME

3 | Foundations of Talent Management

3. After you click the CREATE (▢) button, you'll be presented with a window that lets you assign one organizational unit to another. Select the relationship, and click the CONTINUE (✔) button.

In Figure 3.8, you can see that the organizational unit creation screen contains many different tabs and areas.

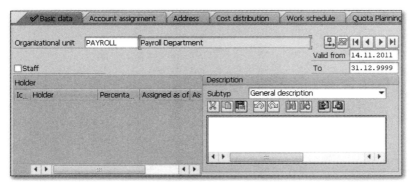

Figure 3.8 Creating a Sample Organizational Unit

There are many areas of SAP where organizational planning is used, and it is very expansive. Remember that OM isn't just for the Talent Management module but will also be used throughout many of SAP's other modules. But within Talent Management, the OM module is key to leveraging and fully using the functionality. Your talent management systems will run much more smoothly if you have set up solid and accurate organizational unit structures that mirror your enterprise structure. This also makes additional Talent Management modules easier to implement if you choose to do phased implementations.

3.1.6 Positions

To fulfill staff assignments to an organizational unit, you must populate the organizational unit by assigning positions that will later be filled by employees. A *position* is defined as a placeholder object for a person, central person, business partner, or user that has responsibility for a certain set of tasks within an organization. Though positions aren't the actual employee or user object—for that, we use the person object, which will be discussed in the next section—they are a representation of your personnel capacity, or headcount. By assigning positions to organizational units, you can get an accurate snapshot of the current organizational structure.

All of the objects within OM are tightly integrated and have relationships with one another. Positions play a very important role in linking all of the objects to one another. They are essentially instances of a job, which we'll also be discussing later in the chapter. It is important to understand the relationship between jobs and positions, as positions have inherited attributes directly from a job.

Not only do positions inherit attributes from a job, but they also have important relationships to organizational units. To make a complete organizational plan, you must assign positions directly to your organizational unit. An organizational unit can, and is supposed to, contain many positions, as shown in Figure 3.9.

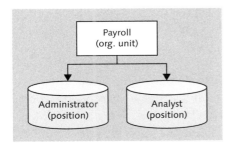

Figure 3.9 Multiple Positions Under a Single Organizational Unit

Note that a position "belongs to" an organizational unit and the same organizational unit "incorporates" the position, as shown in Figure 3.10.

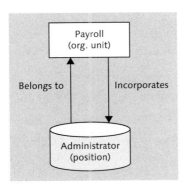

Figure 3.10 Relationship Between an Organizational Unit and a Position

Before we look at assigning positions to organizational units, let's explore how positions are used within the system itself. By assigning statuses to positions, you can determine how to fill your staff assignments, as well as get a good reading of the current state of the organizational unit or the organizational plan as a whole.

The following list details the main statuses that a position can have. They each have their own unique meaning and visual representation in the system:

- **Occupied**
  This position has an employee or user assigned to it.
- **Vacant**
  An employee is currently being sought for this position.
- **Unoccupied**
  No employee is currently being sought to fill the position.
- **Obsolete**
  This position is no longer being used.

Like an organizational unit, you assign positions an object type as well. The object type S represents a position within the OM module. Also like an organizational unit, the position object type has many different relationships to many other object types. The following are the most common and important object types for a position:

- Organizational unit (object type O)
- Job (object type C)
- Person (object type P)

Next, let's explore the relationship between an organizational unit and a position.

Just as SAP provides many ways to create organizational units, it also provides many ways to create your own positions. Again, one of these methods is using Transaction PPOME.

For this example, let's create a position under the Benefits department organizational unit by following these steps:

1. Click the CREATE ( ) button, and the same window appears as if you were creating another organizational unit and lets you easily create and assign a position.

2. Select the relationship INCORPORATES, and click the CONTINUE ( ) button. Figure 3.11 shows you where you'll edit information about the new position.

Organizational Management | 3.1

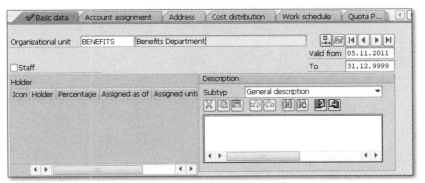

Figure 3.11 Creating a Position Under an Organizational Unit

The position creation screen, shown in Figure 3.12, looks very similar to the organizational unit screen. You can use the various screen areas and tabs to enable cross-module support.

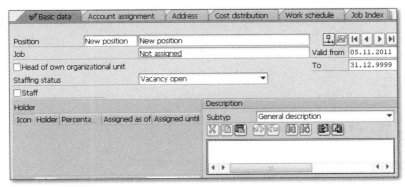

Figure 3.12 Creating a Position

Now that you have a position assigned to an organizational unit, let's take a look at the overall object structure you've created. In Figure 3.13, you can see the full relationship of Payroll employees in an organizational structure. By adding positions to the Payroll organizational unit, it becomes part of the larger HR department organizational unit as well because Payroll has a direct relationship to the HR department.

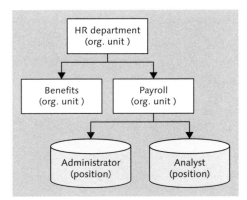

Figure 3.13 Object Structure of Organizational Units and Positions

Transaction PPOME shows you how this full structure looks in the SAP ERP HCM system. By using a graphical depiction of each object type, you can easily see the relationships of organizational units and positions, as shown in Figure 3.14.

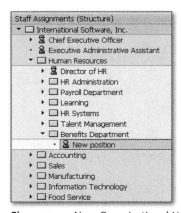

Figure 3.14 New Organizational Unit and Position in the Structure

Figure 3.14 shows how this new position appears in the organizational structure. Now that the organizational units and position are set up, you need to assign a manager to this organizational unit by using the system's chief position flag.

3.1.7 Chief Positions

Chief positions are important in a Talent Management organizational plan. They are defined as a managerial position within an organizational unit that has direct reports (e.g., a Payroll manager within the Payroll department). You can flag a position as a chief position directly in the detail area in Transaction PPOME by checking the HEAD OF OWN ORGANIZATIONAL UNIT box, as shown in Figure 3.15.

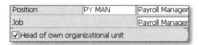

Figure 3.15 Chief Position

Checking this box means that the position should have direct reports and is the manager of this particular organizational unit.

> **Tip**
>
> Although SAP allows you to have multiple chief positions in one organizational unit, one best practice is to only have one chief position per unit. Because the business workflow looks at the chief of an organizational unit and assigns the subordinate positions as employees to that manager, it's important to keep your manager positions aligned with these chief positions. This assignment has a downstream impact on the rest of the Talent Management suite. For example, in the Performance Management module, the chief position dictates which employees are managers and which employees fall under these managers. This will determine which employee can perform appraisals, and can cascade goals to employees.

3.1.8 Person

Now that we understand the basic structure of OM, let's explore the last piece of the puzzle: assigning an employee or a user to a position. Even though you may assign other object types to a position (central person, business partner, or a user), the concept is the same. In this example, we'll use the person object as a holder for a position. This step will complete the basics of setting up the organizational plan and, as a result, enable full use of the Talent Management functionality.

The person object is very important in OM because it is the link that combines an actual employee in your company to an organization. By assigning the person object, you can now see the entire picture of where exactly an employee is assigned relative to your employee structure, and you can view and assign managers to chief positions. With the person object assigned to a position object, all of the necessary components are in place to complete an organizational plan.

The person object (object type P) represents an actual employee in your system, so it will have a relationship to the position object. You can keep your data consistent by maintaining one-to-one relationships between persons and positions even though SAP lets you assign multiple persons per position. Figure 3.16 shows that where one person holds one position, that position is occupied by one person.

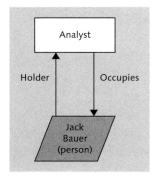

Figure 3.16 The Relationship Between a Person Object and Position Object

We'll cover how to create a person object later in this chapter in Section 3.2, which discusses PA. For the purposes of completing our organizational plan, we'll assign a holder to a position object using the same transaction as before: Transaction PPOME.

1. Within Transaction PPOME, choose the position that you want to assign a holder.
2. Click the ASSIGN ( ) button, and a new window will appear that displays all of the relationships that are available to the position object, as shown in Figure 3.17.

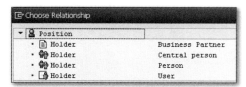

Figure 3.17 Available Relationships to the Position Object

3. To fill the position, choose the HOLDER relationship of PERSON, CENTRAL PERSON, BUSINESS PARTNER, or USER.

   After successfully assigning someone to a position, you can see that this position is now filled within the organizational structure with that individual's name.

In Figure 3.18, the person JACK BAUER is now the holder of the ANALYST position, which is part of the PAYROLL DEPARTMENT.

Figure 3.18 A Person Assigned to a Position in the Organizational Structure

Notice that the PAYROLL DEPARTMENT in Figure 3.18 also has a chief position assigned to it as well—the PAYROLL MANAGER.

> **Tip**
>
> Be very careful when assigning relationships manually with Transaction PPOME. The system allows you to assign a person object to a position even if that person is otherwise occupied (assigned to another position), but because each person can only be assigned to one position at a time, the system delimits the current relationship of the person to the previous position. Manual changes in these transactions could lead to data corruption and strange results in the other Talent Management modules.

Now that we have the last required object to complete the organizational plan, let's explore the organization as a whole, as it appears in the system.

3.1.9 Organizational Management Summary

This section will explore the organizational plan as a whole and will summarize everything described in the previous sections of this chapter. We've covered what it means to have a complete organizational plan and which important objects constitute a complete plan. By assigning each department and division in your company to an organizational unit in your SAP ERP HCM system, you can effectively map out and view your headcount.

Figure 3.19 shows the complete organizational plan. Its organizational units can have additional organizational units that report to them. Within *those* organizational units, we have many positions. These positions can have a person object as a holder.

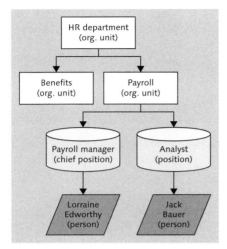

Figure 3.19 Overall Organizational Plan

Figure 3.20 shows what this looks like in your system, triggered by Transaction PPOME.

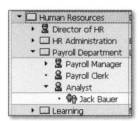

Figure 3.20 Overall View of the Organizational Plan in Transaction PPOME

Now that you have a solid understanding of the foundational concepts of OM, we can move on to explore another important foundational concept: personnel administration.

Understanding how personnel administration fits into the Talent Management foundation is just as important as understanding OM. These objects should be created and maintained properly to achieve a successful talent management system. In the next sections, we'll explore how the Personnel Administration (PA) module integrates with not only Talent Management, but the OM module as well.

3.2 Personnel Administration

Personnel Administration (PA) is an extremely important part of integrating your Talent Management modules with one another. By itself, PA isn't technically its own module (although we refer to it as such) but rather a set of data specific to personnel. In fact, it plays a crucial part in talent management strategy because it can be used to house all of the administrative and personnel data for your employees in your SAP ERP HCM system. This is a central repository that all of the other Talent Management modules can leverage to access, update, and manage employee data.

The following are some of the main integration points of PA with other Talent Management modules:

- SAP E-Recruiting — new hire data
- Performance Management — organizational and personal information
- Compensation Management — transfer of compensation information
- Talent Development/Succession — talent data

PA is used by multiple other SAP ERP modules as well. Its components are used in Payroll, Time Management, Controlling (CO), Financial Accounting (FI), Material Management (MM), and Sales and Distribution (SD). For the purposes of this book, we'll only look at this module as it pertains to the Talent Management modules.

We'll explore a few main areas that are particularly important to Talent Management, as they extend part of the OM module. PA and the OM module leverage each other to share detailed information about the employee.

The following subsections discuss many fields, or data elements, that relate to PA. We'll look at the function of each field and how it relates to Talent Management.

3.2.1 Company Code

The company code field isn't specific to PA; it is also used heavily in the CO, FI, MM, and SD modules. With a company code, you can use some of the following functions:

- Reporting purposes
- Base authorization checks for users off their inherited company code
- Default personnel administration values for employees, such as address and bank data
- Default currency key for an employee's basic pay

PA has its own set of important control data that is used in the Talent Management modules. To create this data, you must first have a company code so that data can be inherited down to lower levels within the organization.

Even if you're not currently using a company code in any of the other SAP ERP modules, you can use this field to represent the highest level of your enterprise structure. This differs from organizational units because company codes are used to identify entirely separate company and legal entities. If you don't have more than one company in your enterprise structure, you may simply use one company code. This will allow you to create the subunits that will be used to classify your personnel.

Next let's look at personnel area and personnel subarea, and how they are used in Talent Management.

3.2.2 Personnel Area

The personnel area field is a way to categorize employees by a logical area. It can be used in Talent Management to organize your personnel and is mainly used for payroll purposes. Because personnel area is a subdivision of company code, you must first establish a company code to create personnel areas and cascade the data that is associated with the company code to all personnel areas that fall within it.

Personnel area is generally used to group employees by geographical region within Talent Management, which can be very useful to global organizations for categorizing their personnel. In Talent Management modules, personnel area information is passed along to the person object. Transaction PP01 is used in the person object to pass information to the employee in the system, allowing you to organize and report on this category of personnel.

Personnel area can be maintained via Transaction SPRO or via the menu path SAP Customizing Implementation Guide • Enterprise Structure • Definition • Human Resources Management • Employee Groups. Figure 3.21 shows how personnel areas look in the system.

Personnel area	Personnel Area Text	
SG01	Plant Singapore 1	Singapore
SG02	Plant Singapore 2	Plant Singapore 2
TH01	Personnel Area TH01	Personnel Area TH01
TW01	Taiwan personnel area	Taiwan personnel area
UN01	NPO Personnel Area 1	NPO Personnel Area 1
UN02	NPO Personnel Area 2	NPO Personnel Area 2
UN03	NPO Personnel Area 3	NPO Personnel Area 3
US01	United States Headquarter	Philadelphia
US02	US Product A	San Francisco
US03	US Product B	Los Angeles
US04	US Subsidiary A	Atlanta
USPS	US Public Sector	Palo Alto
VE01	Area de personal Venezolana 1	Caracas
VE02	Modelo de Compañia II Vzla	
XX01	Personnel area XX01	
ZA01	Head Office - Johannesburg ZA	ZA - Model Personnel Area
ZA02	Factory - Midrand ZA	ZA - Model Personnel Area

Figure 3.21 Maintaining Personnel Areas in Transaction SPRO

3.2.3 Personnel Subarea

As a further categorization of employees, personnel subareas are generally used to differentiate pay scale, wage type structures, and work schedule planning. They group employees into further categories based on geographical location.

For example, within the personnel area for a company's US headquarters, the following are some examples of possible personnel subareas:

- Administration
- Human resources
- Finance
- Sales and marketing
- Manufacturing

These subareas are specific to the personnel area itself and therefore are part of the US headquarters personnel area. By using company code, personnel area, and personnel subarea, you can successfully categorize your employees into detailed areas that closely resemble your enterprise structure.

When creating the person object in Transaction PP01, you can see and maintain the company code (CoCode), personnel area (Pers.area), and personnel subarea (Subarea), as shown in Figure 3.22.

Figure 3.22 Enterprise Structure Information for the Person Object in Transaction PP01

Within the PA module, there are further ways to categorize employees: by employee groups and employee subgroups.

3.2.4 Employee Group

Unlike personnel area and subarea, employee groups are a way to identify and report on employees based on how they fit into the labor force in your enterprise. Employee groups are used heavily in the Payroll module, but we recommend that you also use them when setting up your Talent Management system. The benefits of setting up employee groups include being able to report on your labor force, using them for authorization checks, and viewing the basic pay for an employee.

The following are some common examples of employee groups:

- Active
- Retiree/pensioner
- Interns
- Terminated
- Inactive employees

Figure 3.23 shows other possible employee groups.

Transaction SPRO has its own node to maintain these employee groups, which you can access via the menu path SAP Customizing Implementation Guide • Enterprise Structure • Definition • Human Resources Management • Employee Groups.

Employee group	Name of employee grp
1	Active
2	Retiree/pensioner
3	Early retiree
4	Interns
5	Terminated
6	Inactive Employees
7	Temp/Seasonal
8	Expatriate
9	External employee

Figure 3.23 Defining Employee Groups in the System

Another sublayer of groupings exists within employee groups. Employee subgroups are another way to effectively categorize your personnel within the system and can extend the details of employee groups.

3.2.5 Employee Subgroup

Employee subgroups can be used to divide employee groups into many subsections and to classify employees by wage types. The following are examples of employee subgroups that are already in your system, even if you don't currently leverage this functionality:

- Salaried employees
- Hourly employees
- Pay scale employee
- Apprentice
- Executive
- Partner

On a global scale, these subgroups can be very useful to organize your employees. Like employee groups, subgroups can be used in various system functions. Consider these commonly used functions that subgroups can help manage:

- Identify an employee's remuneration
- Determine wage types
- Restrict eligibility of pay scale
- Determine work schedules

3 | Foundations of Talent Management

Notice that most of these functions are used for the Payroll and Time Management modules. Within Talent Management, they can be used in the Performance Management module to view appraisal documents for subgroups of employees.

Like personnel areas and employee groups, we can maintain employee subgroups within the Implementation Guide (IMG), using Transaction SPRO. Figure 3.24 shows you how employee subgroups can be created, viewed, and maintained.

Employee subgroup	Name of EE subgroup
A0	Non-PS mthly wage AR
A1	Wood mthly wage AR
A2	Commerce mthly wg AR
A3	Confid. mthly wageAR
A4	Wood hrly wage AR
A5	Commerce hrly wg AR
A6	Retiree monthly AR
A7	Juvenile mthly wg AR
A8	Manager mthly wg AR
A9	Ext.profess.mthly AR
AA	Hourly wage earner
AD	Industrial trainee
AE	Monthly wage earner

Figure 3.24 Creation and Maintenance of Employee Subgroups

After you've successfully maintained subgroups that match your personnel structure, you can assign an employee group and employee subgroup to an employee, as shown in Figure 3.25.

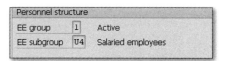

Figure 3.25 View of Employee Group and Subgroup in Transaction PP01

Within Transaction PP01, you can enter an employee group and employee subgroup for an employee. By assigning employees to these groups to match your personnel and enterprise structure, you can effectively organize your workforce using PA.

3.3 SAP Job Architecture

SAP Job Architecture extends the relationships between jobs and positions. In EhP 4, the SAP Job Architecture was enhanced by two new objects: the functional area and the job family. This has produced further segmentation and allows additional flexibility with how qualifications can be aligned within the SAP Job Architecture structure. We'll discuss these qualifications later in the chapter.

You can maintain these new objects in the same way that jobs and positions have traditionally been maintained by using Transaction PP01, as shown in Figure 3.26. SAP has included Transaction HRTMC_PPOM (as well as HRTMC_PPOS and HRTMC_PPOC, which is shown in Figure 3.27) as equivalents to PPOME for working with these new objects and other Talent Management objects and relationships. Finally, Talent Management specialists can develop and manage the SAP Job Architecture with an easy and intuitive visual interface by using the SAP Talent Visualization by Nakisa (STVN) Talent Framework. We'll discuss STVN Talent Framework along with Nakisa Talent Development (Succession Planning), Talent Profile, and Talent Assessment later in the book.

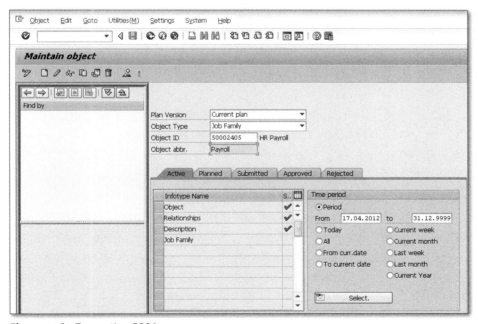

Figure 3.26 Transaction PP01

3 | Foundations of Talent Management

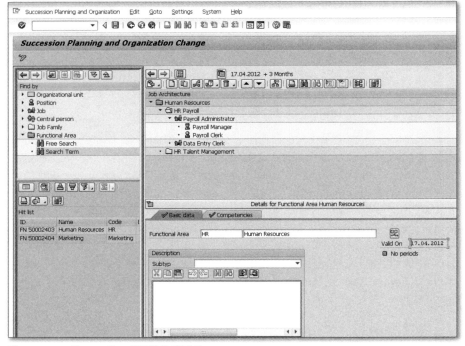

Figure 3.27 Transaction HRTMC_PPOM

3.3.1 Functional Area

A functional area (object type FN) is a collective area of job families that share common attributes and is often aligned to a particular business function. The functional area represents a task area that contributes to the attainment of corporate objectives. Examples of functional areas include recruitment, marketing, production, and administration.

The functional area is independent of job level, company/region, cost center, reports-to hierarchy, HR organizational structure, and so on. Functional areas have related knowledge, skill set, and ability requirements.

The SAP Best Practices for HCM (USA), which provides flexible, reusable business scenarios and content for organizations, is delivered with approximately three functional areas; these can be used as delivered, modified to reflect specific customer needs, or used to provide guidelines for creating and organizing positions within SAP.

Table 3.2 is a sampling of the functional areas provided in the SAP Best Practices for HCM (USA), which can be accessed via Transaction S_AHR_61016497.

Object ID	Name
50000120	Information Technology
50000121	Executives
50000838	Human Resources

Table 3.2 SAP Best Practices for HCM (USA) Functional Areas

The functional area allows users to group one or more job families. This way, you can use the functional area to edit multiple job families and thus jobs and positions collectively. Users use Transaction PP01 to create functional area objects, relationships, and descriptions. We've created a functional area called "Human Resources" (see Figure 3.28) as an example.

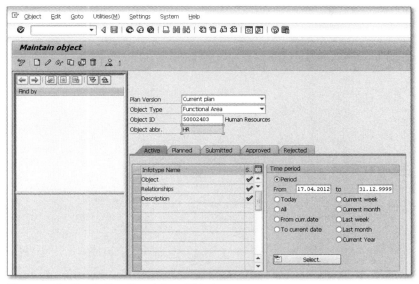

Figure 3.28 Create Functional Area Object

We'll now create relationships to the job families "HR Payroll" (shown in Figure 3.29) and "HR Talent Management" (shown in Figure 3.30). Relationships to job families are created when creating functional areas based on the principle of inheritance: each job family, job, and position for which you create relationships will inherit the competencies (qualifications) from each level above it. The final step is to create descriptions for each functional area object. Figure 3.31 shows an example for the HUMAN RESOURCES functional area.

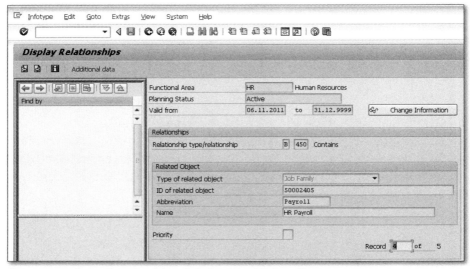

Figure 3.29 Create Functional Area Relationship—HR Payroll

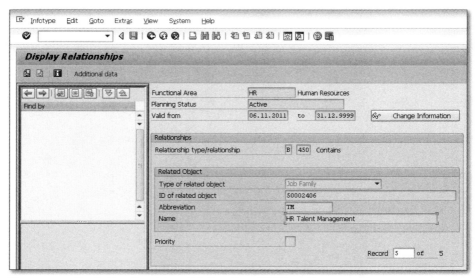

Figure 3.30 Create Functional Area Relationship—HR Talent Management

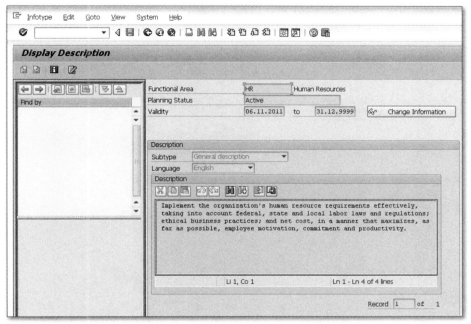

Figure 3.31 Create Functional Area Description—Human Resources

3.3.2 Job Family

Job family is a further breakdown of the job architecture and defines the nature of the work being performed. It's a group of jobs involving work of the same nature—that is, the same or relatively similar work is being performed and similar skill sets are required—but requiring different levels of skill and responsibility levels. For employees, it's often possible to move within a job family with minimal training. For example, business analyst and senior business analyst are in the same job family.

A job family (object type JF) is assigned to functional areas and is a cross-organizational grouping of positions; we use it in Talent Management to plan the distribution of employee potentials within an organization.

The SAP Best Practices for HCM (USA) is delivered with approximately eight job families. Like the functional areas, they can be used as delivered, modified to reflect specific customer needs, or used to provide guidelines for creating and organizing positions within SAP.

Table 3.3 offers a sampling of the job families provided in the SAP Best Practices for HCM (USA), which can be accessed via Transaction S_AHR_61016497.

Object ID	Name
50000118	Programmers
50000119	Applications Analysts
50000122	Accounts Payable Analysts
50000123	Recruiters
50000600	Directors
50000833	Database Administrators
50000839	HR Management
50000841	Network Specialists

Table 3.3 SAP Best Practices for HCM (USA) Job Families

The job family consists of the following data:

- Name
- Description
- Qualifications (contains the qualifications, which you can assign from the Qualifications Catalog, that an employee must have in order to have potential for the job family)

The system saves the job family data in the following infotypes:

- Infotype 1000 (job family)
- Infotype 1002 (description)

The system saves the relationships between the job family object and the other objects in Infotype 1001 (relationships), as illustrated in Table 3.4.

Object	Relationship	Name
Central person	A744/B744	Has potential for/Is a potential of
Position	A450/B450	Belongs to/Includes
Qualification	A031/B031	Requires/Is required by

Table 3.4 Job Objects, Relationships, and Names

Recall that the job families that we created are HR PAYROLL (shown in Figure 3.32) and HR TALENT MANAGEMENT (shown in Figure 3.33).

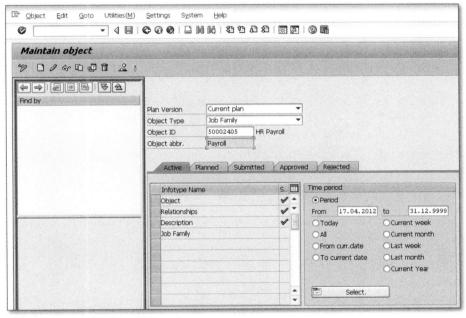

Figure 3.32 Job Family—HR Payroll

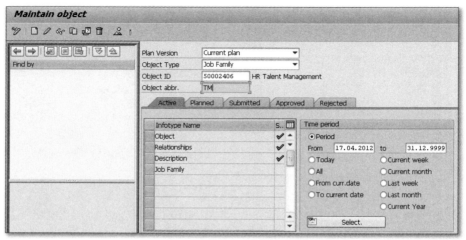

Figure 3.33 Job Family—HR Talent Management

Job families can be subsequently divided into levels:

- Hierarchy (e.g., senior management, middle management)
- Expertise (e.g., entry level, intermediate, experienced, advanced, expert)

Dividing a job family along these lines simultaneously divides *all* job families into identical levels. You use the levels, for example, to divide the positions that you want to assign to a job family into a hierarchy. If you want to use levels, you should follow these steps before using job families for the first time.

1. Select Transaction OOSC. You'll be presented with the Change View Scale: Overview window, as shown in Figure 3.34.

2. Choose NEW ENTRIES, and create a scale for the QUALITY SCALE category, as shown in Figure 3.35.

3. Assign proficiencies to the scale (as shown in Figure 3.36), which will be used later to describe the levels of your job families.

> **Note**
>
> If you want to divide the job families into a hierarchy, you must create the proficiencies so that the lowest hierarchy level has the smallest numeric proficiency (ID). Don't use the entry "0" as a numeric proficiency.

4. Save your entries.
5. Call Report RHTM_T77TM_JF_Level.
6. Enter the scale you created.
7. Run the report, as shown in Figure 3.37.

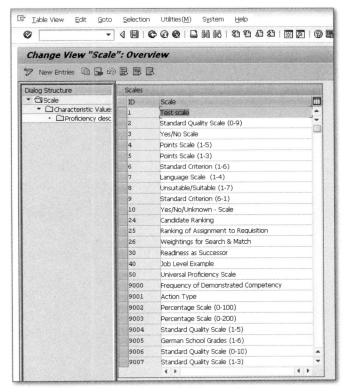

Figure 3.34 Transaction OOSC

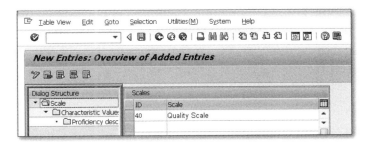

Figure 3.35 New Entries

3 | Foundations of Talent Management

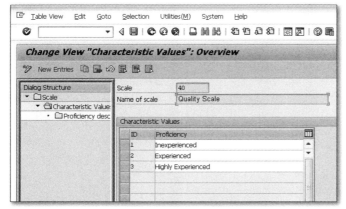

Figure 3.36 Proficiencies

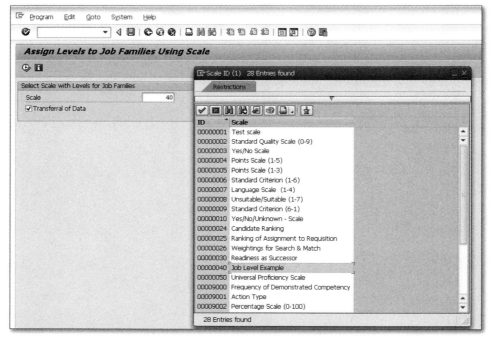

Figure 3.37 Report RHTM_T77TM_JF_Level

3.3.3 Jobs

Jobs (object type C) are assigned to job families and are a classification of functions in an enterprise. They are defined by the tasks and characteristics assigned to them, and serve as a template for creating positions when creating an organizational plan.

Although many people use the terms *job* and *job description* interchangeably, there is a distinct difference between the two. Attributes of the job include the job title, organization job code, salary grade/broad band, live-in code, representation status, Fair Labor Standards Act (FLSA) status, and job family (if applicable). Job description, on the other hand, is a generic summary of the key responsibilities of a job. It includes the general nature of the work performed, the level of the work performed, the skills and knowledge required for competent performance of the job, and other elements. Job descriptions apply to different positions with similar tasks and characteristics.

SAP Best Practices for HCM (USA) is delivered with more than 40 jobs. Just like functional areas and job families, these jobs can be used as delivered, modified to reflect specific customer needs, or used to provide guidelines for creating and organizing jobs within SAP.

Table 3.5 is a sampling of the jobs provided in SAP Best Practices for HCM (USA), which can be found by going to Transaction S_AHR_61016497.

Object ID	Name
50000040	Chief Executive Officer
50000041	Executive Administrative Assistant
50000042	Director of HR
50000046	HR Manager
50000047	HR Administrative Assistant
50000048	Senior Recruiter
50000052	Director of Accounting

Table 3.5 SAP Best Practices for HCM (USA) Jobs

Object ID	Name
50000053	Controller
50000054	Accounts Payable Manager
50000055	Accounts Payable Analyst
50000060	Director of Sales
50000061	Customer Service Manager
50000062	Customer Service Representative
50000063	Director of Manufacturing
50000068	Materials Manager
50000069	Production Manager
50000070	Production Supervisor
50000071	Labeler
50000072	CD Maker
50000078	Security Administrator
50000079	Network Administrator
50000080	Technology Manager
50000081	Senior Programmer
50000082	Application Analyst
50000083	Applications Manager
50000084	Director of Information Technology
50000840	Junior Programmer
50001400	Officer
50001812	Super User
50001813	Administrator
50001814	Manager

Table 3.5 SAP Best Practices for HCM (USA) Jobs (Cont.)

Object ID	Name
50001815	Analyst
50003597	Utility Worker
50003598	Ground Worker
50003600	Electrician
50003601	Mechanic
50003602	Field Worker
50003603	Work and Resource Coordinator
50003606	Electrical Systems Manager
50004526	Engineering (Mega)

Table 3.5 SAP Best Practices for HCM (USA) Jobs (Cont.)

In addition to the object definition and relationships to positions, jobs in the SAP Best Practices for HCM (USA) are also delivered with additional information attached. When you create the Infotype 1610 EEO/AAP (Equal Employment Opportunity/Affirmative Action Policy) category, the EEO, AAP, and FLSA designations for each job are stored. This information is associated with any employees assigned to a position that is related to the job. In this way, EEO and AAP reports may be run, and overtime calculations may be made based on FLSA status. The FLSA status indicator is reflected on the employee's organizational assignment infotype (0001).

Infotype 1005 (Planned Compensation) has also been defined for salaried (exempt and non-exempt) jobs. This includes the pay grade type, area, grade, and level. If integration is activated, this information defaults in PA, Infotype 0008 (Basic Pay).

We'll now create new jobs to align with the "Human Resources" functional area and the "HR Payroll" job family. We'll use Transaction PP01 to create PAYROLL ADMINISTRATOR and DATA ENTRY CLERK, as shown in Figure 3.38 through Figure 3.45.

3 | Foundations of Talent Management

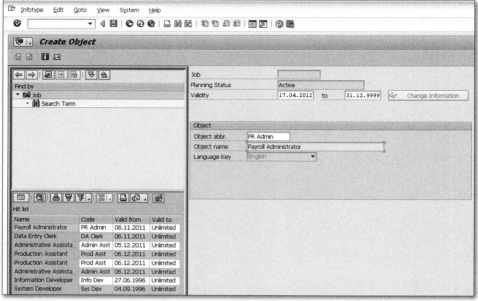

Figure 3.38 Create Job Object—Payroll Administrator

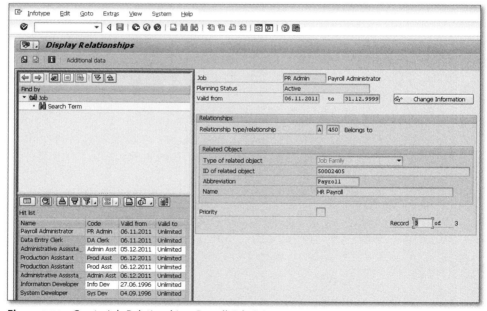

Figure 3.39 Create Job Relationship—Payroll Administrator

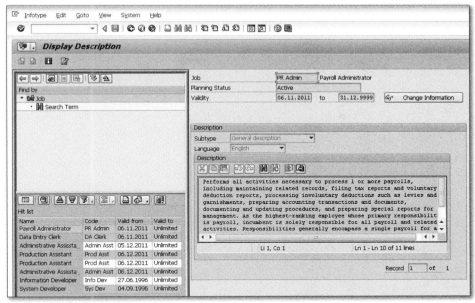

Figure 3.40 Create Job Description—Payroll Administrator

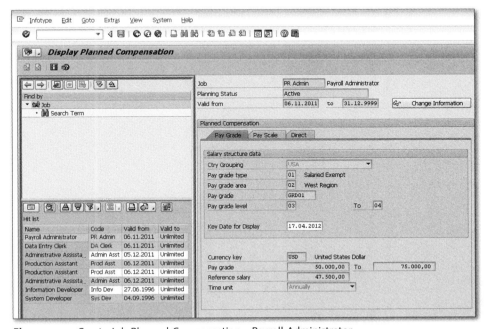

Figure 3.41 Create Job Planned Compensation—Payroll Administrator

3 | Foundations of Talent Management

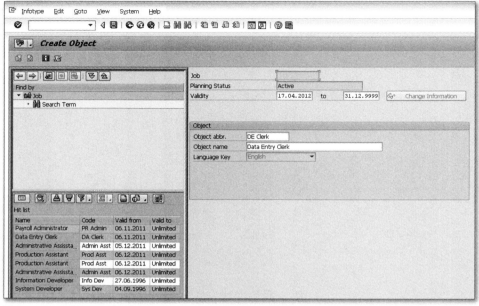

Figure 3.42 Create Job Object—Data Entry Clerk

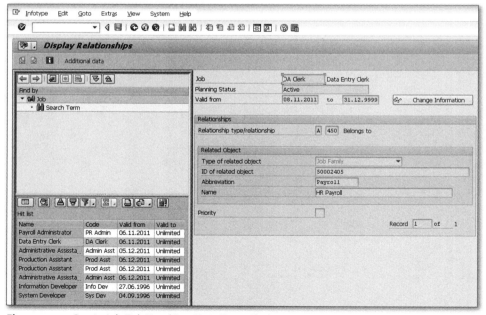

Figure 3.43 Create Job Relationship—Data Entry Clerk

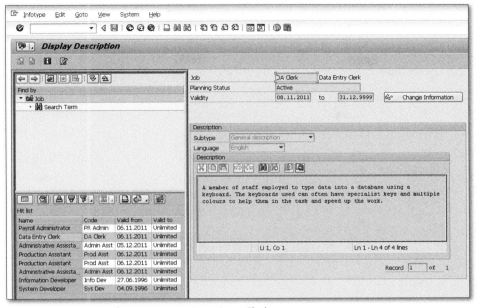

Figure 3.44 Create Job Description—Data Entry Clerk

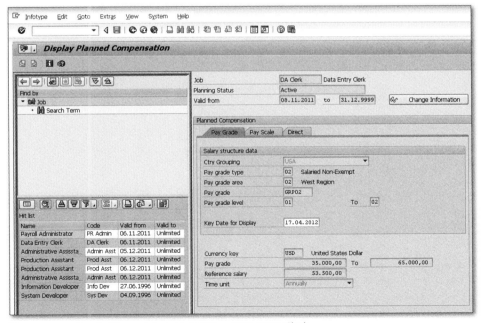

Figure 3.45 Create Planned Compensation—Data Entry Clerk

You follow these same steps to align new jobs with the "Human Resources" functional area and the "HR Talent Management" job family.

3.3.4 Position

From an SAP perspective, jobs are general classifications or groupings for sets of tasks or functions an employee is required to perform within an organization. In that way, the "job" describes a position.

When creating a new position (e.g., an administrative assistant in the Finance department), you can relate it to a job that already exists in the SAP Job Architecture (e.g., administrative assistant). Through this relationship, the position (object type S) automatically inherits the tasks and characteristics of the job. This significantly reduces data entry time because tasks and characteristics don't have to be assigned to each position separately. Instead, they are inherited via the descriptive job. But note that specific tasks and characteristics can also be assigned to positions. Please refer to Section 3.1 on OM for more information on creating positions.

3.3.5 The Importance of SAP Job Architecture

Although the majority of companies that use SAP end up implementing the OM module and PA, most of those organizations overlook the hierarchical functions of SAP Job Architecture and the Qualifications Catalog. The Qualifications Catalog will be discussed later in this chapter, so let's take a look at some of the implications of failing to fully implement a job architecture or implementing one that is poorly designed.

Organizations that don't implement a full job architecture usually find themselves creating one job for every position. This proliferation of jobs and positions can make the following objectives challenging:

- Meeting corporate objectives due to the inability to align the workforce with organizational goals
- Effectively attracting, developing, and leveraging talent
- Aligning talent management efforts with corporate objectives
- Implementing innovative reward strategies (pay for performance and competency, variable pay plans, and long-term incentive programs)

- Efficiently identifying, developing, and tracking high-potential employees best suited to fill certain positions
- Retaining key talent due to the lack of clearly defined career and development plans and personalized learning opportunities
- Effectively gaining useful insight into the workforce to manage human capital, track costs, and determine ROI associated with HR projects
- Deploying the right resource based on skills and availability
- Monitoring scheduling and progress on projects, tracking time, and analyzing results for strategic decision making
- Aligning the right learning paths for employees
- Supporting the movement (mobility) of talent within the organization
- Ensuring transparency regarding opportunities for all employees
- Clarifying expectations (roles and responsibilities) using a common language across the organization

Finally, by not taking the time upfront to implement a job architecture along with OM, PA, and qualifications, organizations can expect increased time and costs in the following areas:

- Job code maintenance
- Implementing SAP workflow
- Implementing OM, PA, and qualifications
- Rework in any or all of the foundational areas
- Ongoing maintenance of the job inventory and monitoring of local job consistency
- Developing a strict governance model for the ongoing job structure

Let's now shift our focus to the Qualifications Catalog.

3.4 Qualifications Catalog

In SAP, organizational competencies are maintained within the Qualifications Catalog. However, before we can talk about the contents or details of the Qualifications

Catalog in SAP ERP HCM, we must first understand the importance of competencies to any Talent Management framework.

3.4.1 Organizational Competencies

Core competencies can be defined on an individual or organizational basis. At an organizational level, core competencies are deep proficiencies that differentiate an organization from its competition. They enable an organization to deliver unique value to its customers, which, in turn, create a company's competitive advantage in the marketplace. In addition, core competencies represent an organization's collective learning. They can take various forms, including technical or subject matter expertise, a reliable (patented) process, and close relationships with customers and suppliers. Understanding core competencies allows companies to invest in the strengths that differentiate them from their competitors and select strategies that unify their entire organization. Organizations should ask what is the underlying skill, ability, knowledge, experience, technology, or process that enables them to provide a unique set of products or services. As a final note, few companies are likely to build world leadership in more than five or six fundamental competencies.

3.4.2 Individual Competencies

At an individual level, core competencies are those that everyone (from the CEO to the mail room clerk) is expected to exhibit on a daily basis. They are used to evaluate individual, team, and organizational performance, and they are the driving force behind successful job performance. They contribute to increased productivity through improved performance, increased ability to use and adapt existing skills to meet new demands, and increased ability to see, create, and exploit new opportunities. Core competencies are also personal attributes or underlining characteristics that enable the successful performance within a job. They state the expected areas and levels of performance and outline what is appreciated and rewarded. Of course, other factors (such as personal values, motivation, and type of work) also play their part in job performance, but those are typically not defined at an individual level.

3.4.3 SAP ERP HCM Qualifications Catalog

Organizations need to structure competencies in a logical way to make them meaningful. To that end, the Qualifications Catalog in SAP ERP HCM contains all of the organizational and individual competencies that are of interest to an organization.

These competencies are used in every application within Talent Management (Learning Solution, SAP E-Recruiting, Enterprise Compensation Management, Performance Management, and Talent Development/Succession Planning). Consider the following competency tenets from an SAP perspective:

- A competency is a knowledge, skill, ability, or experience that allows an employee to perform his or her job. Therefore, a job can be described by its competencies.
- A job inherits its competencies from the job family that describes it and can have additional competencies.
- A position inherits its competencies from the jobs that describe it and can have additional competencies.
- A person's abilities may be described by the competencies they fulfill.

The qualifications and requirements component can be used to define, structure, and manage the Qualifications Catalog. The combination of the qualifications and the organizational structure allow profiles to be created. These profiles can then be used to manage, evaluate, and compare object characteristics and to show both the requirements of a position and the qualifications and career goals (preferences) of a person. You can run profile matchups to find out how suitable certain employees (persons) are for a specific position within the organization.

The Qualifications Catalog contains all of the qualifications that are of interest to an employer. It forms the basis for working with essential subprofiles, including qualifications, requirements, preferences, and dislikes. The following are some of the key features of the Qualifications Catalog:

- **Qualification groups**
  Qualifications can be grouped together into groups based on similarity and then organized hierarchically.
- **Proficiency scales**
  Different proficiency scales can be assigned to each qualification group.
- **Proficiency texts**
  Descriptive texts can be stored for the individual proficiencies of each qualification.
- **Alternative qualifications**
  One or more alternative qualifications can be assigned to a qualification.

- **Depreciation meter**
  The depreciation meter lets you simulate scenarios in which qualifications become outdated or are forgotten if they aren't used. If a qualification for which the depreciation meter information has been defined is assigned to a person, the proficiency of the qualification will change automatically as time passes.
- **Validity period**
  You can specify a validity period for qualifications, which lets you show that certain qualifications expire and have to be renewed at regular intervals (such as licenses, for example).

> **Key Point**
> The validity is calculated separately based on the relationship period. If a qualification is assigned to a person for whom a validity period has been defined, the qualification is automatically deleted from the person's subprofile when the validity period expires.

- **Qualifications overview**
  The historical record of each qualification can be displayed, which provides information on the qualification group, scale, and validity periods.
- **Where-used list**
  A where-used list for each qualification group can be displayed along with every qualification. This helps to supply information on the objects related to the qualification (group) in question.

We'll focus our attention on scales, qualification groups, qualifications, and qualification blocks as they relate to the Qualifications Catalog.

Scales

Scales describe the level of proficiency required for a competency. The following is a list of things to remember about scales:

- Scales are defined by specifying three things: a unique numeric identifier, a unique name, and proficiencies for each scale.
- At least one proficiency scale needs to be defined before qualification groups can be created.
- Quantitative or qualitative scales can be used.

- The worst score should be 1, and the best score should be the highest number on the scale; there should be no gaps in the values.
- Both the Qualifications Catalog and the Appraisal Catalog use scales. Note that the Appraisal Catalog will be covered in more detail in subsequent chapters.
- You can maintain scales using Transaction OOSC.

> **Key Point**
>
> Scales don't always transport well—that is, they don't always arrive at the landscape clients, such as Production, successfully—so double-check to make sure that the scales are set to be transported correctly.

Let's examine the two basic types of scales: quality scales and quantity scales.

Quality Scales

With quality scales, you must define and name every proficiency. You can define up to 9,999 proficiencies per scale, but each needs to have its own user-defined proficiency text.

Table 3.6 provides some examples of quality scales.

Scale	Proficiency
Language Scale	Basic proficiency
	Limited proficiency
	Adequate proficiency
	Full proficiency
	Resident proficiency
3-Point Scale	1-point
	2-point
	3-point
Yes/No Scale	Yes

Table 3.6 Quality Scale Examples

> **Key Point**
>
> Remember the following about Qualifications Catalogs and Appraisals Catalogs:
>
> - In the Qualifications Catalog, a Yes/No scale only needs one proficiency (Yes). However, the Yes/No scale needs both proficiencies (Yes and No) in the Appraisal Catalog.
> - In the Qualifications Catalog, you cannot use the proficiency "0" for rating qualifications or requirements. However, in the Appraisals Catalog, "0" can be used to mean "doesn't exist."
> - You can enter text to describe the individual elements in a quality scale. These proficiency descriptions are then passed on as defaults for every element in the Qualifications Catalog and Appraisals Catalog that is assigned to the scale in question.

Consider these recommendations when creating quality scales:

- The more proficiencies a scale has, the less meaningful the scale becomes, so try not to define any more than 20 proficiencies for a scale.
- Create at least one proficiency for each quality scale. Define it using a unique numeric identifier and a descriptive proficiency text.
- Ensure that all your scales are sorted in ascending order—that the highest proficiency ID value is used for the highest or best proficiency. This will ensure that the suitability percentage is calculated correctly.

We'll now create an example of a quality scale (including proficiencies and descriptions) that will be associated with qualifications in our Qualifications Catalog. The scale will include the characteristics and proficiencies shown in Table 3.7.

Characteristic	Proficiencies
Novice	- Has limited situational perception - Displays rigid adherence to rules or plans - Treats all attributes separately and with equal importance
Competent	- Sees action in terms of longer-term goals - Demonstrates conscious, deliberate planning - Has standardized and routine procedures
Proficient	- Sees what is most important in a situation - Perceives deviation from the normal pattern - Varies decision-making process according to the situation

Table 3.7 Universal Proficiency Quality Scale Characteristics and Proficiencies

Characteristic	Proficiencies
Expert	▶ No longer relies on rules or guidelines
	▶ Has an intuitive grasp of situations based on deep understanding
	▶ Uses an analytical approach when problems occur

Table 3.7 Universal Proficiency Quality Scale Characteristics and Proficiencies (Cont.)

To create the Universal Proficiency quality scale, follow these steps:

1. After logging in, use Transaction OOSC, as shown in Figure 3.46.

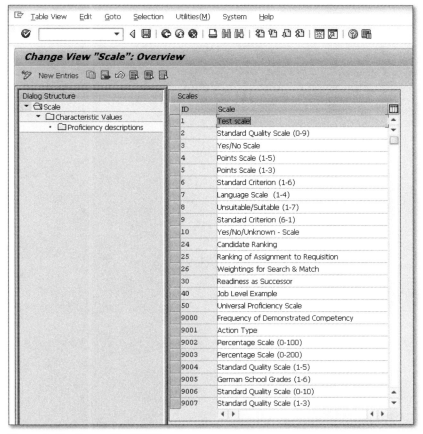

Figure 3.46 Transaction OOSC

2. Select the NEW ENTRIES button, and then enter the ID and the name of the scale. In this case, name the scale "Universal Proficiency Scale," as shown in Figure 3.47.

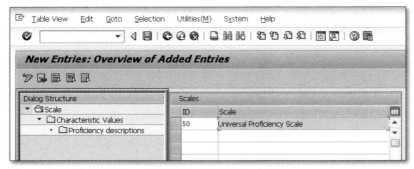

Figure 3.47 New Entries—Create New Scale ID and Name

3. After the scale has been created, highlight the new row and double-click on the CHARACTERISTIC VALUES folder in the left-hand navigation window. Here you'll decide whether to create a quality scale or a quantity scale. Click QUALITY SCALE to create a quality scale, as shown in Figure 3.48.

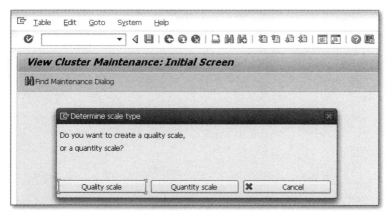

Figure 3.48 Determine Scale Type

After you select the scale type, you can start creating the proficiencies, as shown in Figure 3.49.

Qualifications Catalog | 3.4

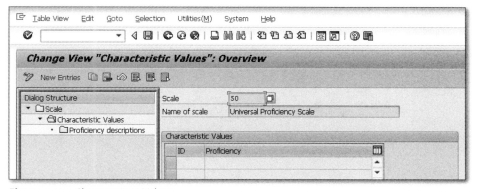

Figure 3.49 Characteristic Values

4. Select NEW ENTRIES, and enter the ID and proficiency name. Save the entries, as shown in Figure 3.50.

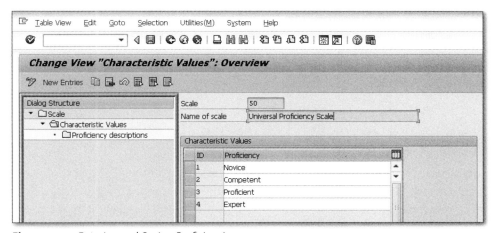

Figure 3.50 Entering and Saving Proficiencies

5. Now you need to create the proficiency descriptions. Highlight the row of the proficiency that you want to create a description for and double-click the PROFICIENCY DESCRIPTIONS folder in the left-hand navigation window shown in Figure 3.51. You then repeat this step for each proficiency.

89

3 | Foundations of Talent Management

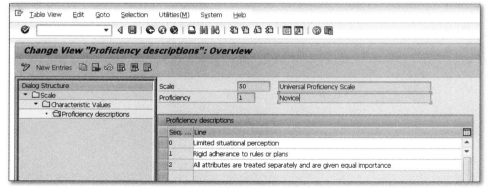

Figure 3.51 New Entries—Proficiency Description

Quantity Scales

For quantity scales, every scale that gets defined also needs to define its highest and lowest proficiency, the interval range, and the unit used to rate the proficiencies.

> **Key Point**
>
> Remember that quantity scales can only be used in the Appraisals Catalog. As mentioned previously, quantity scales and the Appraisals Catalog will be covered in more detail in subsequent chapters.

Qualification Groups

Qualification groups are used to structure the Qualifications Catalog. They can contain both qualifications and additional qualification subgroups. You must assign each qualification group a proficiency scale, which will be inherited by the qualifications in this group. As mentioned previously, qualification groups can also be organized hierarchically.

Now let's create qualification groups and assign the scales that you just created to these groups. The first qualification group will be for the organization (International Software), which you'll create using Transaction SPRO or the menu path HUMAN RESOURCES • PERSONNEL MANAGEMENT • PERSONNEL DEVELOPMENT • SETTINGS • CURRENT SETTINGS • EDIT QUALIFICATIONS CATALOG (see Figure 3.52).

3.4 Qualifications Catalog

Figure 3.52 Edit Qualifications Catalog

Then use the following steps to create the International Software qualification group:

1. Select CREATE at the top of the screen.
2. In the QUALIFICATION GROUP tab, enter "International Software Qual. Catalog" in the free-form text field at the top of the window, as shown in Figure 3.53.

   Remember that the scale proficiencies for each qualification group can be described in more detail by entering user-defined text.

3. Select UNIVERSAL PROFICIENCY SCALE (created earlier) from the SCALE drop-down menu, also shown in Figure 3.53.

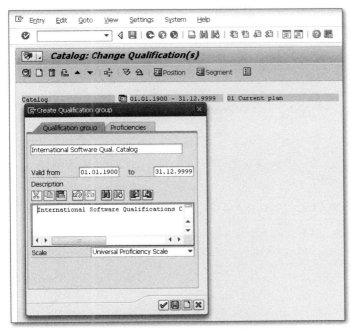

Figure 3.53 Enter International Software Qualification Group

4. Save.

5. Go to the Proficiencies tab. Notice that the proficiencies and descriptions of the corresponding scale (created earlier) have been proposed as defaults. You can overwrite these defaults as required by deselecting the Default checkbox (see Figure 3.54).

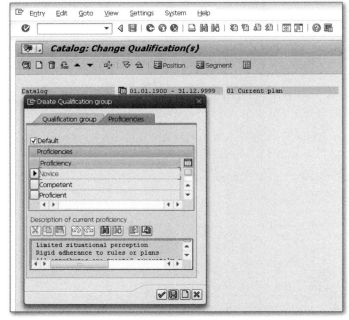

Figure 3.54 Proficiencies Tab with Defaulted Proficiencies and Descriptions

Now let's create another qualification group for the "Human Resources" functional area so that we can eventually align it to the job families, jobs, and positions by taking the following steps:

1. Click the checkbox next to the International Software Qual. Catalog entry.

2. At the top of the screen, choose Entry • Create.

3. Select Qualification Group (see Figure 3.55).

4. In the Qualification Group tab, enter "Human Resources" in the free-form text field at the top of the window (see Figure 3.56).

5. Save.

3.4 Qualifications Catalog

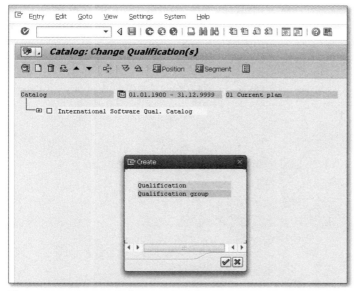

Figure 3.55 Create a Follow-on Qualification Group

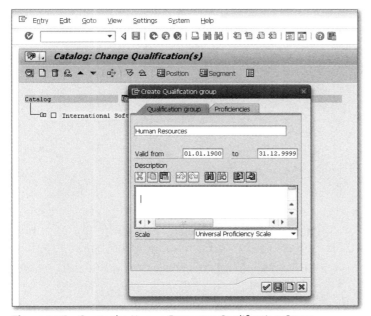

Figure 3.56 Create the Human Resources Qualification Group

Notice that the scale that was created from the International Software qualification group is defaulted into the new HR qualification group, but you can change the scale when or if you create each additional qualification group. This will not be the case when you create qualifications, however.

The proficiencies and descriptions are also defaulted in the PROFICIENCIES tab shown in Figure 3.57.

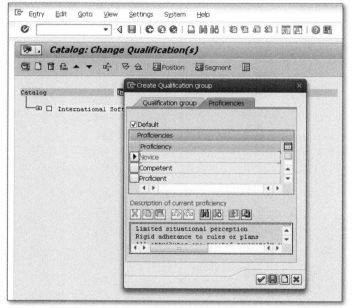

Figure 3.57 Human Resources Proficiencies Tab

Qualifications

Qualifications can include further qualifications, but they can't be inserted directly under the root node of the catalog. Just like with the qualification groups, you can enter additional text to describe the proficiencies for each qualification in more detail. The proficiency descriptions of the corresponding qualification group are defaulted (if there are any); otherwise, the proficiency descriptions of the corresponding scale are defaulted (once again, if there are any). These description defaults can be overwritten based on requirements.

Now, let's create three qualifications in the "Human Resources" qualification group: Personnel and Human Resources, Judgment and Decision Making, Fluency of Ideas.

Use the following steps to create the first qualification (Personnel and Human Resources), and repeat this process for the other two qualifications:

1. Click the checkbox next to the HUMAN RESOURCES entry.
2. Select CREATE at the top of the screen.
3. Select QUALIFICATION instead of QUALIFICATION GROUP.
4. In the QUALIFICATION tab, enter "Personnel and Human Resources" in the free-form text field at the top of the window, followed by the description in the optional free-form text field, as shown in Figure 3.58.
5. Save. Notice that the scale from the previous qualification groups is defaulted and can't be changed.

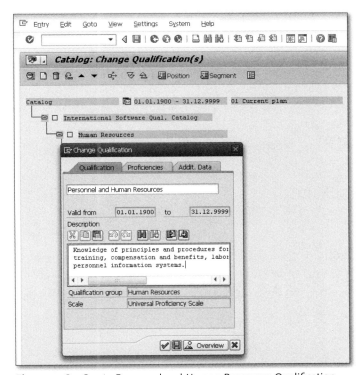

Figure 3.58 Create Personnel and Human Resources Qualification

Just as with the qualification groups, the proficiency descriptions are defaulted in, but they can be removed by deselecting the DEFAULT checkbox, as shown in Figure 3.59.

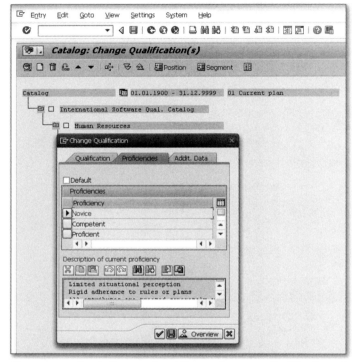

Figure 3.59 Create Personnel and Human Resources Qualification—Proficiencies Tab

There are additional conditions that can be maintained within the qualification, but we won't spend much time on them here:

- **Depreciation meter**
  Situations where qualifications are forgotten if they aren't used regularly, as shown in Figure 3.60

- **Validity period**
  The period in which a qualification is valid without having to be renewed or refreshed, as shown in Figure 3.61

Qualifications Catalog | 3.4

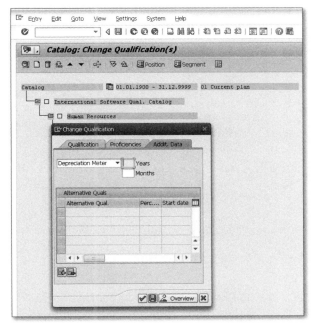

Figure 3.60 Depreciation Meter

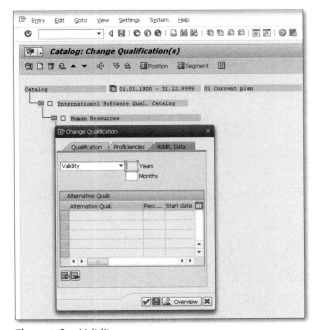

Figure 3.61 Validity

Qualification Blocks

Qualification blocks allow you to bundle together individual qualifications from diverse qualification groups (with different scales) and assign them in a block to other objects to map qualifications and requirements. This serves the same purpose as assigning individual qualifications to other objects but can also significantly reduce maintenance time.

You can define qualification block objects and relationships using Transaction PP01. Qualification blocks can also be assigned to one another there, thus creating a hierarchy of qualification blocks. Using Transaction PPPM, you can assign qualification blocks to persons as qualifications and to positions, jobs, and job families as requirements.

Follow these steps to assign qualification blocks to the job families that were created earlier:

1. Go to Transaction PPPM.
2. Search for job families in the JOB FAMILY folder in the left-hand navigation menu. HR PAYROLL and HR TALENT MANAGEMENT families are displayed, as shown in Figure 3.62.

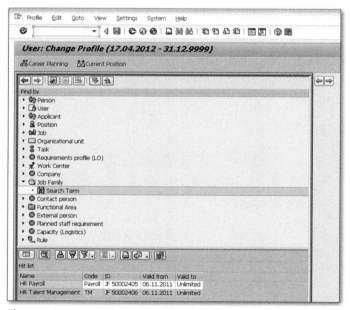

Figure 3.62 Transaction PPPM—Job Families

Qualifications Catalog | 3.4

3. Double-click on the HR PAYROLL job family.
4. Choose REQUIREMENTS • CREATE from the menu bar.
5. Search for qualifications to add to the job family requirements.
6. Select all three qualifications that were created in the previous section (FLUENCY OF IDEAS, JUDGMENT AND DECISION MAKING, and PERSONNEL AND HUMAN RESOURCES), as shown in Figure 3.63.
7. Select a proficiency for each qualification (as shown in Figure 3.64), determine whether it's an essential qualification, and choose the start and end dates for each qualification (see Figure 3.65).
8. Save.

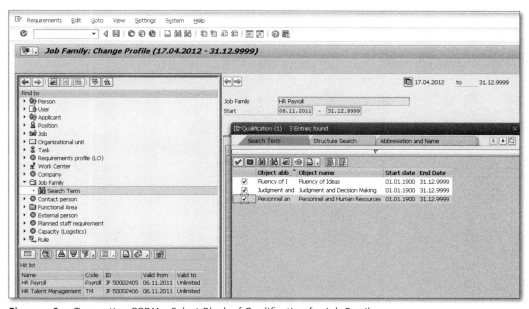

Figure 3.63 Transaction PPPM—Select Block of Qualification for Job Family

3   Foundations of Talent Management

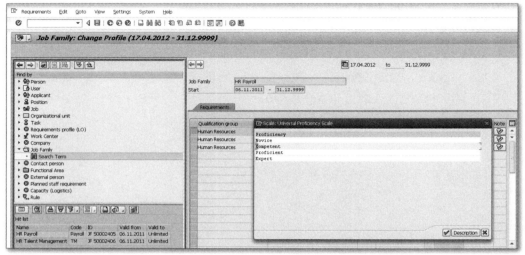

Figure 3.64   Transaction PPPM—Select Proficiency for Each Qualification

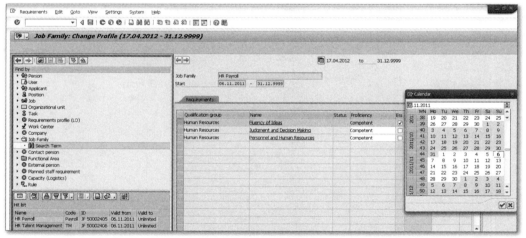

Figure 3.65   Transaction PPPM—Essential Qualifications and Start Date

Figure 3.66 shows that if you repeat the previous steps for job PAYROLL ADMINISTRATOR (created earlier), the qualifications that were added for the HR Payroll job family are now defaulted in the requirements via the inheritance principle.

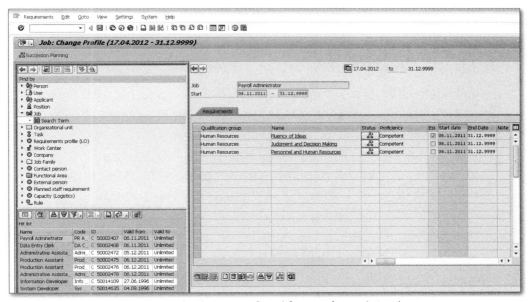

Figure 3.66 Transaction PPPM—Job Inheritance of Qualifications from Job Family

3.5 Summary

In this chapter, we covered the basics of the foundational aspects used in Talent Management. Having a strong OM structure and properly maintaining your PA data are very important factors of a successful Talent Management system.

In the OM module, we explored how you can use the organizational unit objects to create your enterprise structure within the system. Within organizational units, positions and persons are used to populate your organizational plan, making it readily available for the Talent Management modules to use.

We also explored how the SAP Job Architecture was recently enhanced by the functional area and job family, and how these areas further enhance the integration with the Qualifications Catalog to bolster the SAP Job Architecture structure.

With job families, you can classify functions within your enterprise. The job objects reside within these job families. They are defined by the tasks and characteristics assigned to them and serve as a template for creating positions when you create an organizational plan.

This chapter also described core competencies in detail, which is very important because they are used in almost every Talent Management module. They enable an organization to deliver unique value to its customers, which, in turn, creates a company's competitive advantage in the marketplace.

The Qualifications Catalog and scales are essential parts of Talent Management as well. By assigning a proficiency scale to each qualification, you can effectively rank your talent's skills.

We also described many transactions that are used to maintain all of the foundational objects and relationships. Transactions PP01, PPOME, HRTMC_PPOM, HRTMC_PPOS, and HRTMC_PPOC will help you here.

In the next chapter, we'll dive into the core of this book: the SAP ERP HCM Talent Management modules. This is a very important chapter because it will describe the processes that Talent Management follows.

The SAP ERP HCM Talent Management suite is an incredibly powerful set of tools that can not only improve your current HR processes but also ensure maximum integration, solid performance, and information integrity.

4   How SAP Defines Talent Management

Now that you have an understanding of the foundational components of SAP ERP HCM Talent Management, let's explore how SAP delivers its Talent Management solutions. (Remember that we'll reference SAP ERP HCM Talent Management as Talent Management from here on.)

When we talk about Talent Management, we look at how to properly manage your company's talent using SAP's own technology and frameworks. SAP is widely known for its stability and capability of housing very large amounts of data. The data models and frameworks used in Talent Management are no exception to this standard. It is common for a Talent Management system to house hundreds of thousands of employees, candidates, and users, as well as millions of records.

Talent Management is broken up into individual modules based on common business processes and practices. The division of these individual business processes into their own modules allows customers the flexibility to implement them where needed.

Talent Management consists mainly of five core modules. In this chapter, we'll discuss the SAP E-Recruiting, Performance Management, Enterprise Learning, Enterprise Compensation Management (ECM), and Talent Development/Succession Planning modules and their common business processes. Each module in the system is essentially a set of business functions that need to be imported and activated in your system. These business functions will help you accomplish a certain task within Talent Management. Each follows its own business logic, workflow, and screens independent of the others.

Consequently, the business functions can only be activated and used on an individual basis. You can implement one module at a time and fully use its functionality without activating or using any of the other modules. However, implementing more than one Talent Management module greatly expands your system's functionality and interoperability. The more modules you implement at your company, the more likely you'll be to successfully manage your company's talent.

In this chapter, we'll cover the five core modules, their respective processes, and how they can develop a successful talent management system. We'll also discuss primary integration points to one another. These processes and integration points will be put into practical use in Chapters 5 through 8, which feature real-world examples of these modules in action. Those chapters will walk through the entire lifecycle of an employee, as it relates to Talent Management.

Let's start with the module that brings in outside talent and makes them part of your company.

4.1 SAP E-Recruiting

SAP E-Recruiting, which we'll refer to here as simply E-Recruiting, has come a long way over the past few years. Introduced to the market in 2004, it's now on its third release, which is version 6. Each of the subsequent enhancement packages since its release has greatly improved the functionality and usability of E-Recruiting.

E-Recruiting is based on SAP's most advanced technology and has powerful integration with many of SAP's cutting-edge products, such as SAP NetWeaver Business Client, SAP NetWeaver Portal, and SAP NetWeaver Business Warehouse, as well as the other Talent Management modules. Many great features have been added recently, and E-Recruiting is definitely making its presence known in the market.

E-Recruiting offers support for talent relationship management by giving organizations the ability to develop and draw from a qualified, global pipeline of internal and external talent. Recruiters can take advantage of this talent pool to quickly find the staff they need, collaborating closely with hiring managers throughout the hiring process. This module is used to create job requisitions, source and screen candidates, hire qualified candidates, and coordinate on-boarding activities for new hires.

E-Recruiting also lets users manage all recruiting activities with process templates. Leveraging these process templates makes E-Recruiting a global solution for talent acquisition.

E-Recruiting comes with many flexible tools that can handle high-volume recruiting with efficiency, objectivity, and collaboration from all members involved in the recruiting process. It also uses SAP's Internet Communication Framework (ICF), which allows for web-based interaction for all users and integration with partner solutions. Also, SAP NetWeaver Process Integration (formerly known as Exchange Infrastructure) can be leveraged to enhance the recruiting process with these partner solutions.

> **Related Resources**
>
> All of these functions can be found in great detail in *E-Recruiting with SAP ERP HCM* by Jeremy Masters, Christos Kotsakis, and Venki Krishnamoorthy, which is based on EhP 4 (SAP PRESS, 2010). In this chapter, we'll cover the main recruiting process, as well as some of the main features that are new in EhP 5.

Let's start with the main business processes of E-Recruiting, which drive the core functionality of the system. By exploring the system by process, you can get a good idea of the overall recruiting process as a whole as defined by E-Recruiting. We'll then explore the integration points with the other Talent Management modules. First, let's look at these business processes and how they fit into the talent acquisition process.

4.1.1 E-Recruiting Process

E-Recruiting has many great features, which range from requisition creation approval to candidate offer correspondence. This module also has many different roles associated with it, such as recruiters, candidates, and hiring managers, just to name a few. Many more features are being added with every released enhancement package. So how do we organize these functions?

Instead of looking at E-Recruiting from a role perspective, let's explore this module from an end-to-end business process lens. By splitting up E-Recruiting into processes by function, we can look at some of these functions in the context of use. So, looking at E-Recruiting from a business process point of view, we can break down this module into five processes: requisition, source, screen, interview, and hire.

These five processes will cover the main functions in E-Recruiting. Because the main purpose of the module is to hire a new employee from an Internet application,

4 | How SAP Defines Talent Management

these processes are used in sequence. Stringing them together presents us with the end-to-end course of action, shown in Figure 4.1.

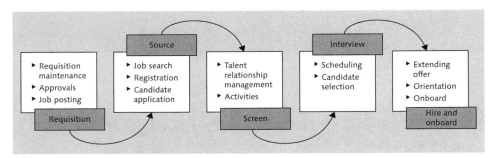

Figure 4.1 E-Recruiting End-to-End Process

In this chapter, we'll look at each process at a high level and cover the new features that are included in the new EhP 5 for E-Recruiting. (Again, we recommend that you reference *E-Recruiting with SAP ERP HCM* for more information.) Let's take a look at the requisition process first, which is the first step to hiring an employee into your company.

Requisition Process

Creating and maintaining a requisition is the first step in the entire E-Recruiting process. Chapter 5 will discuss this process in detail, as there are many areas of the core SAP ERP HCM that factor in to properly creating a requisition.

Requisition is the process of recording the skills and experience that are required by an organization for a specific role. By putting these skills, experience, and requirements into the E-Recruiting system, you can create a requisition, posting, and publication. These three pieces of information will connect an open position to an Internet candidate.

E-Recruiting makes creating and publishing a requisition simple and allows for deep integration with the Organizational Management (OM) module, Jobs Catalog, and Qualifications Catalog. We'll discuss these integration points later in this chapter, but for now, note that by integrating with the position and Jobs Catalog, you can effectively match up the requisition information closely with the position you're hiring for.

Figure 4.2 shows the Create Requisition screen, which shows some of the fields that are used during requisition creation.

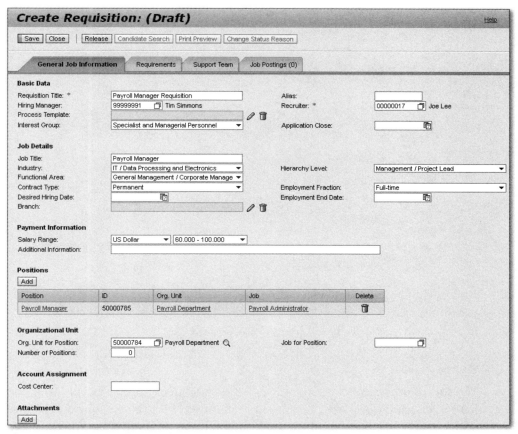

Figure 4.2 Requisition Creation Screen

The purpose of the requisition process is to release a job posting to the Internet. This is done by creating and releasing the requisition, job posting, and publication. The publication can either be released to external candidates or internal candidates, depending on whether your organization wants to post the job to employees, external users, or both. Figure 4.3 shows how flexible the E-Recruiting module is for creating and managing its publication channels.

4 | How SAP Defines Talent Management

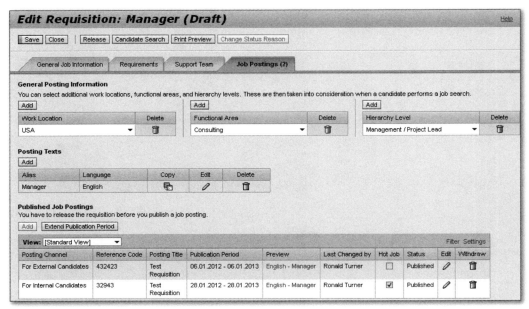

Figure 4.3 Publications Screen in Requisition Process

After the publication has been posted, each candidate will then be able to find the job on the search screen and eventually register in the system. This leads directly into the next step of E-Recruiting: the source process.

Source Process

The source process refers to the procuring of candidates in the system. After you have a requisition in place, the job information will be available for candidates to search on. Depending on which publication channel the job was posted to (i.e., internal or external), candidates can search using a number of criteria fields. After they find a job they want to apply to, the candidate should create a profile and submit an application to the requisition.

For the purposes of this chapter, we'll cover the basics of the source process. Candidates entering the system generally can either go directly to the Search page or immediately create a profile for themselves instead. If candidates search for a job first, they will be taken directly to the Job Search screen, where they can input specific criteria.

After the candidate searches for a job and the results appear, the candidate can perform several other tasks using the following buttons:

- ADD FAVORITE
- SAVE SEARCH QUERY
- TELL A FRIEND

These functions are shown in Figure 4.4, which also offers sample search results.

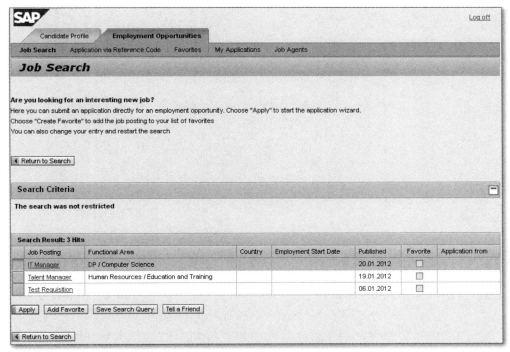

Figure 4.4 Add Favorite, Save Search Query, and Tell a Friend Functionalities

If the candidate finds a job of interest, he can apply to the job directly. But first, the candidate must complete a registration process that allows the candidate to input information about himself, pick a user name and password, and verify his email address.

Once registered, the candidate is now an official user in the system. The candidate can create applications to postings and a candidate profile. These are particularly important because they retain information that recruiters and hiring managers can search, rank, and track.

Let's take a look at the basic Candidate Profile creation screen, shown in Figure 4.5.

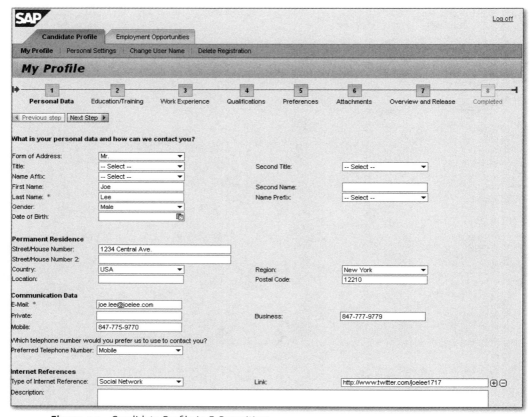

Figure 4.5 Candidate Profile in E-Recruiting

The Candidate Profile and Application screens are nearly identical. However, in the Application screen, recruiters and hiring managers can input Desired Qualifications and Questionnaires to further evaluate the candidate for the requisition. After the candidate has filled out all of the required information in an application, the individual can submit the application and unlock his profile so it can be searched upon by recruiters.

The recruiter can now view the candidate that has just applied to the requisition in order to rank, assess, and perform activities in the next process: the screen process.

Screen Process

The screen process begins with an analysis of application materials submitted by applicants in response to the announcement of an open position. Candidates that apply to a requisition in the system will automatically be added to the recruiter's Power Object Work List (POWL) queries for that requisition. These POWL queries supply recruiters with additional information; at a glance, they can see the candidate count for a requisition, the publications open, and the statuses.

From the POWL queries, you can navigate directly to a requisition and view the candidates that have applied to it. Here, E-Recruiting automatically places candidates into different tabs on the screen according to which phase of the application process they are in. Figure 4.6 shows the Candidate Shortlist for a requisition (in this example, a manager position); the Candidate Shortlist is a tool to sort, view, and compare candidates.

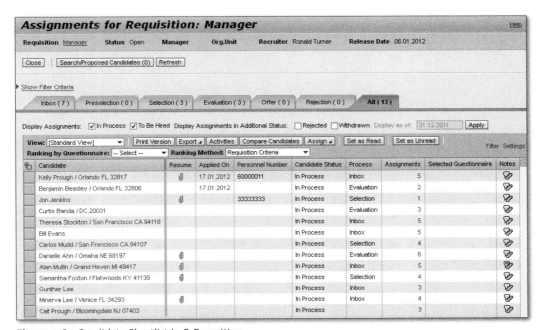

Figure 4.6 Candidate Shortlist in E-Recruiting

In the Candidate Shortlist, you can perform activities on a candidate. Activities are system actions that a recruiter can perform; they help recruiters track, organize, and communicate with candidates. Activities are configurable in the system and can be used to help move candidates along the recruiting process. For example, they can also be used to invite candidates to apply, send candidates for review to a hiring manager, and ask candidates to complete system questionnaires.

You can configure and set up activities by assigning a set of activities to a process template, essentially defining the entire process that recruiters must take to properly categorize or hire the right candidate.

Figure 4.7 shows a list of activities assigned to a process template.

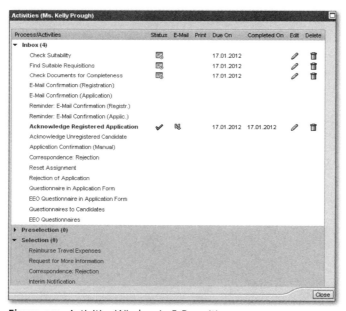

Figure 4.7 Activities Window in E-Recruiting

E-Recruiting facilitates screening candidates and proceeding to the next phase of the recruiting process, which is the interview process.

Interview Process

The interview process is extremely important and differs from company to company. Depending on your company's practices, you can move forward with some interviews even as you continue to track, document, and share the interview process within E-Recruiting. Note that most steps within the interview process take place outside of the E-Recruiting system.

By aligning and defining your interview business process steps within E-Recruiting, you can streamline the process for recruiters. However, for large organizations or even global implementations, your interview process will probably not be the same; however, E-Recruiting's process templates are flexible enough to adapt to custom activities during your interview process to stay in line with your respective business processes.

Recruiters must prepare, execute, and record the steps before deciding to hire any candidate. E-Recruiting allows for these activities to be tracked and documented within the system so that it can be reported if necessary.

Figure 4.8 shows the Job Interview activity, which makes many great functions available for recruiters as they set up an interview.

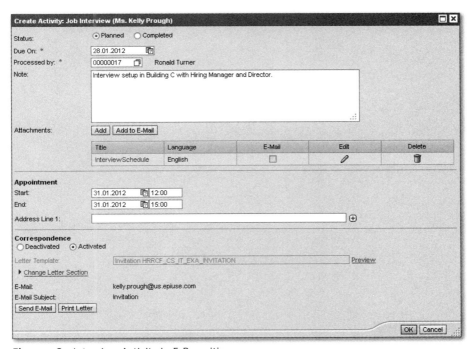

Figure 4.8 Interview Activity in E-Recruiting

When you're ready to hire the candidate, E-Recruiting prepares the appropriate information that is needed to fully onboard your selection.

Hire Process

The hire process involves more than just choosing a candidate to hire. E-Recruiting contains many activities that make rejecting candidates, taking down postings, and closing requisitions easier. These steps are necessary to complete the recruiting process, and E-Recruiting allows recruiters to perform them seamlessly.

After the interview process is completed in the system, recruiters can extend an offer to a candidate directly from the system. Because offer letters generally contain sensitive information, recruiters can compose their own correspondence and send it out through the E-Recruiting system.

Figure 4.9 shows an example of an offer letter.

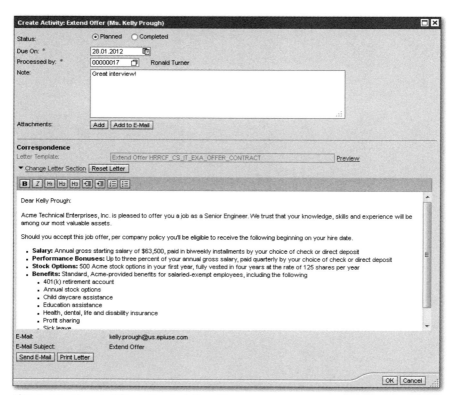

Figure 4.9 Sample Offer Letter in E-Recruiting

Understandably, hiring a candidate to your company requires a lot of administration outside of the E-Recruiting system at the time of hire. This includes all of your onboarding activities, such as seat/cubicle assignment logistics, pre-employment checks, and taxation forms, for example. However, E-Recruiting makes transferring the new hire information to your core HR system as seamless as possible by using the standard data transfer activity. Transferring the data allows for many other Talent Management modules to use and leverage the information collected in E-Recruiting. In Chapter 5, we'll explain where the E-Recruiting information goes after a candidate has been hired.

Now that we've covered E-Recruiting at a high level, let's take a look at some integration points, and then move on to what's new in EhP 5 for E-Recruiting.

4.1.2 Integration Points

E-Recruiting contains many integration points to the other Talent Management modules and systems. By effectively using these integration points, you can increase productivity, interoperability, and visibility to many key functions of the other modules. Let's explore a few of them.

Application Link Enabling

Application Link Enabling (ALE) is a vital part of integration between E-Recruiting and your core HR system. This two-way communication stream is responsible for transferring employees, positions, organizational structures, jobs, and qualifications to your E-Recruiting system. When you hire a new candidate, this interface transfers the new hire information back to your core HR system and populates the new hire's talent profile with the information the new employee previously entered into E-Recruiting. The new employee's profile will be filled out even before their first day on the job, making ALE a significant time saver.

To use ALE, E-Recruiting must be located on a physically different server than your core HR system. See Chapter 9 for more details about the communication between a core HR system and stand-alone E-Recruiting servers.

Organizational Management

As mentioned earlier, your entire organizational structure can be imported via ALE into your E-Recruiting system. If you're implementing E-Recruiting on the same server as your core HR system, the organizational structure will automatically be available.

Organizational units and positions are used at the time of requisition creation and during data transfer back to your core HR system. Organizational unit and position information can be found on the GENERAL JOB INFORMATION tab of the requisition, which tracks the position that you're filling.

Jobs Catalog and Qualifications Catalog

The Jobs Catalog and Qualifications Catalog can also be transferred to your standalone E-Recruiting system as needed. This enhances the E-Recruiting system because you can assign a requisition to a particular job.

Qualifications can also be created in E-Recruiting, which induces an additional level of screening for candidates. Because many qualifications in your core HR system are company-specific, it might not translate well to an outside candidate trying to understand what the "qualification" means. New qualifications created in E-Recruiting fill this gap by allowing you to create more posting-specific qualifications, scales, and proficiencies.

Qualifications, proficiencies, and scales can all be transferred to and used in E-Recruiting, which allows candidates to rank themselves using the qualifications structure. If you decide to hire them, these qualifications will follow them into your system as new employees.

Personnel Administration

A good deal of information gets transferred over to Personnel Administration (PA) after a candidate is hired into the system. The employee's basic information (name, address, phone numbers, etc.) gets transferred along with complex information such as qualifications, education/training, and work experience.

All of this data will appear on the employee's talent profile after the individual is hired into the core HR system, eliminating this step for employees on their first day.

> **Full Personnel Administration Integration**
>
> Within E-Recruiting, several programs new to EhP 5 can be run to sync up the education and work experience information for a candidate/employee in both your core HR system and E-Recruiting. However, to transfer work experience and education/training data to PA from a stand-alone E-Recruiting system to your core HR system, you must have SAP NetWeaver Process Integration (SAP NetWeaver PI) installed. For more information on SAP NetWeaver PI, refer to *SAP NetWeaver Process Integration* (2nd ed.) by Mandy Krimmel and Joachim Orb (SAP PRESS, 2010).

4.2 SAP ERP HCM Performance Management

SAP ERP HCM Performance Management, which we'll refer to as simply Performance Management, allows companies to effectively plan, measure, optimize, and analyze the performance of their workforce from end to end. We'll start with an overview of Performance Management, then move on to the process, new features of EhP 5, and finally integration points.

The main purpose of Performance Management is to set, organize, and deploy goals to entire organizations, teams, and individual employees, as well as track these goals and provide a continuous feedback process. It standardizes a company process for employee review and appraisals, which is critical to successful talent development. It also provides a continuous feedback process that can easily be configured to align with your business process and improve communication between managers and employees.

> **Note**
>
> We'll explore the high-level functions and processes of Performance Management in this chapter. For a much more detailed walkthrough of Performance Management, please refer to *SAP ERP HCM Performance Management* by Christos Kotsakis and Jeremy Masters (SAP PRESS, 2008).

Performance Management consists of a template-based framework. This means that appraisal templates are created and used as the framework to create individual appraisal documents for employees. Appraisal documents are living objects in the system. Throughout the appraisal process, each employee's appraisal document is constantly updated with goals, comments, and notes between the managers and employees. Through customizable roles, additional participants are also able to take part in the appraisal process. You can also set up your appraisal document to require approvals from these extra participants at any point during the process.

SAP delivers two unique solutions for the Performance Management module: the rapid-deployment predefined solution and the highly configurable flexible solution. The predefined solution offers you rapid deployment of appraisal templates for your company, but it doesn't allow for any configuration or customization of these templates. On the other hand, the flexible solution is, as the name suggests, highly flexible in terms of configuration and customization options. The obvious downside of this flexibility is the additional time required to implement it.

Let's explore these two solutions further.

4.2.1 Predefined versus Flexible Solutions

The predefined solution is configured and deployed differently than its counterpart, the flexible solution. The predefined solution is designed to quickly set up, configure, and create appraisal templates and appraisal documents. Its setup is much different from the flexible solution and doesn't have as many features and configuration options.

The predefined solution uses a different graphical user interface (GUI). It incorporates Adobe Flash Islands technology alongside Web Dynpro for ABAP for its appraisal documents. This includes the template creation process, in which the predefined solution uses a step-by-step Web Dynpro for ABAP interface. Predefined templates contain very few configuration options, but they allow for process configurations, which expand the functionality of templates.

Figure 4.10 shows the three-step process of creating a predefined template through which users select checkboxes and rating scales.

The predefined template creation process is straightforward. After a template has been created, a process configuration (shown in Figure 4.11) can then be created to further define what will appear in the predefined appraisal documents.

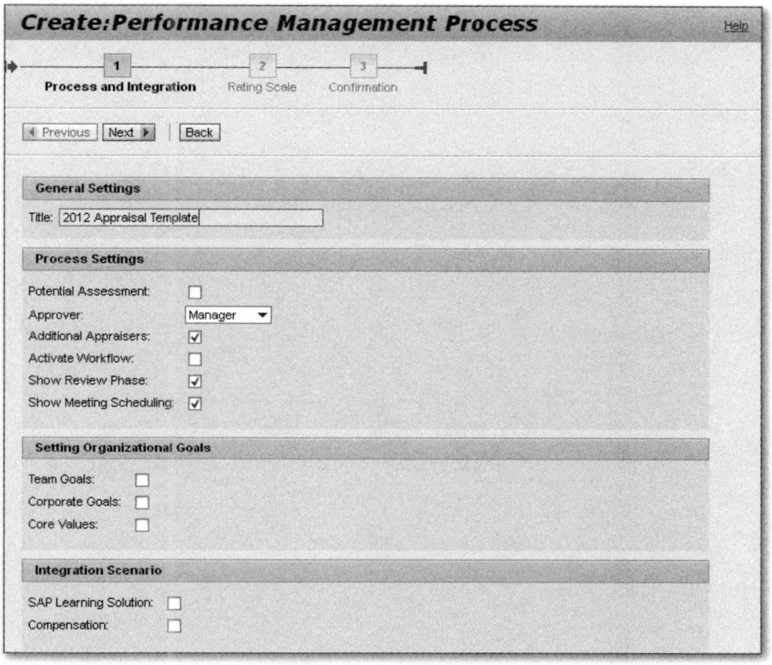

Figure 4.10 Predefined Solution—Template Creation

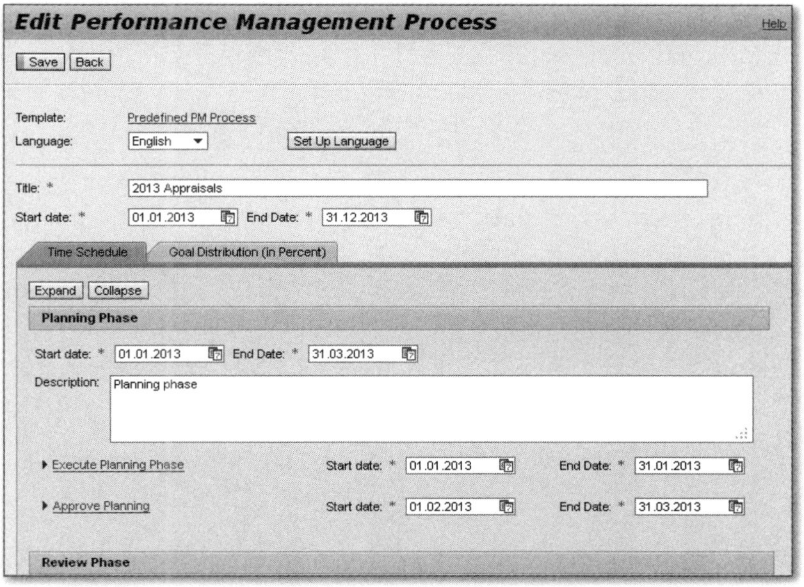

Figure 4.11 Process Configuration for Predefined Templates

Not only is the setup for predefined templates different, but appraisal documents also look different. The resulting predefined appraisal document is shown in Figure 4.12.

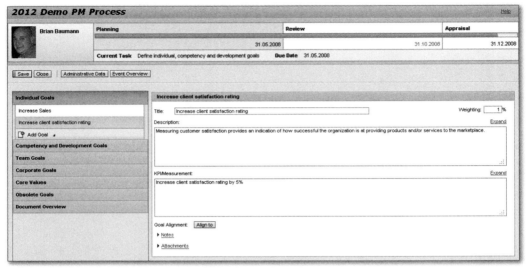

Figure 4.12 Predefined Performance Appraisal Document

The flexible solution's frontend is purely based on Web Dynpro for ABAP, and its template creation and configuration use SAP backend transactions. However, for both solutions, cascading goals uses Web Dynpro for ABAP and Adobe Flash Islands.

Template creation for the flexible solution is a highly configurable process that leaves room for completely custom content. The content is divided into "columns," as shown in Figure 4.13, which also shows how the template creation process for the flexible solution allows for column access and high-level process column configuration.

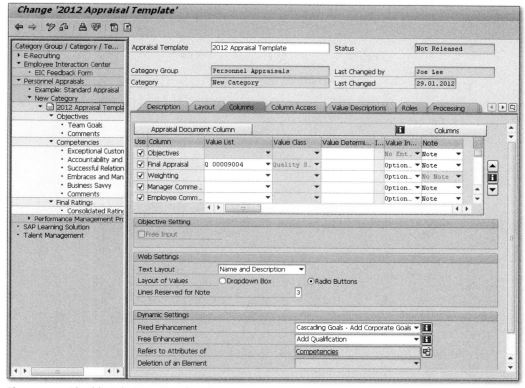

Figure 4.13 Flexible Solution—Template Creation

In terms of the actual appraisal document, only Web Dynpro for ABAP technology is used. The layout, fields, user experience, and process flow are much different as well. But the appraisal document is still highly flexible in that configuration has a huge impact on how the screen looks. If you set up columns and value lists in the template creation, the graphical elements on the screen generate themselves with no need for further customization (see Figure 4.14).

The difference in deployment strategies for each solution is significant. The predefined solution is much more of a rapid-deployment package. It requires minimal setup and contains prepackaged processes for its appraisal document creation, making it a great solution if you need to set up appraisal templates and appraisal documents quickly.

4 | How SAP Defines Talent Management

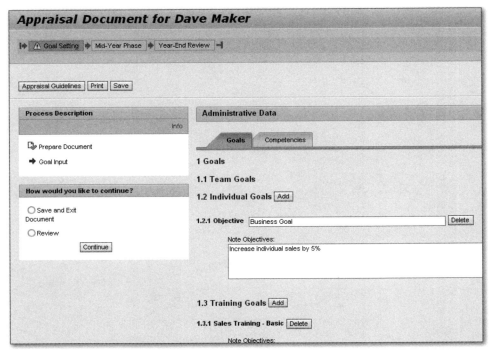

Figure 4.14 Flexible Appraisal Document

We recommend the flexible solution if you want to set up very specific screen elements or highly customize the solution. Because it's based purely on Web Dynpro for ABAP, you can implement customizations easier than with the predefined solution because you wouldn't need to modify Adobe Flash Islands.

However, because the appraisal documents are generated dynamically through configuration, the screen elements and process flow becomes a little harder to customize. Fortunately, Performance Management has many Business Add-Ins (BAdIs) that you can leverage to incorporate any changes you want to implement.

Now that you have a basic understanding of the two solutions, it's important to note that, for the purposes of this book, we'll be using only the flexible solution because it can be highly configured to follow your business process procedures.

So let's now explore the process of Performance Management and the functions of each step.

4.2.2 Performance Management Process

The Performance Management process allows for the creation of appraisal documents that are used to track, review, and set ratings for an employee's yearly performance. Because employee performance tracking is an ongoing process, it's important to use a tool such as Performance Management to make sure that all objectives are organized, monitored, and met. Deploying the Performance Management module and following the defined process both increases the visibility of objectives and promotes communication between managers and employees.

Performance Management is a structured, linear process. That is, you can't move on to the next process before completing the previous. Because appraising employees generally happens cyclically every year, following the process end to end is easy and sequential.

The five processes that make up Performance Management are prepare, plan, review, appraise, and calibrate. In this chapter, we'll look at each process at a high level and cover the new features that are included in EhP 5 for Performance Management.

Figure 4.15 shows some of the highlights of each process step, as well as the end-to-end process.

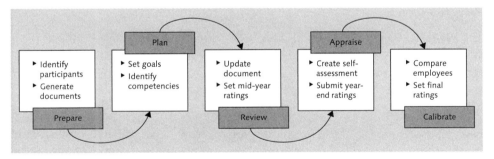

Figure 4.15 Performance Management End-to-End Process

In terms of the actual appraisal documents themselves, four general statuses identify an appraisal's progress through the process. These statuses are configurable, as are the substatuses within each status. Performance Management's configuration is flexible enough to accommodate even the most complex business processes.

In the standard delivered application, there are generally four statuses:

- In Preparation
- In Planning
- In Review
- Completed

These four statuses simply describe the appraisal document itself, not the overall business process of prepare, plan, review, appraise, and calibrate. For example, an "In Planning" status references the appraisal document, not the performance appraisal itself. We'll talk about some of these appraisal document statuses as we go through the main business processes, so let's first take a look at the prepare process, which kicks off the Performance Management sequence by identifying participants and creating appraisal documents.

> **Key Point**
>
> The processes described in the following subsections reflect what is done on the end user side. All Performance Management template creation activities have already taken place, as this should have been done at the time of implementation or before the Performance Management process starts.

Prepare Process

The prepare process involves two very straightforward steps: To start the process of evaluating employees, you must first identify which employees to appraise and then generate the appropriate documents. To this end, Performance Management allows you to easily view employees in your organizational structure and choose which employees to create appraisals for.

Performance Management also allows you to mass-create documents for your employees. By clicking CREATE MULTIPLE on your Performance Management dashboard, a window appears that automatically shows the employees in your organizational structure, as shown in Figure 4.16.

The CREATE MULTIPLE functionality allows managers to define multiple pieces of information in a single step; the validity dates, appraisal template, and employees can all be set in one simple window. Click the CREATE button to create a single appraisal document for these employees.

Figure 4.16 The Create Multiple Screen in Performance Management

If you click on a newly created appraisal document in the dashboard POWL, you'll bring up further administrative information. Here, you can add FURTHER PARTICIPANTS, change the VALIDITY PERIOD, and specify a name for that particular document. You can also change the roles of participants at this time. These fields are shown in Figure 4.17.

Figure 4.17 Creation of an Appraisal Document

After the appraisal documents for your employees have been generated, the next step is to set yearly goals. Goal setting is part of the plan process, which we'll examine now.

4 | How SAP Defines Talent Management

Plan Process

Performance Management's plan process uses intuitive functionality to define, manage, and cascade goals for your employees. As a manager in the system, you can define and push goals to your entire team. After shared goals have been defined, individual goals and competencies are completed for each employee. Chapter 6 goes into further detail about goal setting and assessing, so we'll only cover the basics here.

One best practice is to set four different kinds of goals for employees during this process:

- Corporate goals
- Team goals
- Individual goals
- Training goals
- Competencies

Corporate goals are created by a Talent Management specialist and can be cascaded throughout the organization. An example of a corporate goal is to "Reduce environmental waste." We'll explore corporate goals more in Chapter 6.

As a manager in charge of an entire department, for example, you can also define and cascade specific team goals to all of your reporting employees using Performance Management. Because goal setting is based on your organizational plan, all employees that report to you within the organizational structure automatically appear in the Cascade Goals application, so you can cascade goals with a single click. Figure 4.18 shows the CASCADE TEAM GOALS functionality.

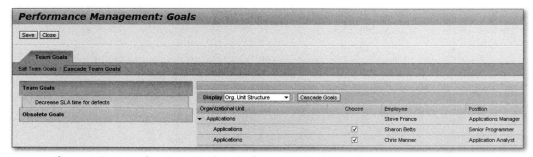

Figure 4.18 Cascading Team Goals in Performance Management

By clicking CASCADE GOALS, you apply the selected goal to the chosen employees, at which point that goal will appear in the applicable appraisal documents.

The plan phase also includes the definition of individual goals. Managers can directly input an employee's goals in their appraisal document, as shown in Figure 4.19.

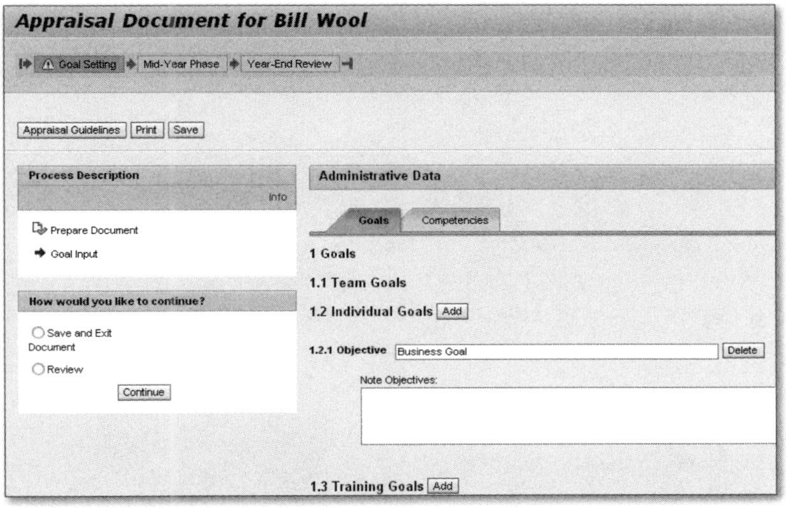

Figure 4.19 Adding an Individual Goal

After individual goals have been added, managers can leverage the integration of Performance Management with another Talent Management module: SAP ERP HCM Learning Solution. This module, which is covered later in this chapter as well as in Chapter 7, organizes and plans ongoing training for employees. In Performance Management, you can browse the Course Catalog to assign courses to the training goals section. For competencies, managers can integrate, view, and add qualifications directly to an employee's appraisal document. Adding target training goals and competencies encourages employees to grow within the company while also strengthening their knowledge for their current tasks.

Now that all of the appraisal documents have been created for employees, and all of the goals have been added to the documents, you can start the review process.

Review Process

After all goals are defined, you can review them before an appraisal takes place. When the appraisal document's status is "In Planning," members involved in the appraisal process have an opportunity to review all goals that will be used to assess performance. This accessibility encourages communication between both the employee and manager, promotes a mutual understanding of goals, and helps set targets and objectives that the employee feels comfortable with attaining. This goal meeting can be done in person or through the system.

Beyond just viewing these goals, managers and employees also have the opportunity to edit them when the review process determines that changes need to be made. You can configure Performance Management to allow these changes before the appraise process.

After all goals have been defined, reviewed, and (if required) edited, the Performance Management process usually waits until mid-year review for any more actions to take place on appraisal documents (see Figure 4.20). Usually, the mid-year review is a midway checkpoint for both managers and employees to assess the progress of the goals and objectives that have been previously set. Managers can rate an employee's progress using configurable drop-down scales and can rank employees based on their performance for the year so far.

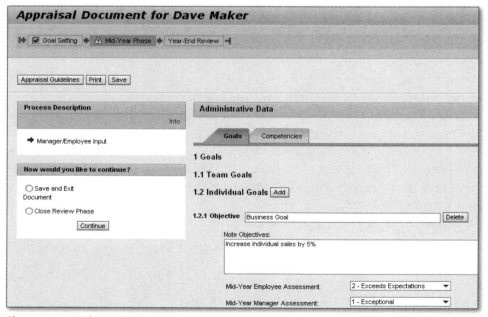

Figure 4.20 Mid-Year Review

After the mid-year review, the document status changes from "In Process" to "In Review." Remember that you can define exactly how the mid-year review process will flow to fit your business process thanks to the highly configurable nature of the Performance Management module.

Appraise Process

Following the mid-year review, the next step in Performance Management is the appraise process. Because this step generally comes at the end of the year for an employee, we'll cover it in detail in the progression phase discussed in Chapter 8.

During the appraise process, the employee gets a chance to create a self-assessment. In this way, employees can document their own achievements and progress toward the defined goals, which promotes communication between managers and employees.

Like the mid-year ratings, managers and employees can complete year-end ratings at this time. This is a configurable field that allows them to leverage and define the scale, making the ratings and rankings more meaningful for both managers and employees (see Figure 4.21).

Each goal and competency can be rated individually during the year-end rating, which is also known as the final appraisal. You can configure the system to incorporate a final appraisal, which is essentially an overall rating for that employee for the entire year. If you properly set up the integration, this rating can be used in the Enterprise Compensation Management (ECM) module to determine merit increases.

In the standard system, the status of the document gets changed to "Completed" after the year-end rating is finished. This means that no more changes can be made to the document, and the appraisal process is complete for the flexible solution.

However, for the predefined solution, one more process step exists. This step is very useful for managers and is a great way to compare the performance of all employees at the same time.

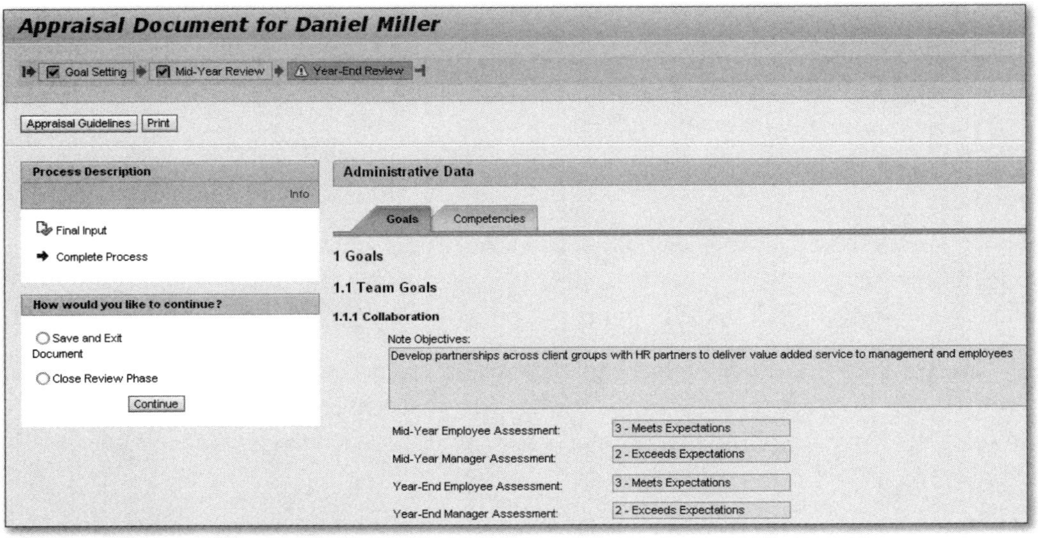

Figure 4.21 Year-End Review

Calibrate Process (Predefined Only)

The calibrate process is the additional step that follows the year-end review for Performance Management's predefined solution. It lets managers view and compare all of their employees' appraisal document ratings at once based on two chosen criteria. These two dimensions can then be viewed in either a graph or a chart format based on Adobe Flash Islands technology, as shown in Figure 4.22.

The calibrate process is useful when companies use Performance Distribution Models. When a manager must only give a certain percentage of employees a top-tier rating, this tool allows for the manager to easily view all of their employees side by side based on the defined dimensions. After the manager has determined the performance distribution, the manager can branch directly to the employee's appraisal document and edit the valuation.

Figure 4.22 Calibrate Process

4.2.3 Integration Points

Performance Management contains many integration points to the other Talent Management modules. Because Performance Management refers to your employees' achievements and tracks their progress through your company, SAP heavily uses the information in the other modules so that managers are able to make the best determination possible for their employees' goals, competencies, and ratings throughout the year.

Each of these integration points will be discussed further in Chapter 6 and Chapter 8. Because this module is a crucial part of Talent Management, we'll explore how data flows through this module in more detail in the later chapters.

Organizational Management

Performance Management seamlessly integrates with the OM module; you can see this when employees and other organizational units that report to you automatically appear in the CASCADE GOALS list. Another time Performance Management and the OM module coincide is when managers use the CREATE and CREATE MULTIPLE functions during appraisal document creation.

Personnel Administration

When choosing employees to cascade goals to or create appraisal documents for, the information that is provided is technically a cross between PA and OM. An employee's name and organizational assignment information is derived from PA.

Talent Development

The final appraisal within Performance Management touches many areas of Talent Development and the Talent Profile. It can be displayed in the following areas, which we'll discuss in Section 4.5:

- Talent Profile for Managers and Talent Management Specialists
- Talent review meeting
- Talent assessment—manager calibration
- STVN SuccessionPlanning

SAP Learning Solution

You can directly add training courses as actionable items within an employee's appraisal document, depending on how you configure your appraisal template. Fixed enhancements enable you to automatically import required or booked courses for employees.

For goals that are set up to integrate with the SAP Learning Solution, clicking the ADD button on an appraisal document will directly link to the Course Catalog and allow you to add a course type for a goal. This can be done through both the predefined and flexible solutions.

Jobs and Qualifications Catalog

Much like the integration with the Course Catalog, qualifications can be added to an employee's appraisal document. These will appear in the appraisal document under the COMPETENCIES tab. When you add a competency, the Qualifications Catalog supplies you with the qualification options. After a qualification is set to a competency, the coordinating proficiency scale comes along with it. A manager can then set the proper proficiency for that qualification during the appraisal process. Refer to Chapter 3 for more details on qualifications and proficiencies.

Enterprise Compensation Management

The calibrate process integrates with Enterprise Compensation Management (ECM) within the predefined solution. After employees have been evaluated and calibrated, managers can see all of their employee's salaries, deviation percentages, and percent increase or decrease. You can display this information in bar or chart format, along with proposed compensation based on ratings.

4.3 SAP ERP HCM Learning Solution

SAP ERP HCM Learning Solution, or simply Learning Solution for short, is the SAP module for managing, tracking, and deploying a variety of learning courses. Organizations use this module to align learning courses and programs with overall organizational objectives.

Learning Solution is an online-based learning management system that provides for a variety of learning delivery methods. By leveraging different delivery methods in a stable management platform, learners can acquire qualifications and competencies based on the content provided in Learning Solution.

Learning Solution fits into the Talent Management model by providing a means for employees to achieve company goals, align with the company strategy, adhere to regulatory standards, and promote progression within an organization. It accomplishes these tasks by leveraging the foundational components of Talent Management, making it a powerful, integrated tool that manages employees' learning development.

Learning Solution relies on many different components to deliver effective training. The process to set up and deliver these courses is intuitive, and SAP provides the tools to allow for maximum productivity with this module.

Before we look at the process of Learning Solution, it's important to understand the variety of delivery methods that are supported. To understand how it effectively delivers content, let's take a look at the different types of courses that can be delivered and managed through Learning Solution:

- **Training that occurs at a specific time and place**
  This includes both web-based courses and instructor-led training courses at a physical location.

- **Training at a certain time only**
  An example is a virtual classroom session, where an instructor teaches a course through an Internet session.

- **Training anytime or anywhere**
  This includes web-based courseware independent of time and location, as well as online testing, external web courses, and static web-based training.

- **External learning services**
  These are direct links to any other online courseware, virtual classroom, or testing service hosted outside of your organization.

A combination of courses with different delivery methods can be grouped together as a curriculum or as a course program.

Learning Solution is a bit different from the rest of the Talent Management modules. To effectively deliver the content, Learning Solution bases itself on a few key components:

- **Learner Portal**
  This online tool allows the learner to view current courses, complete, book or search courses, review required training and qualifications, and view training history.

- **Instructor Portal**
  This tool allows instructors to manage course participation and activities and view course information.

- **Training Administrator Portal**
  This portal allows administrators to perform their day-to-day training activities and manage all courses with Learning Solution.

- **Training Management**
  This controls learning processes and manages course offerings and extends the functionality available in Training and Event Management; the latter controls training logistics and reporting.

- **Authoring Environment**
  This allows for testing and publishing learning content created in the Authoring Environment or via content creation tools for web-based courses. It supports both the Shareable Content Object Reference Model (SCORM) and Aviation Industry CBT Committee (AICC) standards.

- **Content Management System (CMS)**
  This stores and manages learning content.

- **Online content player**
  This delivers the published learning content to the learner in a web browser when a course is launched from the Learner Portal and communicates the progress back to the SAP system. The content player puts the course together on the basis of learning objectives already achieved by the learner and presents it to the learner in the browser. The learner can navigate forward and backward through the proposed learning path or jump to specific learning units from the table of contents as needed.

- **Offline distribution**
  This enables the packaging of learning material for offline access.

- **Offline content player**
  This enables learners to download offline courses from the Learner Portal. These locally stored courses are listed in the course list, and learners can sync up the offline learning process with their Learner Portal.

Figure 4.23 shows how these different components fit together. You'll also see many of these components in Chapter 7, when we walk an employee through the process.

4 | How SAP Defines Talent Management

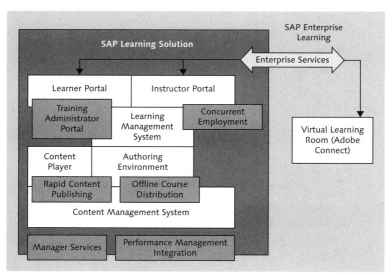

Figure 4.23 SAP Learning Solution Components

As you can see in Figure 4.23, SAP Learning Solution is technically a part of what is known as SAP Enterprise Learning. The main difference between Enterprise Learning and Learning Solution is the Virtual Learning Room, a feature that uses Adobe Connect and requires a separate license. However, Enterprise Learning still uses the core components of Learning Solution and interfaces via Enterprise Services, which acts as the bridge between them.

> **Related Resources**
>
> For detailed information on both SAP Learning Solution and SAP Enterprise Learning, we recommend that you turn to *SAP Enterprise Learning* by Prashanth Padmanabhan, Christian Hochwarth, Sharon Wolf Newton, Sankara Narayanan Bharathan, and Manoj Parthasarathy (SAP PRESS, 2009).

Now let's take a look at the overall Learning Solution process so that you can understand how courses get set up and how learners can access the courses, as well as grasping certain administration functions.

4.3.1 Learning Solution Process

The Learning Solution process involves an end-to-end methodology that begins with creating and uploading content and ends with closing out a course after all participation has been completed. Because Chapter 7 offers a practical use of each process and takes an employee through the end-to-end process, we'll cover each process at a high level at this time.

Based on groupings of similar functions, the main processes within Learning Solution are content, catalog, profile, schedule, participation, and close-out. Like the rest of the Talent Management modules, Learning Solution has many different components working together to deliver a course to an employee. Each process has its own set of features and functions. By following the sequence through the proper processes, you can effectively and efficiently manage this module.

Figure 4.24 shows the Learning Solution cycle from start to finish (i.e., back to the beginning).

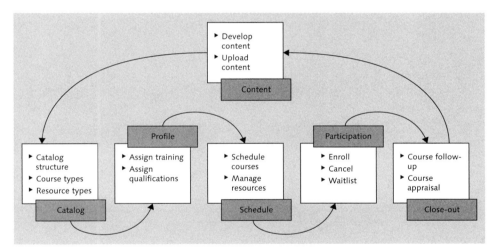

Figure 4.24 Learning Solution End-to-End Process

The Learning Solution process is more of a cycle than a linear process. After the last step is completed, the first step usually repeats soon thereafter. This is usually done on a course-by-course basis. In this chapter, we'll look at each process at a high level. We'll also cover the new Learning Solution features that are included in the new EhP 5.

Content Process

The first phase in the Learning Solution module is to produce and upload content. You can develop content using the SAP authoring tool called the Authoring

4 | How SAP Defines Talent Management

Environment or any of the third-party authoring tools that are available. The Authoring Environment tool shown in Figure 4.25 can be used to quickly and efficiently create course content that can be uploaded to Learning Solution.

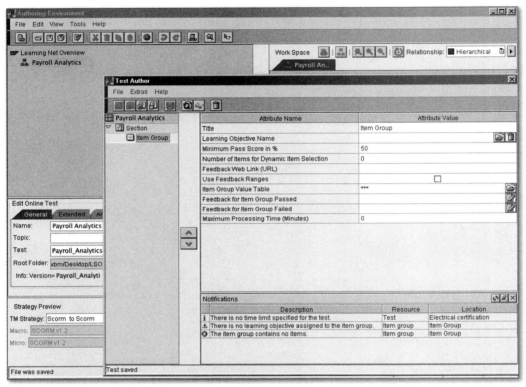

Figure 4.25 Authoring Environment

The content that you upload to Learning Solution must conform to a set of standards, regardless of which authoring tool you use. The most common of these standards are SCORM, SCORM 1.2, SCORM 2004, and AICC.

Standards compliance allows for Learning Solution to track progress, completion status, and comments, as well as many other elements. Content packaged via a third-party content development tool or SAP Authoring Environment can be published to Learning Solution as long as it conforms to one of these standards. Figure 4.26 shows the process of publishing content to Learning Solution.

4.3 SAP ERP HCM Learning Solution

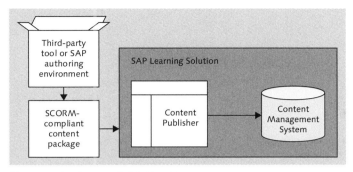

Figure 4.26 Content Publishing Process

After the content has been developed and packaged, Learning Solution gives content administrators an easy way to publish the content. By leveraging these standards, they can transfer data to Learning Solution using the Content Administrator Portal. Figure 4.27 shows CONTENT ADMINISTRATION in the SAP NetWeaver Portal.

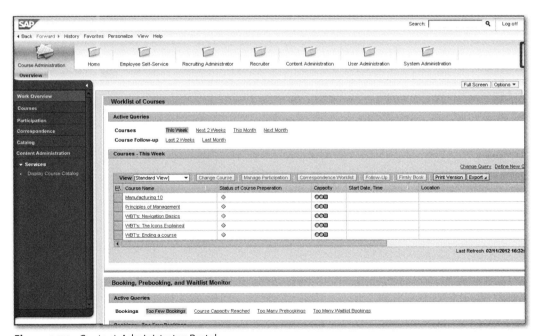

Figure 4.27 Content Administrator Portal

Upon accessing the Content Administrator Portal, the content administrator launches the Rapid Content Publishing tool, inputs the necessary information, and clicks PUBLISH, as shown in Figure 4.28.

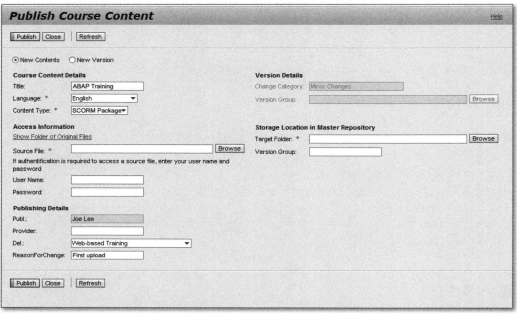

Figure 4.28 Rapid Content Publisher

After the course is published, it becomes part of the CMS and the Learning Solution. Now that we've developed and uploaded the learning content, we can now manage the course type object via the SAP backend using Learning Solution transactions.

Catalog Process

It's now time to catalog the newly created content. You'll need to first assign the content to either a new or existing course type. Transaction LSO_PVCT (shown in Figure 4.29) enables you to see your entire Course Catalog structure, as well as perform functions on course types and course groups. This transaction will also allow you to manage the relationships between all of your courses and groups.

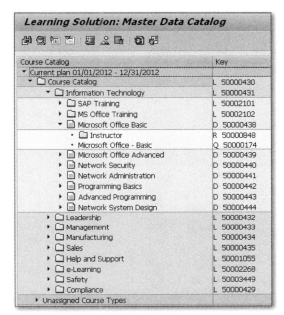

Figure 4.29 Transaction LSO_PVCT

Transaction LSO_PVCT allows you to create course groups and assign course types to them or assign them to a larger course group or Course Catalog. This transaction also shows the qualification that is imparted by the course type, as well as instructor information. By using Transaction LSO_PVCT, you can easily maintain all of the relationships for your entire Course Catalog, resulting in easy and effective maintenance of course types and course groups. Figure 4.30 shows a few of the relationships that can be created and maintained in this transaction such as COURSE GROUP, PERSON, and USER relationships. See Chapter 7 for more details on these specific relationships.

Another important function of this transaction is assigning qualifications to your course types. This allows the automatic transfer of the qualification to employees after they have successfully completed a course. However, this applies only to web-based training. Instructor-led training requires that an instructor manually assigns the qualification to an employee after the instructor decides that the employee successfully completed the course. Chapter 7 offers more details about the end-of-course procedures.

4 | How SAP Defines Talent Management

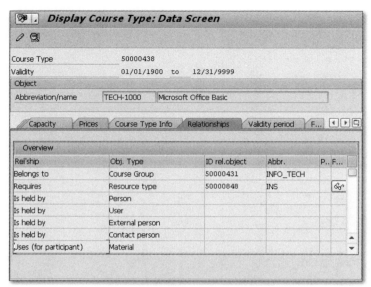

Figure 4.30 Relationships for a Course Type in Transaction PVCT

Profile Process

Learning Solution allows managers to assign mandatory courses for learners—an activity that also assigns the course to the Learner Portal so that employees can easily view, launch, and participate in courses within the system. These courses will be part of the learner's profile.

SAP provides an intuitive frontend application within the Administrator Portal to manage and assign mandatory courses for employees. Administrators use the Manage Required Courses functionality to assign mandatory courses based on individual, position, or organizational criteria. For example, an administrator can assign a mandatory class for one contractor, all contractors, or the Contracting department as a whole. Figure 4.31 shows the Manage Required Courses application.

This application lets you the search by organizational units, jobs, positions, persons, or any combination of those objects. After they have been selected, the application shows the mandatory courses that are assigned to those objects. Figure 4.32 shows an example of required courses for a sample employee, and what it looks like in the Mandatory Required Courses application.

SAP ERP HCM Learning Solution | **4.3**

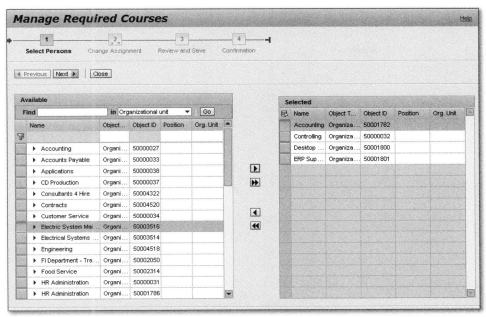

Figure 4.31 Selection of Organizational Units in the Manage Required Courses Application

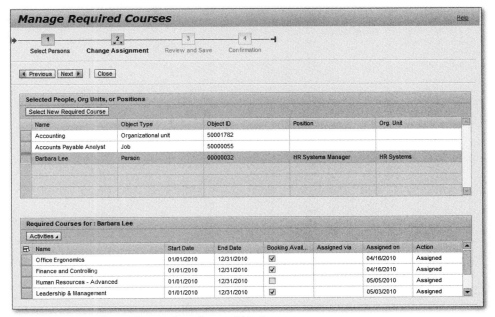

Figure 4.32 Mandatory Courses for a Person Object

Figure 4.32 shows all of the course type information for the mandatory courses on an object. This dashboard displays at-a-glance information so that you can easily determine which courses are assigned, as well as scheduling availability and other assignments.

Other activities can be performed on courses within this application. Administrators can change course validity periods either one by one or en masse, or quickly delete assignments from this screen entirely. After an object has been selected on the Change Assignment screen, you can click the SELECT NEW REQUIRED COURSE button to display and assign courses to an object type. Figure 4.33 shows how a course can easily be assigned to an entire organizational unit, job, position, or person.

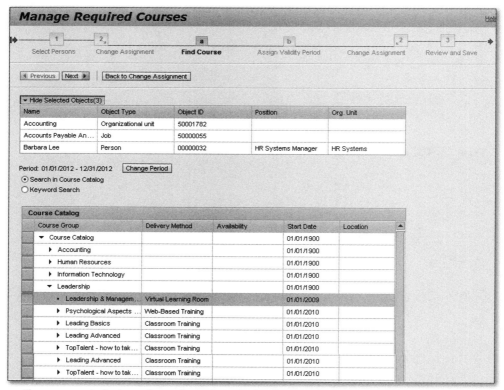

Figure 4.33 Assigning a Course to an Organizational Unit, Job, Person, or Position

After mandatory courses have been assigned to organizational units, jobs, positions, and individual persons, the learner will have a profile that contains all of these courses. Administrators can now book participants to courses, which is done in the schedule process.

Schedule Process

Within the schedule process, the Manage Participants function lets you manage prebooking, individual and mass booking, waitlisting, and cancellation of booked courses.

Much like with the Manage Required Courses application, you can use the Manage Participants application to filter through Organizational Units, Jobs, and Positions to book a Person. You can view booking information or book for individual employees or multiple employees at a time. Figure 4.34 shows the Manage Participants application, along with some of the functions available for that application, such as BOOK NEW COURSE FOR ALL and PREBOOK COURSE.

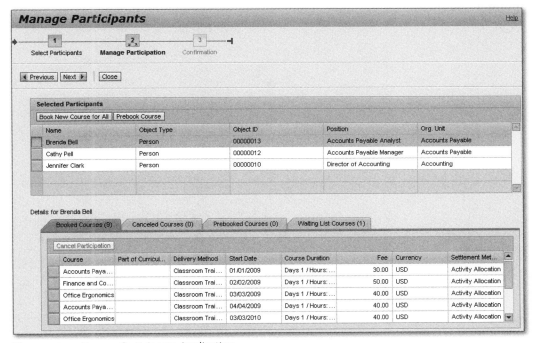

Figure 4.34 Manage Participants Application

You can maintain individual course information in the schedule process using the Administrator Portal. The Course Date application is a graphical tool to manage important course information, such as the course schedule, physical learning space, instructors, and prices. This intuitive application includes many more functions that can be leveraged to manage a successful course. Figure 4.35 shows the Create Course Date application and some of the included functions, such as location management, instructor management, and pricing.

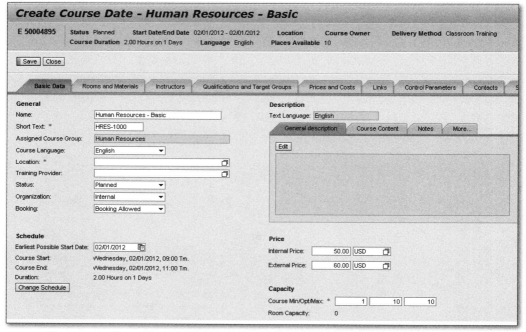

Figure 4.35 Course Date Application

The Course Date application is a robust tool to help administrators properly manage their courses. All of the information that is needed to administer a course is within this application, including qualification information.

The next step is the participation process—the time for the employee to actually take the course through the Learner Portal within Learning Solution.

Participation Process

Within the participation process, managers and learners can both book themselves for courses and then attend them. Within the portal, a manager has the ability to book the reporting employees to a course. As a manager, you can access this application via the menu path TEAM • EMPLOYEE COURSE ASSIGNMENT • MANAGE PARTICIPATION. Figure 4.36 shows the Manage Participants application for managers.

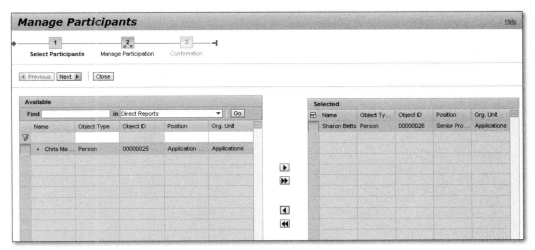

Figure 4.36 Manage Participants—Manager View

Just like administrators, managers use the Manage Participants application to book employees to courses. However, this application will automatically default the assignment of the course for any employee reporting to that manager. This makes it very easy and efficient to book employees to a course.

Employees can also manage all of their learning and enroll themselves in a course using the Learning Portal, which is shown in Figure 4.37. Within the Learning Portal, an employee can see mandatory training (MY REQUIREMENTS), history of courses (MY HISTORY), and current courses they are enrolled in (MY TRAINING).

Employees can also search the catalog structure for courses. This search is similar to what administrators and managers see when they look for a course. When an employee finds a course of interest, clicking on the link brings up all of the course information. Scheduling, booking, and course information can all be viewed by employees. Figure 4.38 shows a STATIC WEB-BASED TRAINING course, as seen by the learner.

4 | How SAP Defines Talent Management

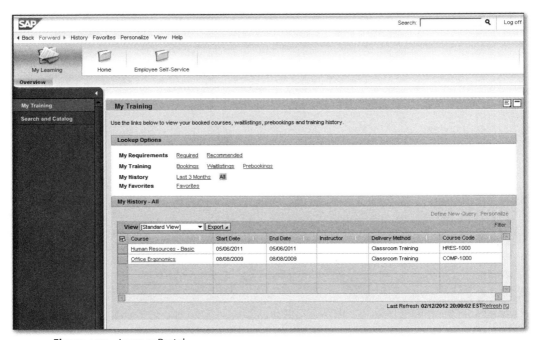

Figure 4.37 Learner Portal

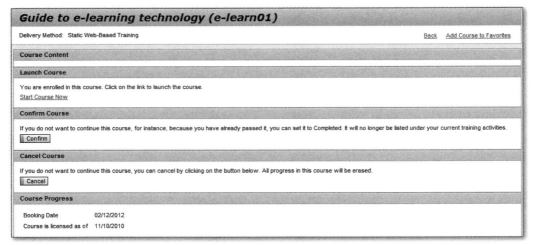

Figure 4.38 Course Information for an Employee

Employees can confirm or cancel their enrollment for a course and also directly launch any web-based training from within the Learner Portal. This can be any web-based content, whether it's hosted by the SAP CMS, or an externally hosted course.

After an employee has taken a course—whether instructor-led training or web-based training—the results are kept in the Learning Solution system. The employee will also earn any qualifications that were associated with that particular course.

Close-Out Process

After a learner completes a course, the results are recorded as a permanent record in Learning Solution. However, depending on the kind of course taken, the way that this information gets into Learning Solution varies. Static web-based courses usually record results immediately because the system immediately leverages the SCORM standard for this interface.

For instructor-led training, SAP provides a separate application, the Instructor Portal, to allow instructors to book participants, follow up, and manage their courses. Figure 4.39 shows the overview for the Instructor Portal.

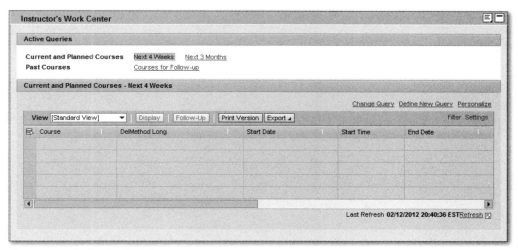

Figure 4.39 Instructor Portal

The Instructor Portal overview screen for instructors shows a number of standard-delivered POWL queries that allow instructors to see which courses, dates, and delivery methods they have assigned to them. After a course is completed, the instructor can do follow-up for a course using the Instructor Portal. This last step for instructors allows them to confirm attendance for participants that were enrolled in the course. After attendance has been confirmed, the instructor is able to pass or fail any participants via the Evaluate Participants screen. Lastly, the instructor can then transfer the qualifications to the participants that were enrolled in the course.

Figure 4.40 shows the Course Follow-Up screen of the Instructor Portal.

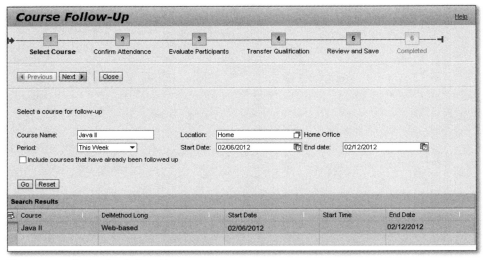

Figure 4.40 Instructor Follow-Up

Another function of the close-out process is the ability for the participants to appraise the course based on a variety of criteria and provide feedback to the instructor. Figure 4.41 shows the Course Appraisal application.

So far we've covered the Learning Solution process from end to end. Let's consider the intersection points between Learning Solution and other Talent Management modules.

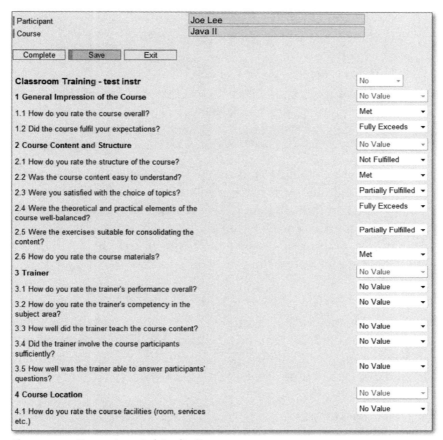

Figure 4.41 Course Appraisal Application

4.3.2 Integration Points

Learning Solution, like the other Talent Management modules, integrates with the core foundational components such as the OM module, jobs, and qualifications.

Organizational Management

The OM module plays an integral role in Learning Solution. By correctly setting up and using the OM module, managers can quickly and easily assign courses to their employees without having to search for them individually. This also allows managers to view all of their reporting employees' progress for their mandated courses.

Jobs and Qualifications Catalog

The Qualifications Catalog is an important part of the Learning Solution. Each course can be assigned multiple qualifications, and when learners successfully complete a course, those qualifications can be imparted to the learner. This is done seamlessly for web-based training and during the follow-up application for instructors.

The Jobs Catalog also plays an important part within Learning Solution. Not only can you assign mandated training to your organizational structure, but you can mandate training based on each job as well. This cascades training to all positions that are related to that job. Consider, for example, a standard electrician course for all electricians in your company. You can assign this course to the job level, and all subsequent positions would receive this course.

Talent Development

Within Talent Development, mandated training can be assigned to employees directly through the talent profile. This integration makes it very easy for managers to assess training and qualifications gaps in an employee's profile and directly assign courses to that employee as necessary.

Performance Management

Like Talent Development, Performance Management allows for the direct assignment of training and qualifications within an employee's appraisal document. This is done in the standard TRAINING GOALS appraisal column; managers have the ability to search through the Course Catalog and assign training for that employee.

4.4 SAP ERP HCM Enterprise Compensation Management

SAP ERP HCM Enterprise Compensation Management (ECM) is a Talent Management module used to budget, track, and update employee compensation. It allows organizations to implement a strategic compensation plan for their employees, basing each employee's compensation on that person's individual performance, bonuses, and long-term incentives (LTIs).

> **Related Resources**
>
> For more detailed information about ECM, refer to book *Enterprise Compensation Management with SAP ERP HCM* by Jeremy Masters and Christos Kotsakis (SAP PRESS, 2010).

Unlike Compensation Management, ECM is an all-inclusive solution combining both the backend transactions and the Web Dynpro frontend functions. In contrast, Compensation Management is strictly backend technology that has no integration with Employee Self-Service (ESS) or Manager Self-Service (MSS) applications. Migration between Compensation Management and ECM can be done if you ever choose to upgrade to ECM, but SAP doesn't currently have any standard tool to do so.

Within ECM, you can create effective compensation plans for your organization using many features, currencies, and regions. The following are a few of the main components that make up the ECM module:

- **Budgeting**
  Creating compensation plans based on monetary and non-monetary budgets can be done directly within ECM through multiple methods, which we'll discuss in this section of the chapter.

- **Job pricing**
  Employee salary data can be exported from ECM for participation in external salary surveys. You can also import salary survey data to create market composite results, which allows you to compare and adjust your company pay structure if required.

- **Compensation planning**
  This allows managers and administrators to plan compensation packages for employees, including tailoring base pay, bonuses, LTIs, and other configurable types of pay to fit your business. Configurable eligibility rules based on performance, guidelines, and approval cycles can all be implemented during planning.

- **Long-term incentives (LTI)**
  Many different types of LTIs can be integrated into a compensation plan for employees.

In this section, we'll explore some of these main components and how they fit in an end-to-end process. Many of these components, such as LTIs and job pricing, can be very complex. For the purposes of this book, we won't go into detail of some of these areas but instead will be exploring the high-level process.

4.4.1 Enterprise Compensation Process

The ECM process is supported by an integrated, powerful, and easy-to-use solution that you can leverage to create accurate and efficient compensation plans for your organization. Like the other modules within this chapter, we'll explore the functions of this particular module by walking through the enterprise compensation process.

The main enterprise compensation processes are budgeting, review, controlling, approval, and payroll. Each process has its set of unique functions that work together to achieve an effective compensation plan. Figure 4.42 shows these processes in sequence, which we'll examine so that you understand the core functions of ECM and how it can be leveraged effectively.

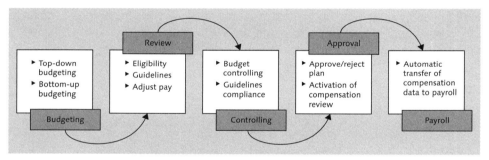

Figure 4.42 SAP Enterprise Compensation Management End-to-End Process

We'll also explore the integration points of this module with the other Talent Management modules. Let's start by taking a look at the first process in ECM.

Budgeting Process

The first step in creating a compensation plan is to create a budget in which you define how assets will be distributed during the compensation plan. Budget units are the SAP objects used to define monetary and non-monetary units. Generally, each organizational unit has its own budget unit created for the fiscal year.

After a budget unit is generated for a specific time frame for a specific organizational unit, ECM provides a web-based tool to administer the process. The Budget Maintenance tool, which is shown in Figure 4.43, is based on Business Server Page (BSP) technology and can be launched by compensation specialists from the backend.

SAP ERP HCM Enterprise Compensation Management | 4.4

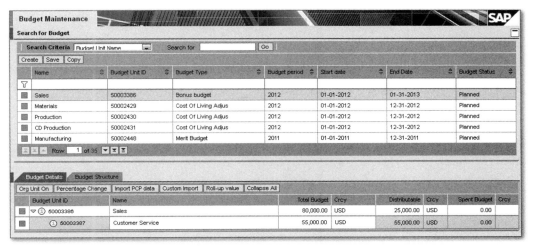

Figure 4.43 Budget Maintenance Tool in ECM

The user-friendly Budget Maintenance tool effectively allows for the distribution of budgets. Through this tool, you can perform top-down or bottom-up budgeting. Both methods will enable you to create an effective budget plan.

Top-down budgeting refers to budgeting that is first completed on a high-level organizational unit. Compensation specialists can first define an overall budget for an entire organizational unit, as well as the distributable amount based off that budget.

After a distributable amount has been defined for the top-level organizational unit, the reporting organization's budget must stay within that threshold. Figure 4.44 gives an example of how top-down budgeting works in a Production department using the Budget Maintenance tool.

Budget Unit ID	Name	Total Budget	Crcy	Distributable	Crcy	Spent Budget	Crcy
50003380	Production	100,000.00	USD	13,000.00	USD	0.00	
50003381	CD Production	10,000.00	USD	10,000.00	USD	0.00	
50003382	DVD Production	30,000.00	USD	30,000.00	USD	0.00	
50003383	Blu Ray Production	47,000.00	USD	47,000.00	USD	0.00	

Figure 4.44 Top-Down Budgeting Model

155

4 | How SAP Defines Talent Management

As you can see in Figure 4.44, the PRODUCTION organizational unit has a total budget of $100,000. Each of the reporting organizations' budgets is within this limit, and their total does not exceed the distributable amount set. We can see that the PRODUCTION organization still has $13,000 to distribute after all of the report organizations have set their budgets. By starting with a bigger budget at the top and distributing budget all within this screen, you can efficiently create a working budget for your organizations.

The bottom-up budgeting model takes a different approach. Instead of starting with a higher-level organization's budget and distributing downward, the budget is determined and set at the personnel level and rolled up into a final budget.

You can do this by leveraging the Personnel Cost Planning (PCP) functionality in the system. To use this functionality, start by creating a cost plan. Figure 4.45 shows a detailed PCP in the SAP system.

Cost Items per Cost Object

Plan: BPC - Test Cost Plan (01 C00001)
Planning Period: 01-01-2012-12-31-2012

Cost Unit	Text	Cost Object	Cost Item Text	Crcy	Σ Amount Qu 1 / 2012	Σ Amount Qu 2 / 2012	Σ Amount Qu 3 / 2012	Σ Amount Qu 4 / 2012	Σ Total Amount
Learning		Learning	Special Payments	USD				551.78	551.78
			ER Social Insurance Contribution	USD				113.12	113.12
		Mr Patrick Morrison	Wages and Salaries	USD	27,000.00	27,000.00	27,000.00	27,000.00	108,000.00
			Special Payments	USD				1,021.78	1,021.78
			ER Social Insurance Contribution	USD	5,535.00	5,535.00	5,535.00	5,744.47	22,349.47
		HR Learning Administrator	Wages and Salaries	USD	8,853.60	8,853.60	8,853.60	8,853.60	35,414.40
			Special Payments	USD				551.78	551.78
			ER Social Insurance Contribution	USD	1,815.09	1,815.09	1,815.09	1,815.09	7,260.36
			ER Social Insurance Contribution	USD				113.12	113.12
		Payroll Training Instructor	Wages and Salaries	USD	14,296.45	14,296.45	14,453.55	14,453.55	57,500.00
			Special Payments	USD				551.78	551.78
			ER Social Insurance Contribution	USD	2,930.77	2,930.77	2,962.98	3,076.10	11,900.62
				USD	60,430.91	60,430.91	60,620.22	63,846.17	245,328.21

Figure 4.45 Personnel Cost Planning

A PCP contains detailed cost information on a per-organization basis. It displays all of the objects that are assigned to that particular organizational unit and the cost per quarter for those position and person objects.

After a PCP is completed, there is a function in the Budget Maintenance tool to directly apply the PCP to the bottom-up budget. A compensation specialist can easily apply a PCP to a budget by clicking the IMPORT PCP DATA button, as shown in Figure 4.46.

SAP ERP HCM Enterprise Compensation Management | **4.4**

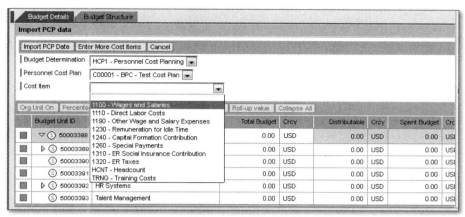

Figure 4.46 Applying a PCP for Bottom-Up Budgeting

After you've applied a PCP, the Budget Maintenance tool will display the total budget. Figure 4.47 shows an applied PCP to an organization. After you import the PCP, the budget automatically reflects the amount set in the TOTAL BUDGET and DISTRIBUTABLE columns.

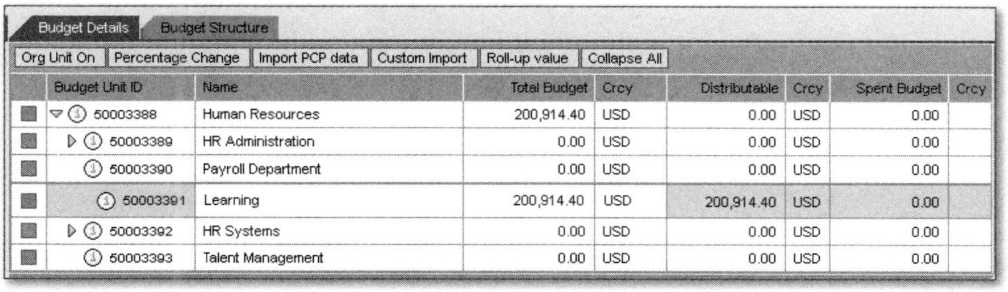

Figure 4.47 An Imported PCP in the Budget Maintenance Tool

After a PCP is applied, its budget is automatically rolled up into the top-level organization's budget. Recall that this distribution is known as bottom-up budgeting because you start with individual objects within an organizational unit and roll the budget upward.

Other functions are also available before completing a budgeting plan. If you already have a defined plan, the Budget Maintenance tool lets you make adjustments to that budget. For example, you can use the APPLY PERCENTAGE CHANGE button to quickly and efficiently apply a percentage change to a budget plan. Figure 4.48 shows the APPLY PERCENTAGE CHANGE function.

157

4 | How SAP Defines Talent Management

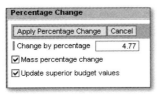

Figure 4.48 Applying a Fixed Percentage Change

The Apply Percentage Change button will apply that percentage to the selected organizational unit, along with the options selected in that window. This functionality is useful for all types of budget plans, including base pay and bonuses.

Another useful function is the Check and Release Budget application. After a budget has been saved, a compensation specialist can use it to first verify that budget values are consistent and then release the budget. Figure 4.49 shows the Check and Release Budget application, which has functions such as Release Budget and Check Values.

Budget Unit ID	Name	Total Budget	Crcy	Distributable	Crcy	Spent Budget	Crcy
50003379	Materials	120,000.00	USD	20,000.00	USD	0.00	USD
50003380	Production	100,000.00	USD	60,000.00	USD	0.00	USD
50003381	CD Production	10,000.00	USD	10,000.00	USD	0.00	USD
50003382	DVD Production	30,000.00	USD	30,000.00	USD	0.00	USD
50003383	Blu Ray Production	0.00	USD	0.00	USD	0.00	USD

Figure 4.49 Check and Release Budget Application

Checking the values for a budget eliminates inconsistencies in your plan, such as a budget outside your guideline range. When you finally release the budget plan, the involved managers can leverage ECM in the next phase, the review process.

Review Process

The review process contains many useful compensation tools to analyze, distribute, and view compensation for employees that managers can access directly from the MSS portal.

The first tool we'll look at is the Compensation Planning tool for managers. Managers first need to select the Compensation Review link in the portal, and the appropriate employees based on criteria displayed in the Employee Selection drop-down list. Figure 4.50 shows the first step of the Compensation Planning tool, which filters employees based on the determined criteria.

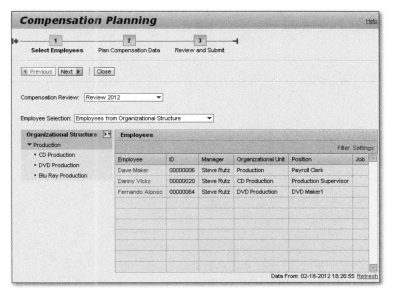

Figure 4.50 Selection Criteria for Compensation Planning

Figure 4.50 shows just one of the displays (EMPLOYEES from the organizational structure) that can be used to filter the correct set of employees to plan for; many different views of employee selection are available (such as by direct reports and organizational unit).

After employee selection is completed, the Plan Compensation Data screen is displayed (see Figure 4.51). These plans are configurable, as are the currency, budgets, and analytics.

This screen can be configured to display the different types of plans, such as bonus, LTIs, salary, and so on. In this example, the MERIT/SALARY PLAN and REGULAR BONUS tabs are displayed, along with a configured OVERVIEW tab. The tabs will display according to which plan you have configured.

As you can also see in Figure 4.51, the first employee, Dave Maker, doesn't have any compensation information available. Configuration can be added to allow eligibility guidelines for compensation plans. In this example, Dave Maker doesn't have an appraisal document final rating completed, making him ineligible for compensation review at this time. You can see that the other employees have their documents complete in the final rating (EXCEEDS and MET) given in the second APPRAISAL DOCUMENT column. With integration to Performance Management, you can click on the link in the APPRAISAL DOCUMENT column to link directly to the appraisal document for that employee.

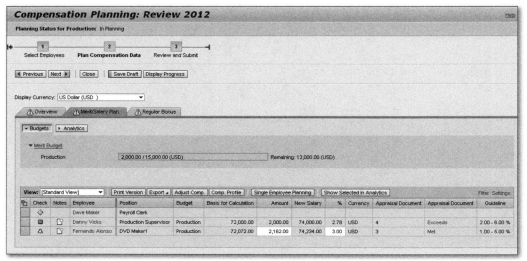

Figure 4.51 Compensation Planning Screen

After you determine eligibility, you can apply the configured guidelines to each employee's compensation plan. You can manually enter in a set amount to increase or a fixed percentage directly on this screen. However, we recommend that you use the guideline functionality, which is a best practice. Guidelines can be configured based on employee performance or, in this case, the appraisal document final rating. You can see the guideline percentages in the GUIDELINE column in Figure 4.51.

By selecting an employee and clicking the ADJUST COMP. button, you can see the four options for adjusting an employee's compensation, as shown in Figure 4.52.

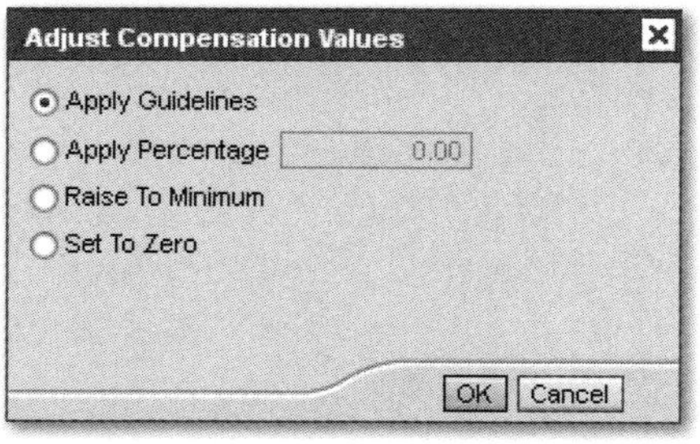

Figure 4.52 Adjust Compensation Values

This figure shows that you can apply guidelines, apply a fixed percentage, raise compensation to the minimum guideline amount, or allow for no compensation. After you have chosen which value to apply, the results are reflected immediately on the Compensation Planning screen.

Figure 4.51 shows the Budget function on the Compensation Planning screen. A graphical representation appears that lets managers know how much and what kind of currency is available for this compensation plan. After you adjust compensation values, the budget function is also updated, showing the amount distributed and the amount remaining.

You can also click the ANALYTICS button while you're in the Compensation Planning screen; this will show applied amounts and percentages for selected employees, letting you see where the dispersed compensation is going. These analytic charts can be toggled to display or hide on the screen. Figure 4.53 shows the ANALYTICS page for the Compensation Planning screen.

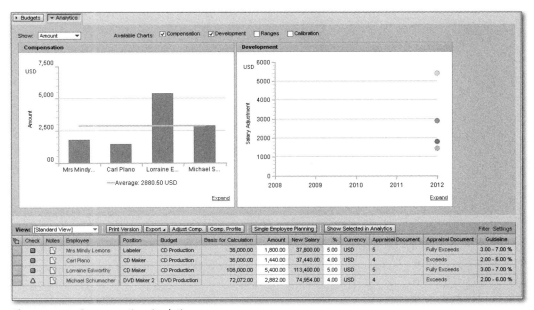

Figure 4.53 Compensation Analytics

After you've determined compensation for your employees on all of your compensation plans, you can review and submit the plan. Clicking the NEXT button on the Compensation Planning screen takes you to the REVIEW AND SUBMIT page, where you can see an overview of the compensation changes that you have made, as shown in Figure 4.54.

You can also include LTIs besides budget and bonus information in your compensation plan, such as granting shares to employees through the Compensation Planning screen. However, compensation specialists must first configure LTIs in the backend via Transaction PECM_EVALUATE_GRANT.

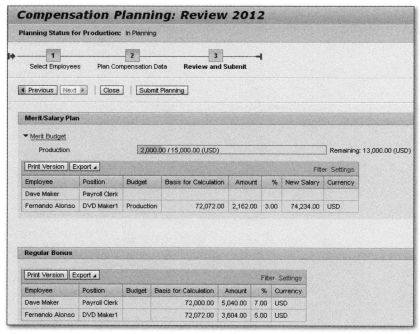

Figure 4.54 Review and Submit Screen

It's also possible to print or export the changes for each plan and see the graphical distributed and available budgets. After you've reviewed the changes, you can click the SUBMIT PLANNING button to submit the plan for approval. This leads into the controlling process.

Controlling Process

Compensation specialists can monitor and control planned budgets to ensure that guidelines are in compliance. So the controlling process should take place after planning and before budget plans are approved. SAP provides many tools to ensure that guidelines are met and that progress is tracked. Figure 4.55 shows the Administer Compensation Process Status tool, which shows the current status of organizations (and any ineligible employee) in regards to budget planning.

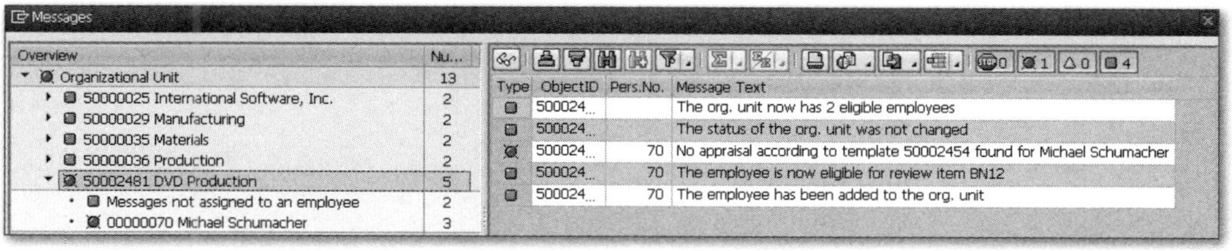

Figure 4.55 Administer Compensation Process Status

The Administer Compensation Process Status tool is used to display budget planning status at a glance. This also allows compensation specialists to recalculate the budget for any given organizational unit. Another very useful tool to display progress is the Compensation Planning Progress transaction, shown in Figure 4.56.

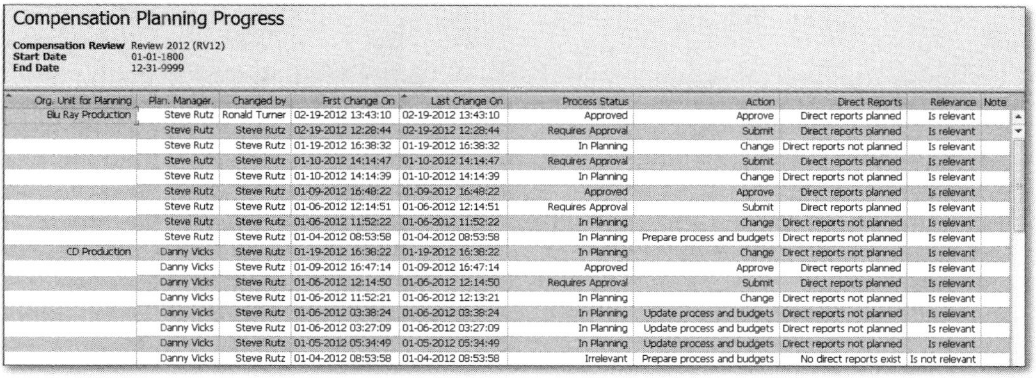
Compensation Planning Progress

Compensation Review Review 2012 (RV12)
Start Date 01-01-1800
End Date 12-31-9999

Org. Unit for Planning	Plan. Manager.	Changed by	First Change On	Last Change On	Process Status	Action	Direct Reports	Relevance	Note
Blu Ray Production	Steve Rutz	Ronald Turner	02-19-2012 13:43:10	02-19-2012 13:43:10	Approved	Approve	Direct reports planned	Is relevant	
	Steve Rutz	Steve Rutz	02-19-2012 12:28:44	02-19-2012 12:28:44	Requires Approval	Submit	Direct reports planned	Is relevant	
	Steve Rutz	Steve Rutz	01-19-2012 16:38:32	01-19-2012 16:38:32	In Planning	Change	Direct reports not planned	Is relevant	
	Steve Rutz	Steve Rutz	01-10-2012 14:14:47	01-10-2012 14:14:47	Requires Approval	Submit	Direct reports planned	Is relevant	
	Steve Rutz	Steve Rutz	01-10-2012 14:14:39	01-10-2012 14:14:39	In Planning	Change	Direct reports not planned	Is relevant	
	Steve Rutz	Steve Rutz	01-09-2012 16:48:22	01-09-2012 16:48:22	Approved	Approve	Direct reports planned	Is relevant	
	Steve Rutz	Steve Rutz	01-06-2012 12:14:51	01-06-2012 12:14:51	Requires Approval	Submit	Direct reports planned	Is relevant	
	Steve Rutz	Steve Rutz	01-06-2012 11:52:22	01-06-2012 11:52:22	In Planning	Change	Direct reports not planned	Is relevant	
	Steve Rutz	Steve Rutz	01-04-2012 08:53:58	01-04-2012 08:53:58	In Planning	Prepare process and budgets	Direct reports not planned	Is relevant	
CD Production	Danny Vicks	Steve Rutz	01-19-2012 16:38:22	01-19-2012 16:38:22	In Planning	Change	Direct reports not planned	Is relevant	
	Danny Vicks	Steve Rutz	01-09-2012 16:47:14	01-09-2012 16:47:14	Approved	Approve	Direct reports planned	Is relevant	
	Danny Vicks	Steve Rutz	01-06-2012 12:14:50	01-06-2012 12:14:50	Requires Approval	Submit	Direct reports planned	Is relevant	
	Danny Vicks	Steve Rutz	01-06-2012 11:52:21	01-06-2012 12:13:21	In Planning	Change	Direct reports not planned	Is relevant	
	Danny Vicks	Steve Rutz	01-06-2012 03:38:24	01-06-2012 03:38:24	In Planning	Update process and budgets	Direct reports not planned	Is relevant	
	Danny Vicks	Steve Rutz	01-06-2012 03:27:09	01-06-2012 03:27:09	In Planning	Update process and budgets	Direct reports not planned	Is relevant	
	Danny Vicks	Steve Rutz	01-05-2012 05:34:49	01-05-2012 05:34:49	In Planning	Update process and budgets	Direct reports not planned	Is relevant	
	Danny Vicks	Steve Rutz	01-04-2012 08:53:58	01-04-2012 08:53:58	Irrelevant	Prepare process and budgets	No direct reports exist	Is not relevant	

Figure 4.56 Compensation Planning Progress Report

In terms of controlling budget and guidelines, the Audit Report for Budgets tool displays the changes that were implemented by managers for their organization. Compensation specialists can see whether managers are keeping in line with the guidelines that were set up. Figure 4.57 shows the summary of changes report.

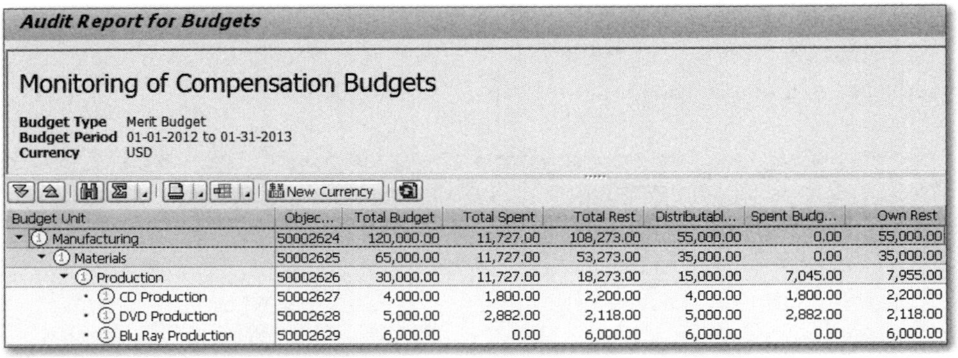

4 | How SAP Defines Talent Management

Figure 4.57 Audit Report for Budgets

Consulting this report can help ensure that managers are in compliance with the guidelines that were established during the budgeting process. Another function that compensation specialists can use is to mass-adjust budgets using the Adjust Compensation Process Records transaction, which will adjust entire budgets based on selected criteria. Figure 4.58 shows an example of adjustments for a given organizational unit.

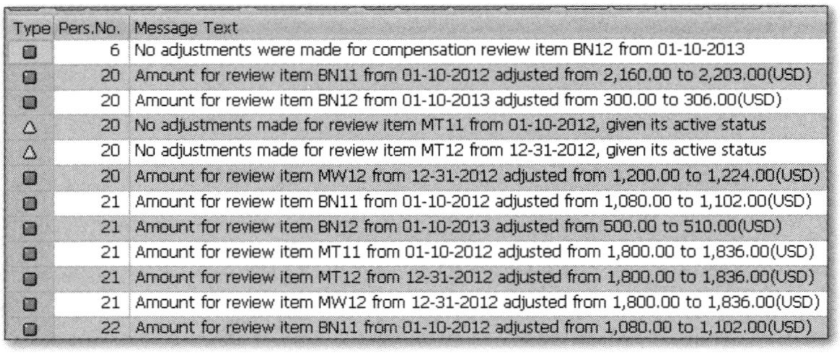

Figure 4.58 Mass-Processing Budgets

After the controlling process is completed, the next step is for an upper-level manager to approve the budget plans completed by reporting managers in the approval process.

Approval Process

Upper-level managers can approve budgets directly in ECM within the MSS tool using the Planning Overview application, shown in Figure 4.59.

4.4 SAP ERP HCM Enterprise Compensation Management

![Planning Overview for Ronald Turner screen]

Figure 4.59 Planning Overview in MSS

Managers can easily view, compare, and approve budgets from this screen. Clicking the APPROVE or REJECT button directly from this screen will set the status of that budget plan accordingly. If you approve the budget plan, it can be moved to active status, at which time the data can be processed by the Payroll module.

Active status allows the ECM data to be processed in the Payroll module. Activating budget plans can be done in the backend by compensation specialists. Transaction PECM_CHANGE_STATUS lets you change the status in budget plans. Figure 4.60 shows the selection screen for activating budget plans that have been approved.

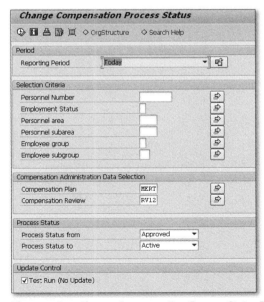

Figure 4.60 Change Compensation Process Status Transaction

165

Activation is the final step that needs to be completed directly in the ECM process. After the plan is active, the payroll process can then be run, updating Payroll module infotypes with ECM data.

Payroll Process

To push the compensation to Payroll, you must first configure the integration between ECM and the Payroll module. This can be done through the IMG path PERSONNEL MANAGEMENT • ENTERPRISE COMPENSATION MANAGEMENT • COMPENSATION ADMINISTRATION • PLAN ATTRIBUTES • ASSIGN COMPENSATION PLAN PAYROLL DATA.

Within ECM, Infotype 0759 (compensation process) contains all of the compensation data. When you activate a plan, the records stored on Infotype 0759 (compensation process) with the status approved are set to active, and the Payroll module infotypes are updated with the data in the ECM infotype. Depending on the category of the plan, this can update one of the following infotypes: 0008 (basic pay), 0015 (additional payments), 0267 (additional off-cycle payments), or 0761 (LTI granting).

We won't go into further detail about the payroll process for the purposes of this book. After the Payroll module infotypes are updated with ECM data, the ECM process is completed end to end.

4.4.2 Integration Points

ECM has heavy integration with the foundational components of Talent Management. Without a solid foundation, ECM couldn't function at all. Let's take a look at some of the important integration points of ECM with other Talent Management modules.

Organizational Management

ECM is highly dependent on a solid organizational structure. Everything from budgeting, planning, and approvals rely on a well-defined organizational structure. Having chief positions assigned to organizational units allows for the hierarchy of plans and approvals of compensation.

Also, job pricing is an important feature in ECM. By integrating with the OM structure, you can use the job pricing feature to plan for compensation for a particular job or position.

Performance Management

When setting up eligibility for ECM, Performance Management plays an important role. Merit-based salary increases, bonuses, or both can be based on each employee's performance. Their final appraisal rating, as well as a direct link to the employee's appraisal document can be easily integrated into ECM and used to determine compensation.

Remember that you can configure defined guidelines to determine compensation based on how well an employee performed during a given time period. The percentage increase can directly correlate to the final rating of an appraisal document.

Personnel Administration

PA infotypes also play an important role in ECM. PA can supply the name and organization assignment information that is displayed for an employee.

Payroll

Although the Payroll module isn't a Talent Management module, it, too, has an important impact on ECM. When you're activating compensation plans, the Payroll module infotypes can be updated to reflect the ECM changes. This integration is an important part of the ECM process not only for salary but also for bonuses and LTI information.

4.5 SAP ERP HCM Talent Development and Succession Planning

Talent Development and Succession—shortened here to Talent Development but also known as Succession Management—covers the development of the workforce and identification of successors for critical positions relevant to the goals and needs of the organization. This is what SAP calls the Talent Management core; it encompasses profiling, assessment, review, succession planning, and employee development. Most often, this focuses on the top-performing and high-potential employees, but in many organizations, it covers a fixed population of employees at higher levels of the organization.

4.5.1 Talent Development Process

Talent Development is an end-to-end process usually performed over a period of 12 months by Talent Management specialists, managers, and employees. Due to the sensitivity of the Talent Development process, not all processes are performed with employee involvement, and the results of some processes are intentionally designed to be inaccessible by the employee.

The end-to-end process includes the following steps:

1. Maintenance of talent profile by employees (ongoing)
2. Cascading of corporate and team goals by Talent Management specialists and managers
3. Performance appraisal by managers and employees
4. Talent assessment by managers
5. Planning and execution of talent review meetings by Talent Management specialists and business stakeholders
6. Succession planning by Talent Management specialists
7. Creation or update of development plans by Talent Management specialists and managers

In addition to these processes, Talent Development includes such ongoing activities as reporting and maintenance of talent Groups.

Talent Profile

To provide Talent Management specialists with a comprehensive overview of all talent-related information of an employee, SAP provides the talent profile. The talent profile comes in two guises: the self-service Talent Profile for Employees that can be maintained by an employee, the employee's manager, or a Talent Management specialist, and the detailed, extended Talent Profile for Managers and Talent Management Specialists that can be viewed by an employee's manager or a Talent Management specialist.

The Talent Profile for Employees allows the user, primarily the employee, to maintain information about an employee. This information includes internal projects in the organization, work experience at previous or other organizations, education, accomplishments and achievements, career goals and likes/dislikes, and mobility preferences. It also displays organization assignment data in the header and in the INTERNAL WORK EXPERIENCE tab.

Beginning with EhP 6, employees will be able to maintain qualifications directly in the Talent Profile for Employees and also access an overview of their learning activities.

The Talent Profile for Managers and Talent Management Specialists provides the user with an extensive overview of the employee, including the information maintained in the Talent Profile for Employees. In addition to the information maintained in the Talent Profile for Employees, the Talent Profile for Managers and Talent Management Specialists also displays the following information:

- Talent group nominations
- Organization assignment and employee's manager
- Succession plan assignments
- Up to five previous performance assessment ratings
- Up to five previous potential assessment ratings
- Core competency assessment ratings
- Derailer assessment ratings
- Language competency ratings
- Overview of future development plan steps
- Résumé summary
- Risk assessment
- Development plan

Beginning with EhP 6, it will be possible to display the appraisal documents from the Performance Management appraisal process in the talent profile.

Figure 4.61 shows the overview page of the Talent Profile for Managers and Talent Management Specialists in the SAP NetWeaver Portal, giving Talent Management specialists and managers fingertip access to key talent data about employees.

4 | How SAP Defines Talent Management

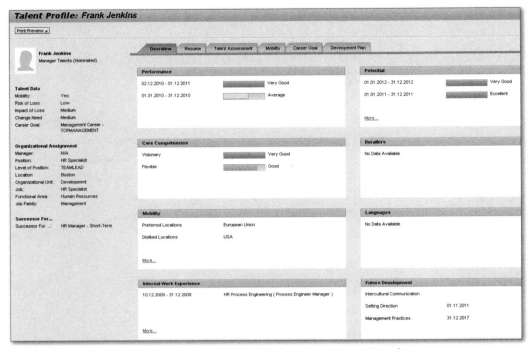

Figure 4.61 Talent Profile for Managers and Talent Management Specialists

Corporate Goals and Values

SAP lets Talent Management specialists create corporate goals and values that can be cascaded into performance appraisal documents. These align the individual's goals with the goals of the organization. This can be particularly useful to ensure that employee self-development matches the strategy and direction of the organization.

Though setting corporate goals is usually a driver for increasing an organization's financial performance, it can also be used to drive that organization's developmental needs to ensure that employees are developing skills that are required for the long-term growth and sustainability of the organization.

SAP's Corporate Goals and Values application lets you create corporate goals, core values, or both for given time periods. You can add a description of both the goal and the method of measurement. These goals or values can then be cascaded to one or more organizational units within the Talent Management specialist's area of responsibility.

Corporate goals will be discussed in more depth in Chapter 6, which covers Performance Management in more detail.

Figure 4.62 shows the creation of a corporate goal in the Corporate Goals and Values application in the Talent Management specialist role in the SAP NetWeaver Portal.

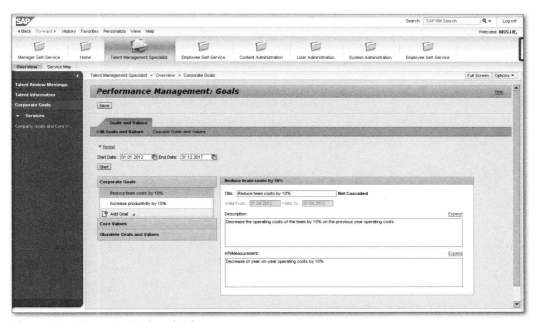

Figure 4.62 Corporate Goals and Values

Talent Assessment

Whereas the performance appraisal is an assessment held exclusively between the manager and employee, the talent assessment is a set of appraisals with which a manager can perform a confidential assessment of talent-related characteristics of an employee. Usually the talent assessment is performed around the same time as or shortly after the performance appraisal is completed to give a complete assessment to the Talent Management specialists.

Importantly, the talent assessment process is where each employee's potential is assessed. Prior to the release of EhP 4, this would have happened during the performance appraisal. Notably, SAP continues to provide enhancements in Performance Management so that organizations that use and prefer this approach are able to continue to use it after implementing EhP 4 or above.

Alongside the assessment of potential, talent assessment appraisals also assess the employee for risks, competencies, barriers to progression (derailers), and nominations for talent groups.

Figure 4.63 shows a talent assessment competency appraisal. Here competencies assigned to the various competency categories can be rated, similarly to the way other talent assessment elements are assessed.

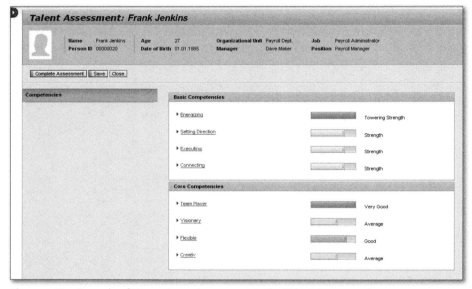

Figure 4.63 Example of Competency Assessment in the Talent Assessment

Talent Review Meeting

After the closure of the annual performance appraisal and talent assessment cycles, a Talent Management specialist can prepare and then conduct review meetings for high-performing and high-potential employees within the organization. The Talent Review Meeting application gives Talent Management specialists a platform to set up, support, and keep records of these meetings.

Talent review meetings are forums in which employees in specific parts of the organization are discussed, compared, and calibrated by Talent Management specialists and managers. They give Talent Management specialists an understanding of the strengths and weaknesses in the workforce, allowing these high-achieving employees to be identified and assigned to talent groups for use in succession and development activities.

The Talent Review Meeting application provides a number of options for preparing and planning meetings. A meeting is scheduled and classified with a category, level, language, and status during preparation. The Talent Management specialist also selects the organizational units that the meeting will focus on, the support team that will administer the meeting, and the attendees who will provide feedback. Handouts can be created to be circulated to the attendees. During planning, the agenda is created, and the employees to be reviewed are selected.

The Talent Review Meeting application can be used to support the meeting by running through each agenda topic. When employees are being discussed, their talent profile can be displayed, either as a summary or as the talent profile for managers and Talent Management specialists. Employees can also be calibrated in the calibration grid, which displays employees in a grid that compares performance and potential. From EhP 5, employees who have not completed the annual performance appraisal and talent assessment cycle can still be added to the grid for calibration. Additional employees can be added to the meeting if they were not added during the planning stage.

Figure 4.64 shows the calibration of employees in a grid during a talent review meeting.

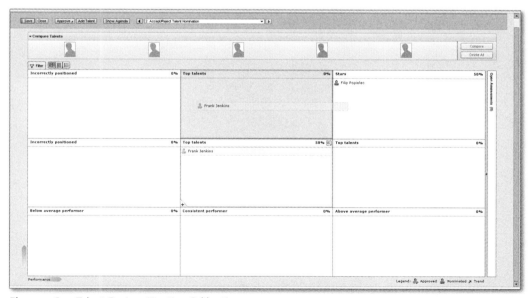

Figure 4.64 Talent Review Meeting Calibration

Succession Planning

Safeguarding critical positions and creating a sustainable future are fundamental issues for organizations as they plan for the future. Recent studies have shown that the modern generations are far more transient and display less loyalty than the baby boomer generation. Succession plans enable organizations to protect their critical positions and ensure that they are covered against an unexpected or unplanned loss of the incumbent. This module was part of SAP E-Recruiting until EhP 4.

To support succession planning, SAP offers a certified solution extension: SAP Talent Visualization by Nakisa (STVN) SuccessionPlanning. It's important to note that SAP doesn't provide an alternative application in the SAP NetWeaver Portal for succession planning, but it does provide a basic transaction in the backend (Transaction HRTMC_PPOM) to perform limited succession planning activities.

STVN SuccessionPlanning has an integrated, graphical frontend for succession management that reads data from and writes data to the backend in real time and leverages the SAP authorization mechanism. It provides an easy-to-use, intuitive interface for identifying key positions, reviewing the bench strength of key and non-key positions, assessing succession plans, assigning successors, and evaluating succession analytics and key performance indicators. Alongside the standard functionality, the application also provides a number of functionalities that aren't otherwise available, such as profile match, successor calibration, and the performance versus potential grid (commonly known as the nine-box grid).

Figure 4.65 shows the organizational structure in STVN SuccessionPlanning. You can see the bench strength view in the structure and the details panel opened for the DIRECTOR OF SALES – NORTH AMERICA position.

Development Plan

The development plan is the final stage of the Talent Development/Succession Planning process. In Talent Management, a development plan is available to the Talent Management specialist and manager to specifically plan the development of talents and successors over a long-term period. This development plan, unlike a development plan in a performance appraisal, can't be accessed by the employee it was created for. The rationale is that the objective is for Talent Management specialists and managers to create long-term, succession-orientated development steps to develop an employee without compromising sensitive succession and talent information. In many instances, it isn't appropriate to inform employees that they are successors for one or more positions within the organization. The development plan also has no fixed end date; it's designed to be a living document that can be used to plan and track development progress over a number of years. This is in contrast to a development plan used in a performance appraisal, as that would only last for the yearly appraisal period for which it was created.

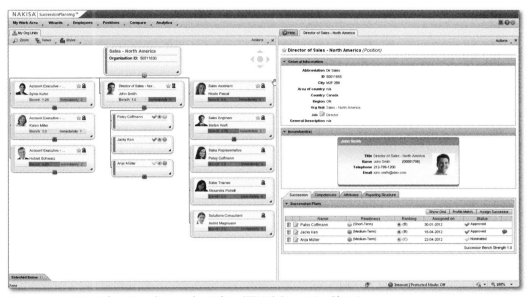

Figure 4.65 SAP Talent Visualization by Nakisa (STVN) SuccessionPlanning

The development plan gives the Talent Management specialist the ability to add one or more development steps, each one with a date period, action description, and note. After the Talent Management specialist has created a development plan, the plan becomes automatically available to the manager of the employee. Both the Talent Management specialist and manager can then update the progress and ranking of each development step in the plan.

After all of the steps in the development plan are complete, the development plan can be closed. The development plan will remain open until a Talent Management specialist decides that the plan is complete or a new plan is required.

Figure 4.66 shows the DEVELOPMENT PLAN tab in the talent profile for managers and Talent Management specialists. Here the development plan progress can be viewed and tracked.

4 | How SAP Defines Talent Management

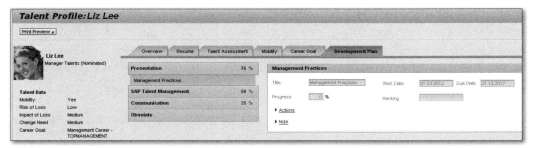

Figure 4.66 Development Plan in the Talent Profile for Managers and Talent Management Specialists

Talent Development in SAP ERP HCM is the cornerstone of identifying and developing talent and creating long-term sustainability for organizations. Through profiling, assessment and review, Talent Management specialists can create development plans and succession plans for their talents and key positions. This long-term strategic planning enables organizations to provide strength and depth in their workforce, for now and for the future.

Now that we've covered the functionality that Talent Management offers to support talent development and succession planning processes, we can look at the integration points of these areas.

4.5.2 Integration Points

As mentioned previously, given that Talent Management is an integrated solution, it's no surprise that there are a number of integration points.

Personnel Administration

As with most SAP HCM modules, the majority of the data used in Talent Management comes from PA. Information about the employee and their organizational assignment is displayed in several locations.

Organizational Management

Most of the other data used by Talent Management comes from the OM module. Talent Management displays data from Infotype 0001 (organization assignment) and 0002 (personal data) of PA, and Infotypes 1000 (objects), 1001 (relationships), and 1050 (job evaluation) of OM. Infotypes 1000 and 1001 are used quite heavily in Talent Management because assignments such as succession plans and talent group memberships are stored as relationships between objects.

Jobs Catalog and Qualifications Catalog

In addition to these standard OM and PA infotypes, Talent Management also uses the Jobs Catalog and Qualifications Catalog. The Jobs Catalog is used within the SAP Job Architecture to display the functional area and job family of the employee. Qualifications and core competencies of employees are displayed, and qualifications are also used for the profile match for successors, which will be discussed in Chapter 8.

Performance Management

As mentioned in the introduction to this chapter, Performance Management is part of the talent development process, but it's also a process in its own right. Talent Management makes use of the performance appraisal result in employee calibration and talent identification.

Analytics and Reports

As of EhP 5, Talent Management reports are available in SAP NetWeaver Business Warehouse, SAP BusinessObjects, Xcelsius, and Crystal Reports. The various extractors use the Talent Management infotypes as well as the PA and OM infotypes used by Talent Management.

4.6 Summary

In this chapter, we have discussed how SAP defines talent management and what functionality SAP offers to support the various Talent Management processes. You should now have an understanding of each of the modules of Talent Management, what functionality is available, and how each module integrates with other areas of SAP. Let's reflect briefly on each module.

4.6.1 E-Recruiting

SAP ERP HCM E-Recruiting is used to recruit candidates via the Internet. This Talent Management module contains many functions that you can configure and leverage to easily manage candidates in your system. Along with strong functionality to recruit candidates and the new features of EhP 5, the integration points of E-Recruiting allow for seamless transfer of data between a stand-alone E-Recruiting system and your core HR system.

4.6.2 Performance Management

The SAP ERP HCM Performance Management module is used to appraise your employee's performance throughout the year. By using either the flexible or predefined solutions, you can effectively define and manage goals for your entire organization.

Due to the highly configurable nature of the flexible solution, this module is designed to accommodate your business process. Many different processes, goals, and competencies can be configured to effectively appraise your employees.

The predefined solution can be rapidly deployed and comes with a very slick UI. You can easily define templates and process configurations using the step-by-step setup interface to get your Performance Management module up and running as quickly as possible.

4.6.3 Learning Solution

SAP ERP HCM Learning Solution contains many useful frontend tools to develop, publish, manage, and deploy learning content throughout your organization. Because it's compatible with multiple delivery methods, as well as tools to manage these methods, Learning Solution can accommodate a variety of learning programs.

Many useful administration tools are also available within Learning Solution. These powerful applications can quickly assign courses to entire organizational units, manage and view mandated courses, administer learning resources, and manage participants within courses.

The integration with the foundational components of Talent Management also makes it a vital piece in an organization's overall talent strategy. By allowing training courses to be assigned to an employee directly through their talent profile or performance appraisal document, managers can quickly and effectively manage their employees' learning in multiple places.

4.6.4 Enterprise Compensation Management

SAP ERP HCM Enterprise Compensation Management is a comprehensive application that combines web-based tools with backend transactions and reports to efficiently set up compensation plans for your organization. With great features such as job pricing and LTIs, as well as integration with Performance Management, managers have the tools they need to accurately compensate employees.

ECM has highly configurable budget and compensation plans. Compensation specialists can apply guidelines to all compensation plans, as well as monitor the progress and changes of managers during the compensation process. With its integration to the Payroll module, ECM can directly update the infotypes that Payroll uses to seamlessly compensate employees based on merit, LTIs, and guidelines.

4.6.5 Talent Development and Succession Planning

SAP ERP HCM Talent Development and Succession Planning covers the Talent Management core and provides assessment, profiling, identification, and reviewing of an organization's talent, as well as aligning the talent strategy with organizational goals. Organizations can manage their talent pipeline and use it to identify and assign successors, so that business-critical positions can be covered against unexpected departures from those positions.

The solutions that SAP provides to support these processes are intuitive and effective enough for Talent Management specialists, managers, and employees to manage the process without needing to use the backend transactions. The STVN SuccessionPlanning solution offers even more functionality than through standard Web Dynpro applications; the features available add strength and depth to the tools that Talent Management specialists can use to effectively plan succession and create sustainability in the organization.

Now that you've glimpsed the five core modules and their respective processes—and how they can develop a successful talent management system—let's put them to use in the upcoming chapters.

Organizations must have a process for identifying, acquiring, developing, and retaining their employees, which makes establishing workforce plans that align with the business strategies a necessity. This is all encompassed in the induction phase. After new employees are hired, they can maintain their talent profile in preparation for the development phase.

5   Induction Phase

Now that you have a deeper understanding of the Talent Management modules from both an EhP 5 and basic integration perspective, let's explore the integration of the Talent Management modules in further detail as we walk through a year in the life of an employee from an SAP perspective. The first of four phases, the *induction phase*, involves creating the new position in SAP and ensuring that the proper qualifications have been assigned.

As soon as the new position has been entered into the SAP system and is available to be filled, either the recruiter or hiring manager enters a new requisition into the system. The candidate then applies for this position, is screened by a recruiter through various activities, and then interviewed and eventually hired—all via the SAP E-Recruiting module (which we'll refer to as simply E-Recruiting).

After the candidate becomes an employee, his journey with the new company continues when he starts maintaining his talent profile. This includes current and previous education, work experience, and career goals. Required qualifications can be viewed in the talent profile, so that the new employee can develop to become qualified for his next position in the company.

However, before we can talk about getting the new position into SAP, we need to first discuss the workforce planning process, which enables organizations to do the following:

- Develop a strategy for allocating resources to meet its staffing goals.
- Prepare a framework for the growth and progress of the organization.
- Proactively anticipate the workforce needs of the company.
- Create a foundation for making strategic business decisions.

Planning for HR needs is one of the greatest challenges facing managers and leaders. To meet this challenge, a uniform workforce planning process that provides a disciplined approach for matching HR with the anticipated needs of the organization is essential.

5.1 Workforce Planning

Workforce planning refers to the method of ensuring that an organization has access to talent and the necessary tools for success. It's a process designed to anticipate and integrate the HR response to an organization's strategic plan. Simply put, workforce planning is the process of placing the right number of people with the right skills, experiences, and competencies in the right jobs at the right time.

Workforce planning is a fluid process that typically takes place on an annual, quarterly, and ongoing basis. Moreover, many companies have created their own processes and terminology for workforce planning, but they are all very much alike and include the following key components:

- Present workforce competency analysis
- Identification of future required competencies
- Comparison of current and future workforce needs to identify competency gaps and surpluses
- Execution of a plan to build the workforce required in the future
- Evaluation processes to ensure that objectives are being met

Workforce planning is also an endeavor for developing information that can help an organization make decisions for both the short and long term, yet allow for flexibility in an ever-changing environment. The plan is intended to help provide solutions to staffing issues that are related to position movement into, around, and out of an organization.

Workforce planning is also a management framework that ties HR decisions to the strategic plan of the organization. It provides managers with a framework for making staffing decisions based on an organization's mission, strategic plan, budgetary resources, and a set of desired workforce competencies. Managers can develop a better understanding of the areas of the organization's workforce that need to be strengthened. This step is the key element in the workforce planning process, and it involves asking questions such as the following:

- Is the organization aligned with strategic business goals?
- Are there certain parts of the organization that experience higher turnover than others?
- What is the right organizational structure?
- Can the organization identify the factors that contribute to turnover?
- Have the skill sets within certain parts of the organization been reduced due to turnover?

Answering these questions helps organizations identify competencies needed in the workforce and determine how recruiting, developing, and training employees can build the workforce of the future.

Workplace planning is of paramount importance because organizations need to ensure they have adequate resources to help fulfill their strategic goals. Because all employers compete for employees from the same labor pool, workforce planning is critical for attracting and retaining the talent required to serve the needs of the organization.

Workforce planning has become increasingly important to organizations over the past several years in large part due to increased retirements, as well as retention and restructuring strategies.

Several relatively recent trends illustrate the importance of workforce planning:

- Aging of the population
- Baby boomers redefining the age of retirement
- Technology trends that are changing the HR function
- Unprecedented growth of job candidates with advanced educational degrees

A key consideration of workforce planning is the benefit it has to managers. Workforce planning provides managers with a solid foundation for making HR decisions. It allows them to anticipate change and provides them with the means for addressing present and future workforce issues.

Some components of workforce planning, such as workforce demographics, retirement projections, and succession planning, are already familiar to managers.

Workforce planning provides transparency and allows managers to better plan by providing more information on changes to be anticipated, the competencies needed within the organization, and key positions that may need to be filled.

Because planning for human capital needs is one of the greatest challenges facing managers and leaders, a uniform process that provides a disciplined approach for matching HR with the anticipated needs of the organization is critical. A workforce plan is a fundamental planning tool important to quality performance; it contributes to the achievement of organizational strategic objectives by providing a basis for justifying budget allocations and workload staffing levels.

An important aspect of workforce planning is position management, which helps organizations ensure that they have adequate resources to help fulfill their strategic goals.

5.2 Position Management

To support an organization's strategic objectives, hiring managers should adhere to position management guidelines that ensure the workforce plan is considered when evaluating vacated positions. Some examples of position management guideline considerations include (but aren't limited to) the following:

- What work needs to be completed?
- Does the position description accurately reflect currently assigned responsibilities?
- Is the vacant position considered a critical position?
- Can the responsibilities be redistributed across the rest of the remaining team members?

Only after these guidelines have been considered should the hiring manager (in consultation with the supervisor and HR specialist) make an informed decision on whether the vacancy should be filled.

At a high level, position management is the continuous and systematic process for determining the number of positions needed, the skill and knowledge requirements of those positions, and the organizational grouping of positions to carry out the work done during the workforce planning process.

Position management is a significant aspect of each manager's personnel management responsibility. To be effective at position management, a conscious effort needs to be made to organize and assign the work in the most efficient and economical way. Each organization should review its position management methods and processes periodically in an effort to make continuous improvements. These reviews should be initiated by upper management to be deemed effective.

5.2.1 Position Management Tools

Like any discipline, position management has tools designed to improve position management methods and processes. To this end, there are established guidelines that use common "symptoms" to help managers diagnose problems. Some examples of these "symptoms" include (but aren't limited to):

- **Layering**
  This occurs when there are too many levels in the chain of command. This can be corrected by asking questions such as "What is the ratio of supervisors to workers?"

- **Unnecessary positions**
  This sometimes occurs when there are "carryovers" from previous operating structures or simply duplicate positions that may not be needed. You can correct this symptom by asking questions such as "Are all administrative assistant positions needed, or can they be shifted, eliminated, or both?"

- **Inaccurate position descriptions**
  This can result in misclassifications, with the incumbents being over-graded or under-graded. Inaccurate position descriptions can be alleviated by periodic review of position descriptions with employees and by rewriting descriptions immediately when changes are required.

- **Fragmentation**
  This is a situation when an organization is needlessly split into many small segments. It requires more supervisors, restricts the development of employees, interferes with communications, and causes over-specialization. This can be corrected by asking questions such as "Are all of these functional areas really necessary?"

Because no two organizations are identical, these types of tools should be used in different combinations to achieve sound position management.

5.2.2 Why Is Position Management Important?

Organizations can gain direct advantages from practicing sound position management, including the following:

- Work can be done more efficiently.
- Processes can be streamlined.
- The organization can be staffed using the available labor market in more effective ways.
- Employees can use their capabilities to the fullest.
- Employee engagement can improve.
- Organizations can provide better career opportunities for their employees.
- Roadblocks such as high turnover can be reduced.

Although these benefits may not be achieved in every organization, you should gain several such improvements after sound position management methods and processes have been implemented. Finally, if position management is used wisely, organizations can be more effective at adjusting their own positions and organizational structures to meet the needs of the enterprise, realize economies of scale, and attain a competitive advantage.

5.2.3 The Cost of Unfilled Positions

Numerous costs are associated with an unfilled position in any company. Many of these costs are difficult to quantify, but they are very real, nonetheless, and can have a negative impact on the company's bottom line. Several organizations calculate the cost of a hire—some even calculate the cost of a bad hire—but few take the time to calculate the cost of a vacant position. Given the fact that many vacancies often exceed 100 days, these are potentially significant financial impacts. Examples of these impacts include the following:

- **Product/productivity**
  Vacancies in key skill positions can mean that products and projects may need to be dropped altogether.
- **Employee impacts**
  Vacancies may cause overworked employees, which may lower productivity or force the affected employees to resign.

- **Increased management time**
  Vacancies often oblige managers to "fill in" for the vacant employee, forcing them to push aside their own responsibilities.
- **Customers**
  Excessive vacancies may cause confusion for suppliers and customers regarding whom they can contact, and might send the message that the organization is getting weak or that it doesn't care about them.
- **Competitive advantage**
  Vacancies in key positions or a large number of vacancies could lead to hiring too quickly and ultimately weaken the corporate culture.
- **Image/recruiting**
  High vacancy rates could send a message to future recruits that the organization isn't able to easily recruit replacements or that no one wants to work there.
- **Out-of-pocket costs**
  Vacancies in key positions could lead to having to hire high-cost consultants as "fill-in help," which could mean higher costs (especially if those consultants are billing hourly).

Organizations that take the time to calculate the cost of vacant positions understand the implications. When they realize the potential significant costs involved, these organizations can create a competitive advantage in the marketplace by using mitigation strategies in their position management methods and processes.

5.2.4 Position Management in SAP

Now that the workforce plan has been created and aligned with the strategic plan of the organization, let's begin the process of walking through a year in the life of an employee from an SAP perspective. The first step in this process is to create a new position in SAP and ensure that the proper qualifications have been assigned.

To this end, you'll create a position based on the following SAP Job Architecture example that was used in Chapter 3:

- Functional Area = Human Resources
- Job Family = HR Payroll
- Job = Payroll Administrator

5 | Induction Phase

Using the steps outlined in Chapter 3, you can now create the position of PAYROLL MANAGER that will eventually be filled by the new employee. Figure 5.1 shows the BASIC DATA tab of the newly created position.

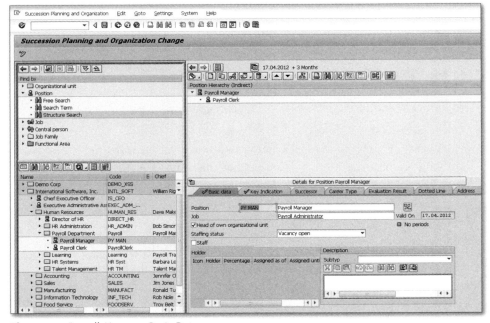

Figure 5.1 Payroll Manager Basic Data

> **Key Point**
>
> There are a handful of frontend (visualization) solutions on the market that allow positions to be created and managed and the organizational structure to be generally managed in a more aesthetically pleasing graphical user interface (GUI). As a result, we're only reviewing the standard SAP transactions for position management.

Now let's establish the relationship between the newly created payroll manager position and the payroll administrator job using Transaction PP01. This will allow the position to inherit the qualifications that have already been assigned to the job within the SAP Job Architecture. Figure 5.2 illustrates the PAYROLL MANAGER position that will be modified.

After you've found the PAYROLL MANAGER position in Transaction PP01, you need to create the relationship to the payroll administrator job. To do this, you highlight

Position Management | 5.2

the RELATIONSHIPS row and select the CREATE icon from the menu in the top left-hand side of the screen in Figure 5.3.

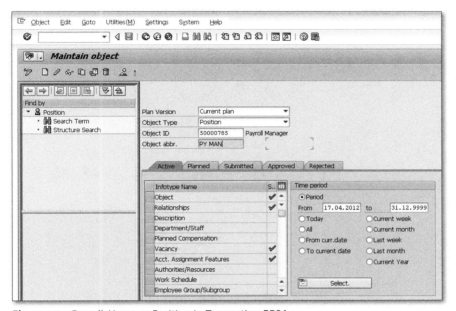

Figure 5.2 Payroll Manager Position in Transaction PP01

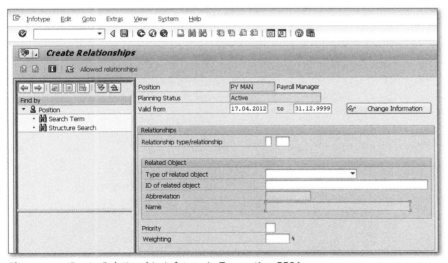

Figure 5.3 Create Relationship Infotype in Transaction PP01

5 | Induction Phase

On the new screen that appears, the first piece of information to be defined is the type of relationship you want to create. In this case, you'll create the relationship B|007 (IS DESCRIBED BY). Figure 5.4 illustrates both the number of relationship options and your selection.

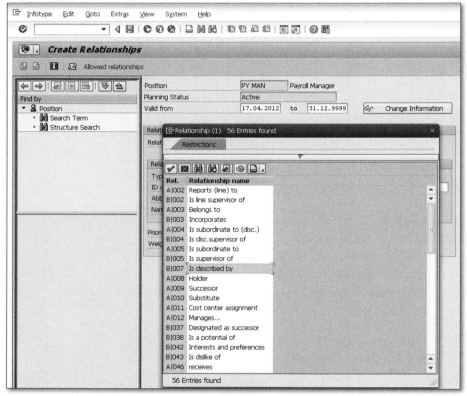

Figure 5.4 Relationship Type B|007 (Is Described By)

You now need to define the type of object that the new payroll manager position needs to be described by. In this case, we want to have the POSITION of PY MAN (PAYROLL MANAGER) described by the job of PAYROLL ADMINISTRATOR (entered in the NAME field), as shown in Figure 5.5.

190

5.2 Position Management

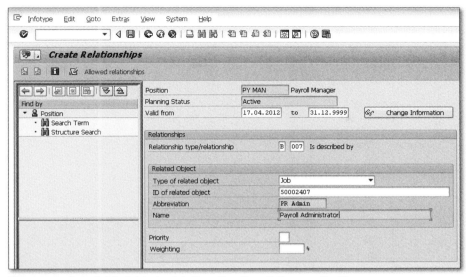

Figure 5.5 Payroll Administrator Job Describes Payroll Manager Position

After the information is saved, you can go to Transaction PPPM to see that the PAYROLL MANAGER position has inherited the qualifications from the payroll administrator job (from Chapter 3), as shown in Figure 5.6.

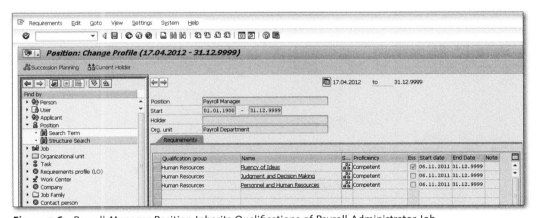

Figure 5.6 Payroll Manager Position Inherits Qualifications of Payroll Administrator Job

The final task within position management in SAP involves indicating whether the position is a "key position." This can be accomplished for individual positions via Transaction HRTMC_PPOM, as well as in STVN SuccessionPlanning. We'll review

5 Induction Phase

Transaction HRTMC_PPOM first. The key position capability for STVN Succession-Planning will be reviewed in more detail in Chapter 8.

The KEY INDICATION tab of the position within Transaction HRTMC_PPOM holds the following fields:

- NOMINATION STATUS
- NOM./APPROV. REASON
- DECIDED BY
- REJECTION REASON
- DECIDED BY
- COMMENT

For the purposes of this exercise, we'll assume that the payroll manager position has been identified and approved as a key position. Figure 5.7 illustrates the information that we've included for the PAYROLL MANAGER position.

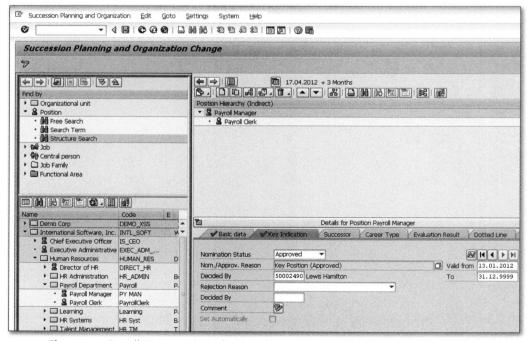

Figure 5.7 Payroll Manager Key Indicator Tab

You can also set a number of key positions in a single transaction by using Transaction SE38 (see Figure 5.8) and running Report RPTMC_SET_KEY_INDICATION.

Figure 5.8 Report RPTMC_SET_KEY_INDICATION

Now that the position has been created and a vacancy has been established, you can use E-Recruiting to find potential candidates to fill the position.

5.3 E-Recruiting

Now that the payroll manager Position has been created in the SAP ERP HCM system, you'll use the E-Recruiting application to begin the process of filling this key position. As mentioned in Chapter 4, E-Recruiting comes with many flexible tools that can handle high-volume recruiting with efficiency, objectivity, and collaboration from all members involved in the recruiting process. To this end, the recruiting process always begins by creating a requisition with the following assumptions:

- The position being recruited for has already been approved and created in the SAP ERP HCM system.
- The position is available in E-Recruiting via ALE from the SAP ERP HCM system. (Refer to Chapter 4 for more information on ALE.)

> **Key Point**
>
> Organizations too often (mistakenly) try to incorporate parts of their workforce planning process into E-Recruiting and contemplate making customizations to the application to help cover up the inefficiencies in their position management process. It may be necessary to analyze how positions are created and approved to avoid costly enhancements to E-Recruiting.

5.3.1 Requisition

Each organization differs in terms of who creates the requisition and how the requisition is created from a process point of view. For the purposes of this book, we'll look at the creation of a requisition from an SAP Best Practice perspective and from the lens of EhP 5.

Manager

With this in mind, let's ask the hiring manager (Dave Maker) to create the requisition using HR HCM Processes and Forms (HCMPF), which leverages the SAP Process Integration (PI) framework via the Manager Self-Service (MSS) functionality in the SAP Enterprise Portal (see Figure 5.9).

First, let's take a moment to talk about HCMPF generally to establish context. The HCMPF framework offers an efficient way to manage cross-role processes involving HR master data. This structure allows organizations to build their own specific processes, irrespective of the data, process flow, and roles.

The HCMPF framework is based on three components:

- **Table configuration**
  This facilitates the implementation of processes without requiring developers to write any code.

- **Adobe Interactive Forms**
  This allows for all business roles to be integrated into processes.
- **SAP Business Workflow**
  This workflow engine enables improved flexibility.

Figure 5.9 Create Requisition Request in Manager Self-Service

Now let's look at the *standard* requisition form for managers specifically. The main sections of the form include the following:

- REQUEST TEMPLATE
  Information from a previous requisition can be used as a template, which saves the manager time.
- BASIC DATA
  Includes REQUISITION TITLE (we'll use "Payroll Manager" in the interest of consistency) and INTEREST GROUP fields. These selections are shown in Figure 5.10.
- CONTACT PERSON
  Includes the HIRING MANAGER, REQUESTER, and SUPPORT GROUP fields.
- ORGANIZATIONAL DATA
  Includes POSITION, ORGANIZATIONAL UNIT, and number of positions.

5 | Induction Phase

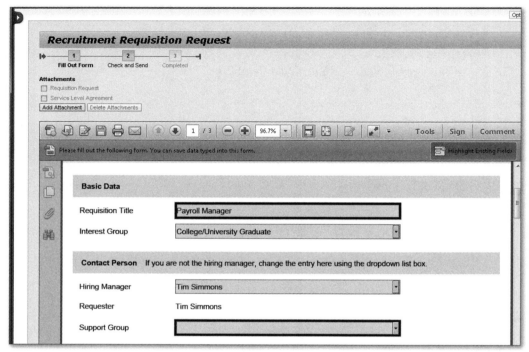

Figure 5.10 Basic Data Information

When the manager creates a requisition based on an existing position, he can see all existing positions that are his direct reports, whether the position is vacant, and the name of the existing position holder if the position is currently filled by an incumbent. The screen that Dave Maker sees is shown in Figure 5.11. Section 1.3 has more information on chief positions. For the purposes of our walk-through, the position of payroll manager will be used in the requisition, which includes the following fields:

- PAYMENT INFORMATION
  Includes salary information (currency, salary range, etc.).

- EMPLOYMENT INFORMATION
  Includes branch, industry, hierarchy level, functional area, work contract type, employment fraction, and employment start date.

- EDUCATION AND TRAINING
  Includes education type, education level, field of education, and subject.
- QUALIFICATIONS
  This is a free-form text field that the manager can use to include required and desired qualifications for the position. Qualifications are defaulted into the requisition based on the job/position brought over from SAP ERP HCM into E-Recruiting via ALE. Any information entered in this field is for informational purposes only.
- JOB POSTING TEXT
  Includes company, department, project, requirements, and tasks.

> **Key Point**
>
> SAP can default posting text into the form from SAP Job Architecture via a delivered BAdI. Refer to Chapter 9, Section 9.5, for more information on BAdIs.

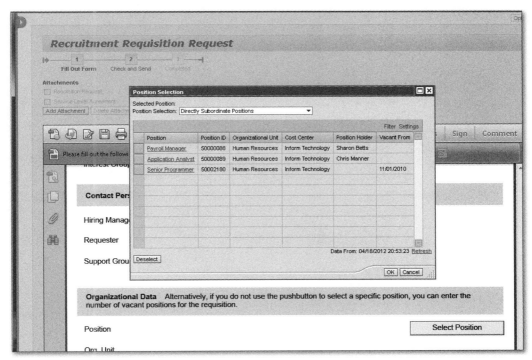

Figure 5.11 List of Existing Positions

> **Key Point**
>
> The E-Recruiting administrator should have already set up corresponding support groups with lead recruiters assigned. This default will control how requisitions created from the manager will appear in the dashboard queries for the lead recruiter after the requisition has been released by the manager. For more information on support groups and other E-Recruiting topics, refer to *E-Recruiting with SAP ERP HCM* by Jeremy Masters, Christos Kotsakis, and Venki Krishnamoorthy (SAP PRESS, 2010).
>
> As discussed earlier, each organization will differ in terms of the necessary fields on the form and the required approval process for requisitions. You can decide how to customize the forms and processes based on your specific business requirements. For more information on HCMPF, refer to *Discover SAP ERP HCM* by Greg Newman (SAP PRESS, 2009).

Now that all of the specific information for the payroll manager requisition has been entered and it has been routed through the proper approval process, an email will be sent to the lead recruiter letting him know that he has a new requisition to review. The lead recruiter then logs into SAP Enterprise Portal and views the new requisition in the My Draft Requisitions query, shown in Figure 5.12. Remember that the lead recruiter was defined in the support group that was selected by the manager, Dave Maker.

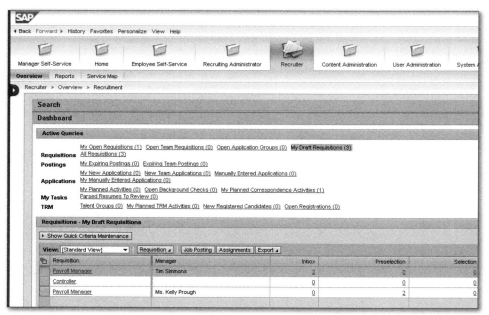

Figure 5.12 Payroll Manager Position in My Draft Requisitions Query

Let's examine the role of the recruiter further.

> **Key Point**
>
> One of the standard SAP roles is a restricted recruiter, who can also start the create requisition process. In this scenario, the restricted recruiter creates the requisition directly in E-Recruiting and then sends it to a recruiter for approval.

Recruiter

Now the recruiter can review or modify the newly created payroll manager requisition so that it can be released and candidates can begin applying. For the purposes of the book, we'll assume at this point that the recruiter and hiring manager have already discussed all of the important information that should go into the payroll manager requisition, so that by the time the recruiter gets the notification, he will be able to make the appropriate modifications.

Notice in Figure 5.13 that all of the information relating to the GENERAL JOB INFORMATION tab that was entered during creation of the payroll manager requisition has been carried over into the recruiter view. Take note of the PAYROLL MANAGER position, as it will increase in importance when we discuss the REQUIREMENTS tab.

The recruiter now reviews the GENERAL JOB INFORMATION tab for the payroll manager requisition. At this point, the recruiter could add additional information that was not included during the initial creation of the requisition such as the following:

- PROCESS TEMPLATE
- BRANCH
- SALARY RANGE/ADDITIONAL INFORMATION
- NUMBER OF POSITIONS
- COST CENTER
- ATTACHMENTS
- JOB FOR POSITION

After completing the GENERAL JOB INFORMATION tab, the recruiter then moves to the REQUIREMENTS tab, shown in Figure 5.14.

5 | Induction Phase

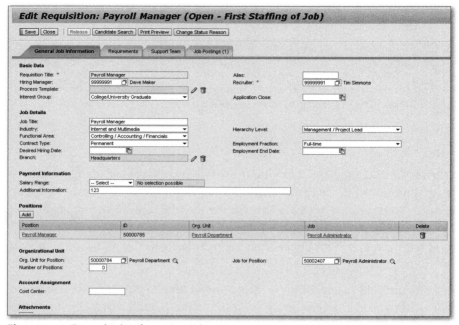

Figure 5.13 General Job Information Tab

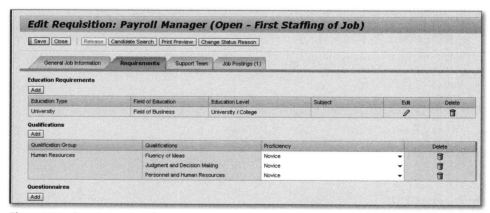

Figure 5.14 Requirements Tab

The recruiter now reviews the REQUIREMENTS tab, which is broken down into three sections:

▶ EDUCATION REQUIREMENTS
This is carried over from when the manager created the payroll manager requisition.

▶ QUALIFICATIONS
These are the same qualifications that were assigned to the payroll manager position in Section 1.2.4.

▶ QUESTIONNAIRES
These could be included on the process template or added here on this tab.

At this point, the recruiter could add additional requirements that were not included during the initial creation of the requisition. After completing the REQUIREMENTS tab, the recruiter then moves to the SUPPORT TEAM tab shown in Figure 5.15.

Figure 5.15 Support Team Tab

Members of the support team will be able to view and modify the payroll manager requisition depending on their role. Recall that the lead recruiter was defined in the support group that was selected by the manager. In addition, the manager that created the requisition is also defaulted in the SUPPORT TEAM tab.

At this point, the recruiter can add additional members to the support team. After the recruiter completes the review of the SUPPORT TEAM tab, he then moves to the JOB POSTINGS tab shown in Figure 5.16.

The JOB POSTINGS tab is broken down into three sections:

▶ GENERAL POSTING INFORMATION
this is information that was initially entered in the payroll manager requisition by the manager.

▸ Posting Text
This contains all of the relevant information that needs to be communicated about the vacancy. This could have been filled in manually by the manager, or (as was mentioned previously) it could be defaulted via a BAdI.

The posting text can be entered before releasing the requisition, but to create publications, the requisition needs to be in a "Released" status.

▸ Published Job Postings
This is the physical release of the of the posting information for a specified period of time. As discussed previously, the recruiter and manager would have already had a discussion regarding the best channels to post the vacancy (job boards, internal career site, etc.).

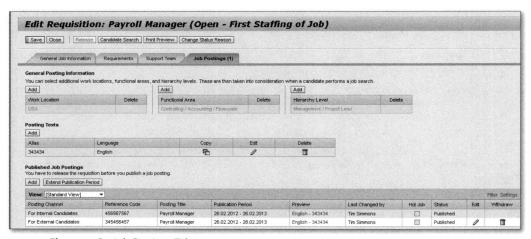

Figure 5.16 Job Postings Tab

> **Key Point**
>
> Many organizations use a job board distributor to post jobs to multiple sites at one time using a single interface. E-Recruiting can be integrated with a job board distributor based on client-specific requirements by using either SAP NetWeaver PI or a custom interface.

After the recruiter has reviewed all of the information and made the required changes, the payroll manager requisition is posted so that candidates can begin applying, which is part of the source process.

5.3.2 Source

The source process begins after the publication has been released. The candidate can search for open jobs, register, and eventually submit an application. In addition, the recruiter can search the talent pool and invite candidates to apply for open jobs.

Now that the requisition is created and posted, let's follow along as a candidate (Frank Jenkins) searches for the newly posted payroll manager position. At this point, the candidate could search on the company's career website, if it's a company that the candidate is targeting, or on various job boards such as Monster or CareerBuilder.

Candidate

For now, we will assume that Frank Jenkins will search on the company's career website for a payroll-related position. His search is shown in Figure 5.17.

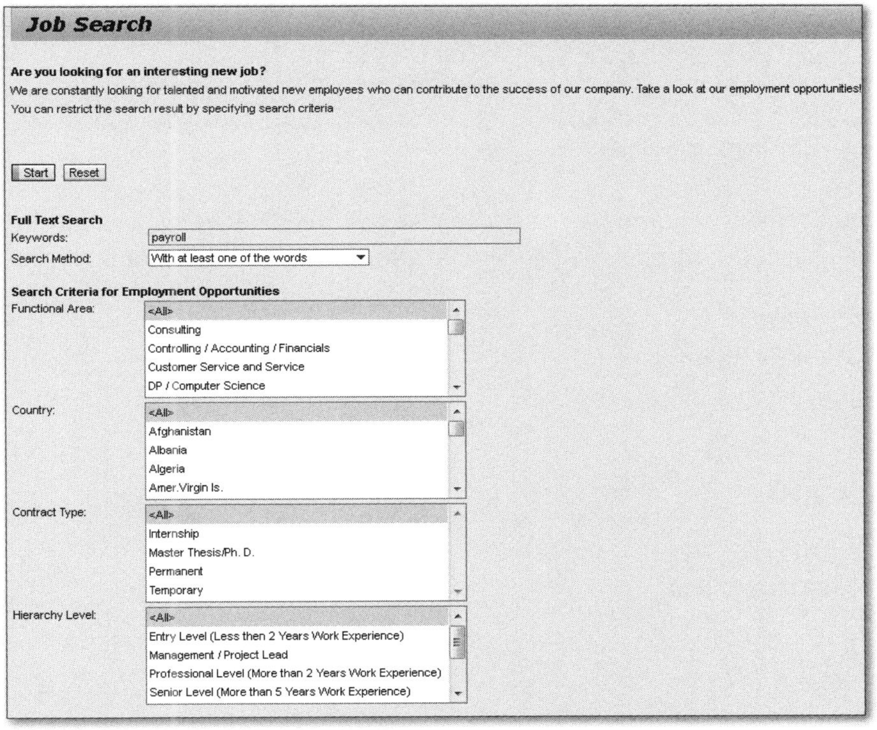

Figure 5.17 Job Search for Payroll Position

5 | Induction Phase

After the results come back from the "payroll" search, Frank finds that the payroll manager position best matches his background, so he chooses to apply. He will now be asked to register with the website using the Application Wizard shown in Figure 5.18. The one major change in the registration screen with EhP 5 is the ability to use an email address as the user name.

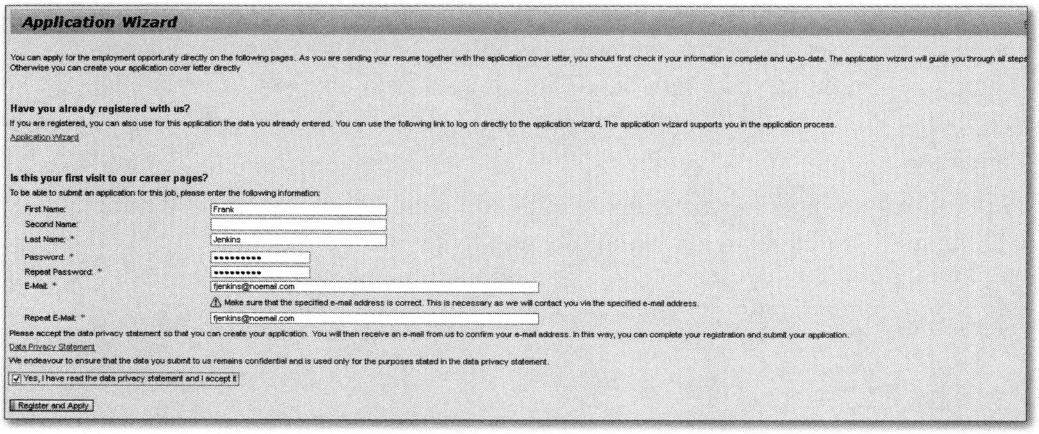

Figure 5.18 New Registration in EhP 5

After Frank Jenkins confirms his registration, he can complete the application. The standard system includes supplying the following data in the application process:

- Personal data
- Education/training
- Work experience
- Attachments
- Qualifications
- Cover letter
- Complete application

E-Recruiting | **5.3**

> **Key Point**
>
> Since EhP 4, E-Recruiting has enhanced the application to allow candidates to parse their résumés, which adds an additional step at the beginning of the process to upload a résumé. After the résumé is uploaded, information can then be parsed into the PERSONAL DATA, EDUCATION/TRAINING, WORK EXPERIENCE, ATTACHMENTS, and QUALIFICATIONS sections. SAP has vendors that have been certified on the résumé parsing interface.

Note the education information entered by Frank Jenkins, as shown in Figure 5.19. This will become important when we discuss the talent profile in Section 5.4.

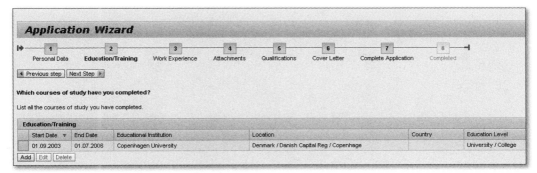

Figure 5.19 Education Information of Application

It's also worth noting that the qualifications that were assigned to the position earlier now appear in the QUALIFICATIONS step of the application process for Frank Jenkins, as shown in Figure 5.20.

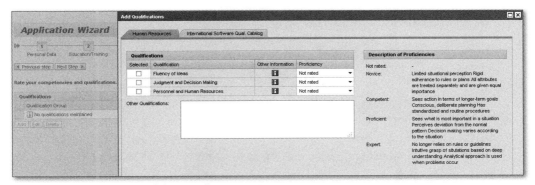

Figure 5.20 Qualifications of the Payroll Manager Position

Recruiter

From a recruiter point of view, the source process consists of two main activities:

- Searching the talent pool
- Inviting candidates to apply

After a recruiter has posted the requisition, a common activity is to search the available (internal or external) candidates within the talent pool that meet the minimum requirements. The talent pool lists the candidates that have released their profile and made themselves available for searches (see Figure 5.21).

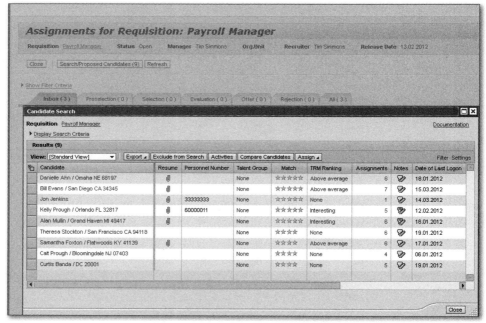

Figure 5.21 Talent Pool

The search function enables the recruiter to comb through the talent pool for suitable skills and assign them to the requisition. The search criterion defaults the structured data that was initially entered on the payroll manager requisition. The search can also be executed using unstructured (free-form text) data, as shown in Figure 5.22.

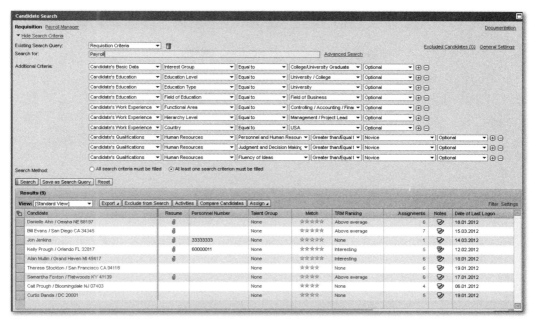

Figure 5.22 Search Criteria for the Payroll Manager Requisition

> **Key Point**
>
> In the United States, organizations are required to follow the guidelines set forth by the U.S. Office of Federal Contract Compliance Programs (OFCCP). As a result, the candidate search functionality usually becomes a major discussion point with the respective organization's legal department during implementation. To this end, companies should consult with their compliance officers or legal counsel during the implementation of E-Recruiting to verify that their recruiting procedures ensure compliance with the OFCCP guidelines and regulations.

After the recruiter has narrowed down the search results to a suitable number of candidates (only those who have not already applied), he can first assign those candidates to the requisition and then invite the same candidates to apply to the posting using the Invite to Apply activity. Figure 5.23 shows the INVITE TO APPLY selection in the PRESELECTION menu, which automatically sends an email message to internal and external candidates. You'll notice that Frank Jenkins doesn't appear in the list of candidates within the INBOX tab because he has already applied.

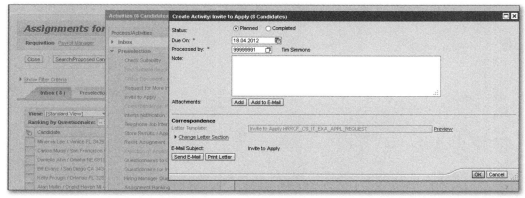

Figure 5.23 Invite to Apply Activity

After the activity has been completed, each candidate will get an email with a link back into E-Recruiting that allows them to apply to the payroll manager posting. After the recruiter finds candidates that meet the minimum requirements, the process then moves on to screening.

5.3.3 Screen

There are typically three main steps in the screening process:

- Suitability check
- Completing assessments (optional)
- Hiring manager review

Let's explore how each character in the E-Recruiting story plays a role in the screening process.

Recruiter

As part of the suitability check, the recruiter typically reviews the candidate résumé, assesses and ranks candidates by completed candidate questionnaires (shown in Figure 5.24 and Figure 5.25), ranks the candidates based on other search criteria, or performs a side-by-side comparison between multiple candidates using the comparison functionality shown in Figure 5.26.

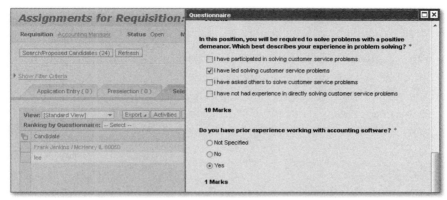

Figure 5.24 Assess Completed Questionnaires

Figure 5.25 Ranking by Questionnaire

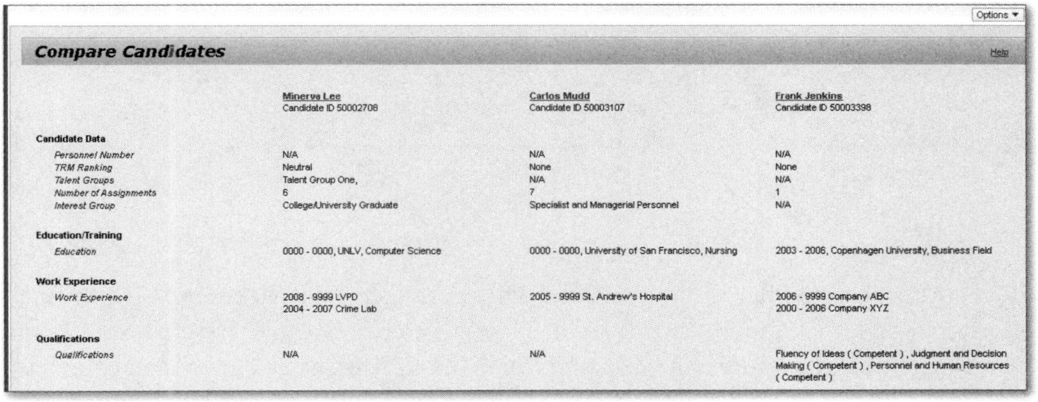

Figure 5.26 Compare Candidates Side by Side

After the recruiter completes the suitability check, he may then choose to conduct phone interviews with those candidates deemed suitable.

There is also an optional step within the screening process that typically takes place outside of E-Recruiting in which the candidate is sent to an assessment vendor for additional screening or processing. Again, this may not be a step that occurs with every candidate that passes the suitability check, but it's worth mentioning.

For our purposes, let's assume that the recruiter has completed a suitability check on all of the applicants and that Frank Jenkins not only meets the minimum requirements but is considered to be one of the top candidates for the payroll manager posting. To this end, Frank will be sent over to the manager, Dave Maker, for review via an activity that the recruiter executes, as shown in Figure 5.27.

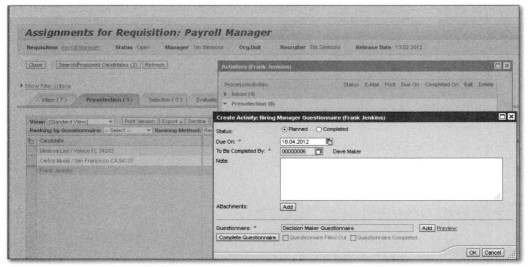

Figure 5.27 Send Candidate to Manager Activity

Manager

After the recruiter completes the activity, manager Dave Maker receives an email letting him know that Frank Jenkins is ready to be reviewed. He then reviews the résumé and questionnaire responses for Frank Jenkins. After Dave Maker completes the review, he finalizes the process by filling out a questionnaire that gets sent back to the recruiter, as shown in Figure 5.28.

If the manager deemed Frank Jenkins to be a suitable candidate, he completes a questionnaire that will be sent back to the recruiter. After the hiring manager has provided feedback to the recruiter on Frank Jenkins, the process then moves on to the interview.

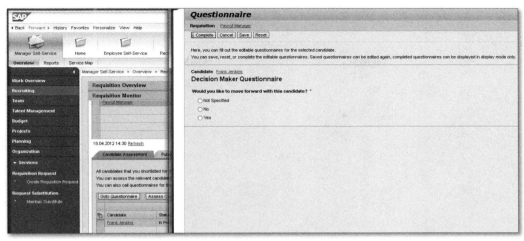

Figure 5.28 Manager Completes Questionnaire

5.3.4 Interview

Most of the interview process typically takes place outside of E-Recruiting and consists of the following steps:

1. Schedule the interview.
2. Conduct the interview.
3. Select the candidate.

The interview process begins with the recruiter scheduling interviews with the candidates that have passed the screening process. The logistics of the interview need to be coordinated and communicated to the appropriate individuals that will be involved in the interview. To this end, a Job Interview (correspondence) activity (shown in Figure 5.29) is executed in E-Recruiting and sent to the candidate, Frank Jenkins.

After the interview has been conducted, the interview team provides feedback about all candidates (including Frank Jenkins) to the recruiter and hiring manager, who choose a candidate to hire. For our purposes, let's assume that this lucky candidate is Frank Jenkins. To let the other candidates down nicely, the recruiter multi-selects the shortlisted candidates *not* selected for hire and organizes them in the system using the status-changing Rejection of Application activity (see Figure 5.30).

5 | Induction Phase

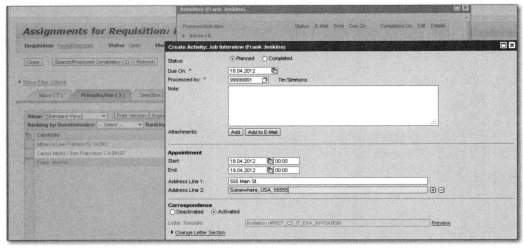

Figure 5.29 Interview Correspondence Activity for Frank Jenkins

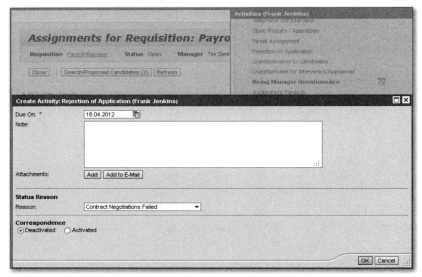

Figure 5.30 Rejection of Application Activity

We'll now move on to the hire process with Frank Jenkins.

5.3.5 Hire

There are typically three main steps in the hiring process:

- Extend the offer.
- Perform pre-employment checks (also known as background checks).
- Hire the candidate.

The recruiter first extends an offer to the candidate that was selected during the Interview process (in this case, Frank Jenkins). In our scenario, we'll generate an offer letter (using a Smart Form correspondence activity) and send it to Frank Jenkins through the E-Recruiting application shown in Figure 5.31.

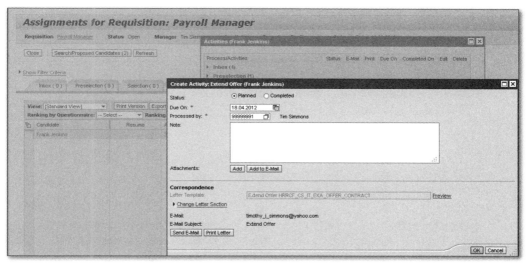

Figure 5.31 Extend Offer Activity

> **Key Point**
>
> Many organizations want to design several offer letter templates, each of them containing tremendous amounts of complex logic and approval workflow. Be careful! This could potentially add significant time and cost to your implementation. Also be sure you have skilled personnel within your project/development team that are familiar with how to build Smart Forms. Refer to Chapter 10, Section 10.2, for additional information on resource considerations.

After the offer is accepted by the candidate, the recruiter then coordinates pre-employment checks. This involves submitting the new hire information to a pre-employment check vendor via a Background Check activity (shown in Figure 5.32). When the results are returned and determined to be favorable, the candidate is then officially hired, and his data is officially transferred into the core SAP ERP HCM system.

Figure 5.32 Background Check Activity

> **Key Point**
>
> As of EhP 4, E-Recruiting has enhanced the application to allow background checks to be sent directly to third-party vendors as part of a pre-built interface; SAP has a vendor that has been certified on the background check interface.

Some examples of information validated in a pre-employment check include (but aren't limited to) the following:

- Education verification
- References
- Substance abuse screening
- Criminal checks

- Driver's license history
- Credit report
- Homeland Security check
- Employment verification
- Federal criminal court searches
- Sex offender registry
- Workers' compensation checks
- I-9 eligibility
- IQ screening
- Professional licenses/certifications

The vendor processes the information for Frank Jenkins and sends the results back to the recruiter for review. After the pre-employment checks have been reviewed to the satisfaction of the hiring organization, the recruiter then creates the Data Transfer For New Employees activity to eventually transfer the information for Frank Jenkins to the core HR (SAP ERP HCM) system. Figure 5.33 shows the Data Transfer for New Employees activity.

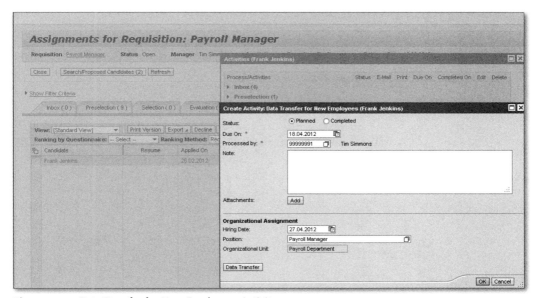

Figure 5.33 Data Transfer for New Employees Activity

As you recall from Section 5.3.1, HCMPF is being used in this process in the SAP NetWeaver PI framework. As a result, the recruiter can take advantage of the enhanced hiring integration with E-Recruiting when hiring Frank Jenkins, especially in relation to talent management and talent development processes. In addition to Frank's basic data such as personal data, position, and organizational unit, an EhP 5 business function (HCM_ERC_CI_4) also enables information about Frank's work experience, education, and qualifications (along with customer-specific fields) to be transferred from E-Recruiting into SAP ERP HCM.

> **Key Point**
>
> Some configuration is required to take advantage of the SAP NetWeaver PI interface because the standard system uses Transaction PA48 as part of the Data Transfer for New Employees activity. System parameters need to be changed in Table T77SO, and periodical service HIRE_REQUEST_VIA_XI needs to be activated and scheduled. For additional information on this new functionality, refer to the HCM_ERC_CI_4 business function documentation.

From a process perspective, the form carrying the new hire information for Frank Jenkins then gets sent to the HR administrator, who verifies that all of the information is correct and passes it to the core HR system (SAP ERP HCM). Frank Jenkins has officially been hired.

Now that Frank Jenkins fills the once-vacant position, the recruiter can begin the process of dispositioning any remaining candidates that weren't invited to interviews and therefore didn't receive the rejection letter.

To close the requisition, you must first withdraw all open publications.

> **Key Point**
>
> If you don't disposition (reject) the other candidates and withdraw open publications, the system will throw an error message, and you won't be able to close the requisition. Note that requisitions where candidates have applied can't be deleted but can be closed.

5.4 Talent Profile

Now that Frank Jenkins has been hired into the organization, he has to create his talent profile in ESS. As mentioned in Chapter 4, Section 4.5.1, the talent profile is where employees can maintain talent-related information that is used in Talent Management processes. If employees can't maintain this information themselves, for whatever reason, then either their manager can maintain this information through MSS, or a Talent Management specialist can maintain this information through the Talent Management Specialist portal role. After Frank has maintained his data, his manager can then review and validate this information. At any stage, a Talent Management specialist can review this information in the same way that Frank's manager can.

5.4.1 Talent Profile for Employees

Frank accesses the Talent Profile for Employees by navigating to CAREER AND JOB in ESS and selecting TALENT PROFILE. Upon launching the Talent Profile application, Frank will immediately see a brief summary of his personal and organizational assignment data in the header section of the application. This information includes his name, personnel ID, age, date of birth, organizational unit, manager, job and position.

Below this are the six tabs where Frank will enter the information about himself:

- INTERNAL WORK EXPERIENCE
- EXTERNAL WORK EXPERIENCE
- EDUCATION
- ACCOMPLISHMENTS
- CAREER GOAL
- MOBILITY

In each tab, Frank can maintain different attributes about that particular area. When maintaining data, Frank can either enter this via a free-text box, or he can select the value from a predefined list of values. In most cases, the latter is the option available to Frank.

The first tab, INTERNAL WORK EXPERIENCE, is open by default and displays a list of organizational assignments within the company. Because Frank is a new employee, he will only see one entry for the PAYROLL MANAGER position that he has just filled. For this assignment, he can view the date period, job, organizational unit, personnel area, and personnel subarea.

Frank can also maintain details of any projects he has been involved in within the organization. This won't be relevant now, but Frank can return later to enter data should he become part of an internal project. When he does, he will have the option to maintain details such as the project title, date period, his role, span of control, project contact, location, and description; he can also upload any relevant attachments.

The second tab, EXTERNAL WORK EXPERIENCE, gives Frank the opportunity to validate the work experience that was brought over from E-Recruiting, which summarizes each of his previous positions outside of the company. With each entry, Frank must validate the name of the employer and the period of employment. Frank can then validate the job title, industry, functional area, hierarchy level, span of control, contract type, working time, location, and description; he can also upload files that support the entries. Frank reviews the details of his previous positions so that the full scope of his experience is accurate.

Figure 5.34 shows Frank's previous employer in the EXTERNAL WORK EXPERIENCE tab of the talent profile for employees.

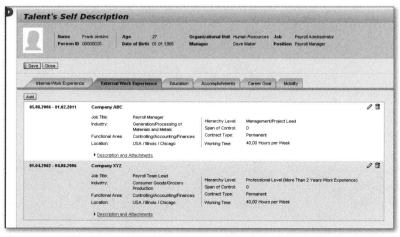

Figure 5.34 The External Work Experience Tab in the Talent Profile for Employees

The next tab, EDUCATION, gives Frank the opportunity to validate the education information that was brought over from E-Recruiting, which summarizes the details about his education and any training he has received. Because so many candidates are high-performing and high-potential individuals with degree-level education, it's no surprise that the EDUCATION tab is focused around this level of education, and most of the entry options reflect this.

Frank can validate institution, period of education, field of study description, education type, field, degree title, grade, degree level, whether this is the highest level of degree, location, descriptions, and any relevant documents that were uploaded to support the entries.

> **Key Point**
>
> Traditionally, education data has been maintained by HR in Infotype 0022. In some countries, this has a legal foundation or is used as the basis for pay grading and salary calculations. SAP introduced Infotype 7404 with EhP 4 to store education data that is maintained by the employee. It's important to note that there is no integration between these infotypes, and no reports exist that allow data to be transferred between the two infotypes. There are various advantages and disadvantages of this data model; whether having two different and separate infotypes is valuable varies from organization to organization.

Figure 5.35 shows the education details that Frank validated in the EDUCATION tab of the talent profile for employees. Note that it's identical to the data entered into E-Recruiting.

Figure 5.35 Education Tab of the Talent Profile for Employees

In the ACCOMPLISHMENTS tab, Frank can enter details about his personal accomplishments and achievements outside of work and education. For each accomplishment, the accomplishment and period in which it was accomplished must be entered, with optional entries for the type of accomplishment, a contact name for verification of the accomplishment, and a description. As with entries on the other tabs, Frank can also upload any relevant documents to support the entry.

As an example, let's say that Frank has been offering financial advice on an informal basis to friends and family, and he is very proud of helping these individuals increase their personal wealth and well-being. He decides to enter this information into his talent profile.

Frank now enters his career goals and job preferences in the CAREER GOAL tab. Frank can select a career type and level, choose his preferred jobs, and enter a note about his career goals. Frank is ambitious and selects a career type of MANAGEMENT CAREER with level TOP MANAGEMENT. He also adds a preferred job, HR VP, which he selects through a series of drop-down boxes based on the following job architecture: FUNCTIONAL AREA, JOB FAMILY, and JOB. Last, Frank enters a note that he is committed to long-term development to meet his goals.

> **Key Point**
>
> A career type is used to identify an employee's career aspiration and also used to define the projected career path of a job or position. Career types also have levels defined so that the career path can be more accurately defined.

Figure 5.36 shows Frank's career goal and job preferences.

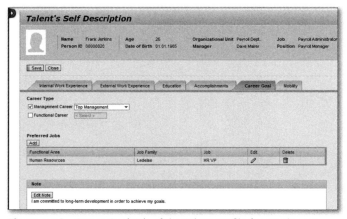

Figure 5.36 Career Goal Tab of the Talent Profile for Employees

The final tab is the MOBILITY tab, as shown in Figure 5.37.

Figure 5.37 Mobility Tab of the Talent Profile for Employees

Here Frank enters his preferences for relocating to other parts of the country or even to other countries, should this be applicable to his organization. First, Frank can specify whether he is willing to relocate, followed by the locations that he would and would not like to relocate to. The level of granularity is such that Frank can select countries, areas of countries, and regions of countries. Frank also has the option to enter a note.

Frank enters that he is willing to relocate and, because he has always liked the idea of living in Europe, enters the European Union as encompassing the countries that he would consider. Frank also enters a note that he needs a notice of six months for relocation.

Now that Frank has completed his talent profile, he reviews all of the information before selecting the SAVE option.

5.4.2 Talent Profile for Managers and Talent Management Specialists

Now that Frank has completed the process of maintaining his talent profile, the data needs to be reviewed and validated by his manager in the talent profile for managers and Talent Management specialists. This is accessed in MSS via TALENT MANAGEMENT • TALENT INFORMATION • TALENT PROFILE. Frank's talent profile can also be reviewed by a Talent Management specialist through the TMS portal role via TALENT INFORMATION • TALENT PROFILE.

Upon opening the talent profile for managers and Talent Management specialists, Frank's manager will be taken to the OVERVIEW tab. On the left side, he will see a brief summary of Frank's personal TALENT DATA and ORGANIZATIONAL ASSIGNMENT data, in much the same way as the header in the Talent Profile for Employees. This information includes his name, talent group memberships and status (nominated or approved), mobility, risks, career goal, manager, position, level of position (career level), location, organizational unit, job, functional area, job family, and successor nominations.

In a similar way to the Talent Profile for Employees, the Talent Profile for Managers and Talent Management Specialists has six tabs that contain different information: OVERVIEW, RÉSUMÉ, TALENT ASSESSMENT, MOBILITY, CAREER GOAL, and DEVELOPMENT PLAN.

> **Key Point**
>
> EhP 5 includes an integration switch for the Talent Profile for Managers and Talent Management Specialists to display the qualifications assigned to the skills profile, rather than just those that are assigned as core competencies. This provides a seventh tab on the talent profile that contains all of the qualifications assigned to the individual.

The following are the category boxes contained in the OVERVIEW tab that provide Frank's manager with a detailed overview of Frank's profile:

- PERFORMANCE
- POTENTIAL
- CORE COMPETENCIES
- DERAILERS
- MOBILITY
- LANGUAGES
- INTERNAL WORK EXPERIENCE
- FUTURE DEVELOPMENT
- ACCOMPLISHMENTS
- CAREER GOALS
- MOBILITY

The PERFORMANCE and POTENTIAL categories both contain the last three performance and potential ratings of the employee so that the manager can track and review the employee's progress over the previous three years. Frank won't have any data at this stage, so the categories will display the text "No Data Available."

Beginning with EhP 6, it will be possible to display the appraisal documents from the Performance Management appraisal process in the talent profile.

The CORE COMPETENCIES category displays the employee's ratings for those competencies that have been assigned as core competencies. By default, these ratings come from the competency assessment of the talent assessment, although from EhP 5, it's possible to display the ratings directly from the employee's skills profile. With this setting, Frank's manager is able to validate Frank's qualifications without needing to request a list from HR. The LANGUAGES category displays the languages that are assessed in the competency assessment.

The DERAILERS category, like the CORE COMPETENCIES category, displays data from the derailers assessment of the talent assessment. The competency assessment and derailers assessment are covered in more detail in Chapter 6, Section 6.2.

The MOBILITY and INTERNAL WORK EXPERIENCE categories display a summary of this data from the talent profile for employees. The last category, FUTURE DEVELOPMENT, displays a summary of the development plan.

The OVERVIEW tab of Frank's talent profile is displayed in Figure 5.38.

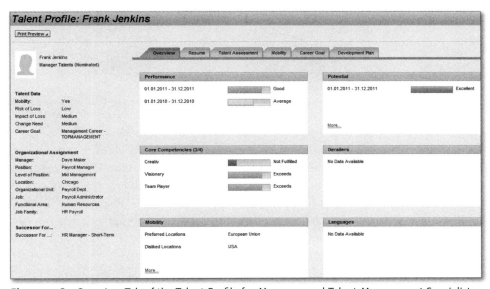

Figure 5.38 Overview Tab of the Talent Profile for Managers and Talent Management Specialists

The RÉSUMÉ tab enables Frank's manager to get a graphical representation of Frank's entire work history, education, and accomplishments. This is Frank's organizational assignment data, plus the data he entered in the INTERNAL WORK EXPERIENCE, EXTERNAL WORK EXPERIENCE, EDUCATION, and ACCOMPLISHMENTS tabs in the talent profile for employees. These tabs are also available for display inside the RÉSUMÉ tab, as shown in Figure 5.39.

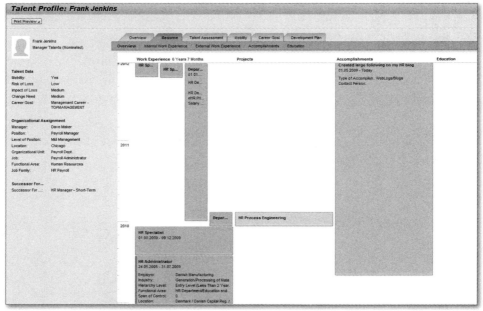

Figure 5.39 Résumé Tab of the Talent Profile for Managers and Talent Management Specialists

In the TALENT ASSESSMENT tab, Frank's manager can display each of the completed talent assessment forms so that he can review Frank's assessment. If an assessment was performed by a different manager during the period, then Frank's current manager can display the assessments performed by that manager. These forms display as they are seen within the talent assessment process, and more information can be found in Chapter 6, Section 6.2.

From EhP 5, the QUALIFICATIONS tab gives a comprehensive view of Frank's qualifications that are assigned to his skills profile. This can be used to verify the qualifications that were assigned from the E-Recruiting system.

Both the MOBILITY and CAREER GOAL tabs display Frank's information in the exact same way as in the Talent Profile for Employees.

The final tab, DEVELOPMENT PLAN, displays Frank's development plan. At this stage, the DEVELOPMENT PLAN tab is likely to be empty, but after the development plan has been created, it can be monitored from here. The information in the tab is displayed in the same way as in the development plan process (more information can be found in Chapter 8).

> **Key Point**
>
> If an employee has been assessed by more than one manager for the talent assessment appraisals, then the talent profile OVERVIEW tab will display the mean value of the assessment values for the potential, risks, derailers, and competencies assessments.

To assist with review or correction, or for assisting talent calibration or succession activities, EhP 5 provides the option to print the Talent Profile for Managers and Talent Management Specialists. Beginning with EhP 6, it will also be possible to get an overview of the learning activities of the employee in their talent profile.

Now that the Frank's manager has reviewed the talent profile, he can pass on any comments to Frank or HR, and the process can continue to the next phase.

5.5 Summary

It's vitally important to have a workforce plan in place that aligns with the strategic goals of the organization because it puts the right number of people with the right skills, experiences, and competencies in the right jobs at the right time, creating a foundation for making strategic business decisions.

After the workforce plan is complete, position management can help determine the number of positions needed, the skill and knowledge requirements of those positions, and the organizational grouping of positions to carry out the work done during the workforce planning process. If used in a disciplined way, position management also provides tools that can be used to improve methods and processes. Finally, numerous costs are associated with an unfilled position within any organization. Many of these costs are difficult to quantify but are very real, nonetheless. Be diligent in your efforts to quantify what the true costs of unfilled positions are for your organization.

SAP position management allows relationships to be built between positions and jobs, which allows those same positions to inherit the qualifications that have already been assigned to the job they are being relationally aligned with. Using the key position indicator enables additional succession planning functionality later in the process. This can be accomplished for individual positions via Transaction HRTMC_PPOM as well as in STVN SuccessionPlanning. It's also possible for organizations to set a number of key positions in a single transaction by using Transaction SE38 and running Report RPTMC_SET_KEY_INDICATION.

The E-Recruiting process always begins with the assumptions that the position being recruited for has already been approved and created in the SAP ERP HCM system, and the position is available in E-Recruiting via ALE from the SAP ERP HCM system. If qualifications are assigned to a position, they are subsequently defaulted in when the recruiter creates, reviews, or maintains the requisition.

As of EhP 5, candidates can use their email address as their user name within the source process, and recruiters can perform side-by-side comparisons as part of the screen process. Most of the interview process takes place outside of E-Recruiting. As part of the hire process, E-Recruiting has enhanced the application to allow background checks to be sent directly to third-party vendors as part of a pre-built interface.

Finally, after an individual has been hired into the company, he maintains his own talent profile. This provides his manager and the Talent Management specialists with a detailed summary of all talent-related information about the individual.

Now that Frank Jenkins has been hired and his manager has reviewed the talent profile, the process can continue. In the next chapter, we'll look at how to set up performance objectives, do a talent assessment, and conduct a mid-year review for Frank Jenkins.

The next Talent Management phase covers steps taken to identify Frank's professional objectives, assess his potential, and provide support and feedback as part of the mid-year appraisal process.

6   Assessment Phase

Talent retention is one of the most important goals for CEOs and executives. More companies are striving to retain their high performers, who drive their organization's performance, productivity, and profitability. One of the most fundamental ways you can retain and develop employees is through a timely performance planning and evaluation process.

The *assessment phase* serves as the foundation for objective setting, talent assessment, and performance measurement. Goals are set successfully when the employee and manager have a shared understanding of the goals, behaviors, and competencies required for the position, as well as the measures that assess whether or not the goals were achieved. When the employee knows what is expected—that is, the basis on which performance is reviewed—then the performance review discussions (both mid-year and year-end) tend to go much smoother.

> **Note**
>
> As discussed in Chapter 4, there are two solutions for SAP Performance Management: predefined and flexible. For the purposes of this chapter, we'll be referring exclusively to the flexible solution.

With Frank Jenkins now officially hired into our fictitious organization, his manager will work with him to begin setting objectives for his new position as payroll manager.

6.1 SAP ERP HCM Performance Management: Objective Setting

The two main components to setting objectives are the prepare process and the planning process. Let's explore each of these further.

6.1.1 Prepare

Recall from Chapter 4 that the prepare process involves two steps:

1. Identifying the participants
2. Generating the documents

Because Frank Jenkins is our main concern from a participant perspective, we'll assume that the appraisal document has already been generated.

> **More Information on Appraisal Documents**
>
> Refer to *SAP ERP HCM Performance Management* by Jeremy Masters and Christos Kotsakis (SAP PRESS, 2008) for additional information on configuring and generating appraisal documents.

6.1.2 Planning

For our purposes, the planning process will consist of the following steps:

1. Setting corporate goals
2. Setting team goals
3. Setting individual objectives

We'll explore each of these in the following subsections.

Setting Corporate Goals

Corporate goals are created by the Talent Management specialist and can be cascaded throughout the organization. This functionality can be used to maintain corporate goals and core values to selected organizational units. After a goal or value (or both) gets cascaded, it's available in the corresponding employee Performance

Management document. Let's create a corporate goal called "Stewardship." Figure 6.1 shows the first screen for creating this new goal, which includes the following elements:

- TITLE
- VALIDITY FROM/VALID TO
- DESCRIPTION
- KPI/MEASUREMENT

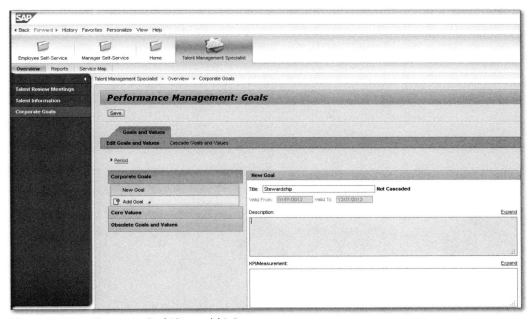

Figure 6.1 New Corporate Goal "Stewardship"

After the new corporate goal has been saved, you need to cascade it to the appropriate organizational units. Figure 6.2 shows the screen in which the Talent Management specialist selects HUMAN RESOURCES from the ORGANIZATIONAL UNIT column and all subsequent organizational units within HUMAN RESOURCES to cascade the corporate goal to. (Notice that FRANK JENKINS is the holder of PAYROLL MANAGER in the POSITION column within this organizational unit.)

6 Assessment Phase

Figure 6.2 Organizational Units for Cascaded Goal

After the goal has been cascaded and saved, a green checkmark will appear next to it, as shown in Figure 6.3. This icon indicates that the goal has been transferred to all respective employee performance management documents.

Figure 6.3 Cascaded Corporate Goal Successfully Saved

> **Key Point**
>
> To add and cascade a core value, the user needs to follow the same process steps as when adding and cascading corporate goals. The only difference is that there is no key performance indicator/measurement for core values.

Setting Team Goals

Team goals are created by managers and can be cascaded to the rest of their teams. This assumes that Organizational Management (OM) has been set up correctly to include chief positions. After a goal gets cascaded from the manager to the members of his team, it's available in the corresponding employee Performance Management document. Let's create a team goal called "Increase Payroll Accuracy." Figure 6.4 shows the new goal being created, including the elements used in the previous goal.

Figure 6.4 New Team Goal "Increase Payroll Accuracy"

After the new team goal has been saved, it needs to be cascaded down to the team members within the manager's organizational unit. Figure 6.5 shows the manager (Dave Maker) selecting the members of his team that he wants the team goal to be cascaded to. (Again, Frank Jenkins is the holder of the payroll manager position within the team.) As with the corporate goal, after the team goal has been cascaded and saved, a green checkmark will appear next to it, indicating that the goal has been transferred to all respective employee Performance Management documents (also shown in Figure 6.5).

6 | Assessment Phase

Figure 6.5 Goal Cascaded to Team Members

> **Key Point**
>
> The manager has the ability to cascade team goals by direct reports, organizational unit structure, or employee structure. In addition, goals can be deleted until they are cascaded. After goals have been cascaded, they can only be set to "obsolete."

Setting Individual Objectives

Now that the corporate goals and team goals have been established, let's set individual objectives for Frank Jenkins. This requires specifying the required levels of performance and identifying the objectives to be achieved. It's important that Frank and his manager (Dave Maker) agree upon and understand each other's expectations of the job. This understanding is the foundation upon which the entire Performance Management process will be built and the reason why it's important that the objective setting is done well. Therefore, before any attempt can be made to review Frank's performance, Frank and his manager must have a common understanding of what constitutes good performance.

After Frank and Dave Maker agree on the objectives that Frank will be evaluated on, Dave can create a new appraisal document for Frank (based on the appraisal document that was already generated in Section 6.1). After Dave confirms that all of the information is correct (validity dates, employee, etc.), the objectives can be established for Frank.

SAP ERP HCM Performance Management: Objective Setting | 6.1

> **Key Point**
>
> We're assuming that the appraisal document generated in Section 6.1 includes placeholders for adding corporate goals, team goals, competencies, and learning/training goals. For the purposes of our discussion in Chapter 6, we'll only be focusing our attention on the first two tabs of the appraisal document: GOALS and COMPETENCIES.

The first tab is the GOALS tab, which allows Dave Maker to view the corporate and team goals and also allows him to add individual and training goals to Frank's appraisal document.

The corporate goal and team goal that were created earlier in the chapter are shown in Figure 6.6.

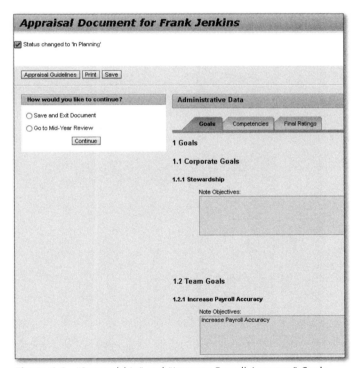

Figure 6.6 "Stewardship" and "Increase Payroll Accuracy" Goals

At this point, you can also add individual goals to the appraisal document for Frank. These can vary depending on the requirements of the individual or for the position. For the purposes of this discussion, we won't go into detail here.

Finally, Dave Maker would like to add goals from the Learning Catalog that pertain to Frank's position of payroll manager. To this end (as shown in Figure 6.7), the following three learning/training goals will be added to Frank's appraisal document:

- Leading basics
- Leading advanced
- Top talent

These goals are expected to be completed prior to the mid-year review, as shown in Figure 6.7. Finally, you'll see these three learning goals again in Chapter 7 and Chapter 8.

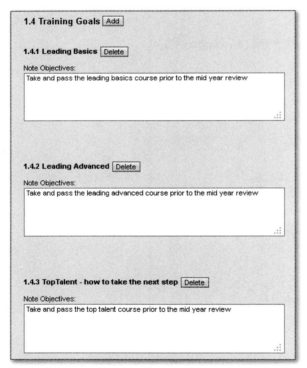

Figure 6.7 Three Training Goals from the Learning Catalog

The second tab is the COMPETENCIES tab, which allows Dave Maker to add competencies from the Qualifications Catalog to Frank's appraisal document. For the purposes of our discussion, we'll be using the same three competencies in Frank's appraisal document that were created and assigned to the payroll manager position in Chapter 3, which include the following:

- Fluency of ideas
- Judgment and decision making
- Personnel and human resources

These three competencies are shown in Figure 6.8.

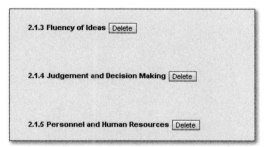

Figure 6.8 Adding Competency Goals from the Qualifications Catalog

> **Key Point**
>
> As discussed in Chapter 4, the Performance Management flexible solution allows for variations in the process. To this end, the application can be configured so that the employee (in this case, Frank) also reviews the goals (established by the manager) and provides comments. For our purposes, however, these steps won't be shown, so you can assume that Frank has completed this part of the process.

Now that the objective setting portion of the appraisal document has concluded, Frank's manager can evaluate Frank's potential through talent assessment.

6.2 Talent Assessment

Manager Dave Maker can now perform an assessment of Frank's talent-related attributes. The outcome of this step provides Dave Maker and the Talent Management specialists with a snapshot of Frank's potential, risks, core competencies, derailers to progression, and possible talent group nominations. This information will help to determine whether Frank can be considered to be a "talent" within the organization.

This assessment is typically performed solely by the manager, so Dave Maker can choose to complete the assessments at any stage of the assessment phase.

When Dave Maker opens the Assessment application, he is presented with all of the talent assessment forms with the status "In process" for each of their employees. Dave Maker also has the opportunity to select all forms that are "Complete," so he can review current and previous assessment forms that are completed.

Because Frank is new to the company, his forms will still be in "In Process" status. There are five forms available for assessing different attributes:

- Potential
- Risks
- Competencies
- Derailers
- Talent groups

The content of the forms will vary for each organization, depending on the organization's talent management strategy. Whereas the talent groups form is standard, the individual elements that can be added to each form in customizing can vary. Some of these elements can be seen in Figure 6.9.

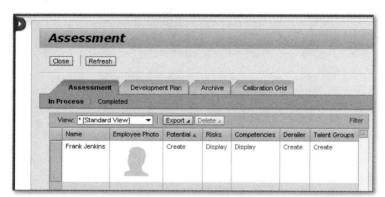

Figure 6.9 Assessment Capability in Manager Self-Services

6.2.1 Potential

Even though Frank is relatively new to the company, Dave Maker must evaluate his potential for growth and progression within the organization. By default, the potential form has one element for Dave Maker to assess the overall potential for Frank, thought it may also have a number of other areas in which to assess Frank's potential. These may include rating potential ability, mindset, and leadership potential. A predefined scale is used to evaluate each of these assessments.

The overall potential rating that is provided is used to calibrate employees in Frank's team, as well as on a performance versus potential grid in the talent review meeting. It will also be used to help identify high-performing, high-potential individuals in the performance versus potential grid in succession planning.

Because Frank was an impressive candidate for the position originally, he is rated as ADVANCED, as shown in Figure 6.10. Frank is also rated positively in the other potential areas.

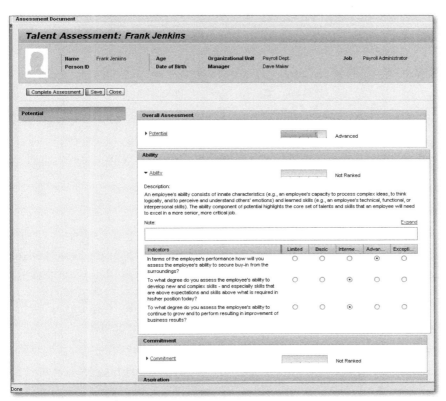

Figure 6.10 Potential Assessment

6 | Assessment Phase

Dave Maker must now assess different risks associated with Frank, such as risk of loss, impact of loss, and change need.

6.2.2 Risks

At present, Frank offers little risk of leaving the organization so he is rated as low risk, but because he was an excellent candidate, it's decided that the impact of him leaving would be of medium risk. For individuals who are influential in the success of the organization, their risk of loss and impact of loss ratings indicate to the Talent Management specialists that action must be taken to retain these individuals within the organization.

But because Frank is new in his payroll manager position, his change need is rated as Low risk, as shown in Figure 6.11.

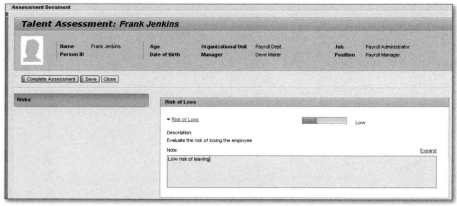

Figure 6.11 Risk Assessment

6.2.3 Competencies

In addition to the competencies that Frank holds via his position, he is assessed on the organization's core competencies. Depending on the organization, the competency groups that are assessed can vary from competencies to specialist competencies to languages to simply core competencies. For the purposes of our scenario, we'll use core competencies, basic competencies, and leadership competencies.

Figure 6.12 shows that the CORE COMPETENCIES include TEAM PLAYER, VISIONARY, FLEXIBLE, and CREATIVE competencies. The BASIC COMPETENCIES include the competencies discussed earlier that are already aligned to the payroll manager position (Fluency of Ideas, Judgment and Decision Making, and Personnel and Human Resources). There will also be leadership competencies, which include team focus, organized, coaching, and change management.

As shown in Figure 6.12, Dave Maker rates Frank on each of these core and basic competencies and enters any relevant notes, such as that development is required or that he is unable to assess Frank at this time.

Figure 6.12 Competency Assessment

These competencies, if they don't already exist, are then created in Frank's skills profile so they are available in the talent profile and to other SAP applications. Any competencies that already exist in his skill profile will have their proficiency rating updated.

6.2.4 Derailers

In additional to those assessments that evaluate how Frank can progress, Dave Maker can now evaluate some attributes that could prevent Frank from developing or progressing further in the organization. Derailers are negative attributes of an individual, such as dishonesty, insensitivity, arrogance, inability to work in a team, inability to delegate, and difficulty adapting.

6 | Assessment Phase

Figure 6.13 shows where Dave Maker makes an assessment of Frank, which in this case is positive.

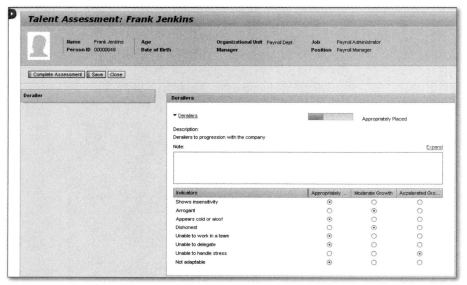

Figure 6.13 Derailers Assessment

6.2.5 Talent Groups

Now that Dave Maker has assessed Frank's talent-related attributes, he has the opportunity to nominate Frank for one or more of the available talent groups in the SAP system. Because Frank's manager has high hopes for Frank, he nominates him for the HIGH PERFORMERS talent group, as shown in Figure 6.14.

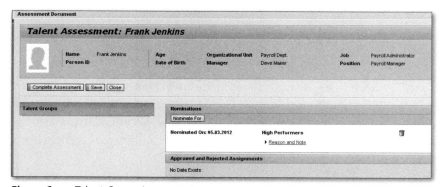

Figure 6.14 Talent Group Assessment

Now that Dave Maker and the Talent Management specialists have a snapshot of Frank's potential, risks, core competencies, derailers to progression, and possible talent group nominations, it's time for the mid-year review. This is when Dave Maker can evaluate Frank's performance relative to the objectives established in Section 6.1.

6.3 SAP ERP HCM Performance Management: Mid-Year Review

As we discussed in Section 6.1, managers should review the performance requirements for all positions within their span of control to help ensure that employees understand what is expected of them. If employees know what is expected of them, know how their performance will be measured, and can receive periodic feedback, then the formal evaluation session itself is less threatening. It can be a productive event because it provides an opportunity for the employee and manager to have a two-way, future-oriented discussion about progress toward meeting the appropriate performance objectives. After those performance objectives are mutually agreed upon, a comparison of actual employee performance becomes the basis for a mid-year performance review.

The objective of the mid-year review is to make sure that performance is on track and to make adjustments to plans that may have changed due to unanticipated events. Employees expect feedback from their managers throughout the performance cycle, so many see the mid-year review as a more formal opportunity to discuss how things are going and avoid any surprises at year end.

> **Key Point**
>
> One way to achieve productive feedback about performance is to encourage employees to document progress toward their objectives and to track their development activities during the course of the performance year. Managers should also document specific examples for their employees.

6.3.1 Manager

Dave Maker will now go into Performance Management to formally document Frank's performance as part of the mid-year review. As discussed in Section 6.1, the first tab is the GOAL tab, which allows Dave Maker to evaluate Frank's performance with regard to corporate, team, individual, and training goals.

The first goal that Frank will be evaluated against is the corporate goal of "Stewardship," which was created in Section 6.1.2. Figure 6.15 shows Dave Maker's mid-year assessment and accompanying comments.

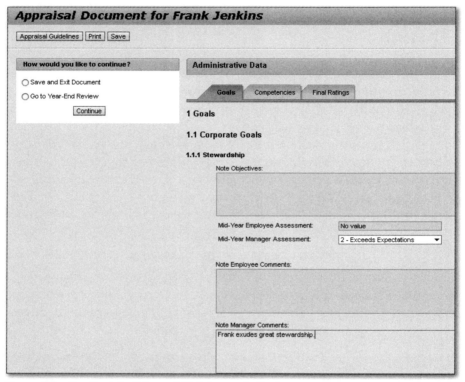

Figure 6.15 Feedback for "Stewardship" Corporate Goal

The next goal that Frank will be evaluated against is the team goal called "Increase Payroll Accuracy", which was also created in Section 6.1.2 (see Figure 6.16).

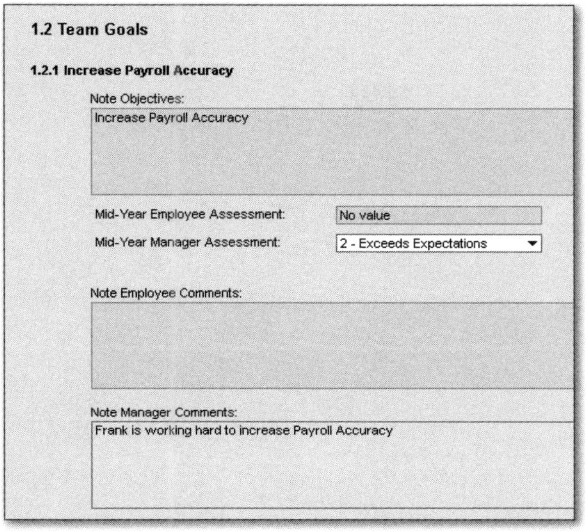

Figure 6.16 Feedback for "Increase Payroll Accuracy" Team Goal

After Dave Maker provides a mid-year assessment and comments for Frank's individual goals, Frank is now evaluated against the goals from the learning catalog, which pertain to his position as payroll manager. Figure 6.17 shows how Dave Maker rated his performance for one of the training goals (LEADING BASICS).

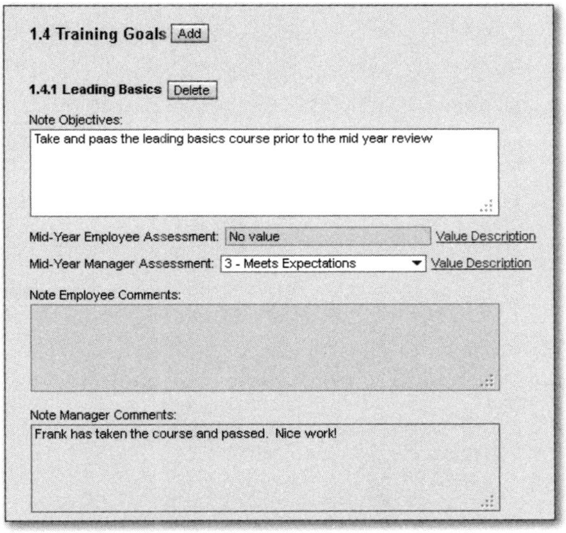

Figure 6.17 Feedback for Training Goals

6 | Assessment Phase

The second tab is the COMPETENCIES tab, which will allow Dave Maker to review Frank's performance on the following three competencies from the Qualifications Catalog: fluency of ideas, judgment and decision making, and personnel and human resources. Figure 6.18 shows how Dave Maker assessed his performance in these areas.

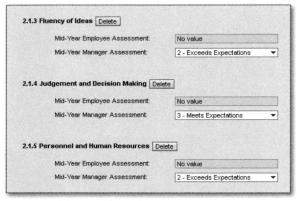

Figure 6.18 Feedback for Competencies

Now that Dave Maker has completed his mid-year review, Frank can provide a self-assessment and comments on his own performance.

> **Key Point**
>
> Performance Management provides several BAdIs that can be modified to meet customer-specific business requirements. To this end, workflow can be tailored to notify both employees and managers at various stages of the process. For the purposes of our discussion, we'll assume that Frank has received a notification that he needs to go into Performance Management and take action on his appraisal document. BAdIs will be discussed in more detail in Chapter 9.

6.3.2 Employee

Frank will now go into Performance Management to formally document his own performance as part of the mid-year review. The first tab is the GOAL tab, which allows Frank to evaluate his own performance.

The first goal that Frank will evaluate himself against is the corporate goal of "Stewardship." As shown in Figure 6.19, Frank can provide a mid-year assessment along with comments.

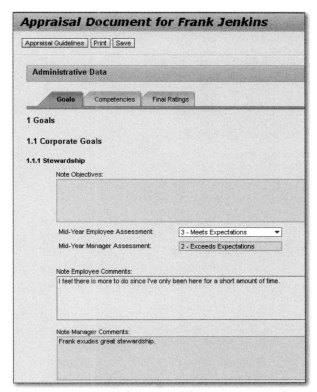

Figure 6.19 Feedback for "Stewardship" Corporate Goal

The next goal that Frank will evaluate himself against is the team goal "Increase Payroll Accuracy," followed by an individual goal (see Figure 6.20).

After Frank provides a mid-year assessment and comments on his individual goals, he is now able to evaluate himself against the goals from the learning catalog, which pertain to his position as payroll manager. Figure 6.21 illustrates his self-assessment for the LEADING BASICS objective.

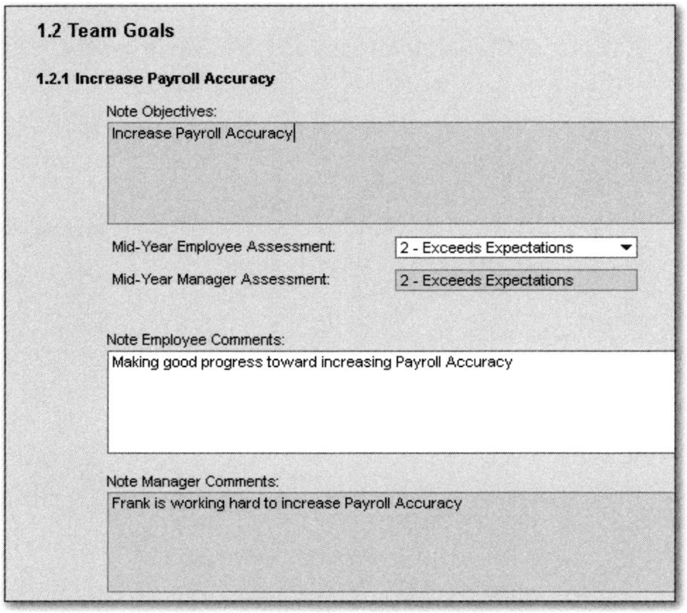

Figure 6.20 Feedback for "Increase Payroll Accuracy" Team Goal

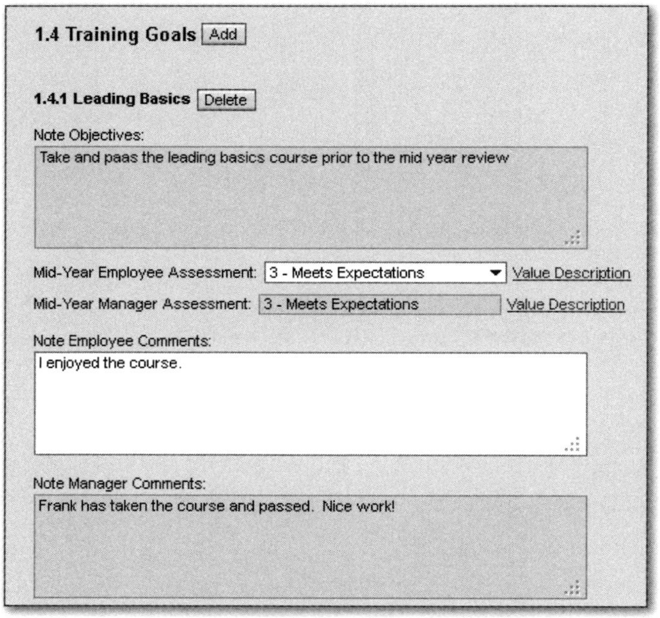

Figure 6.21 Feedback for Training Goals

The second tab is the COMPETENCIES tab, which is where Frank evaluates his performance on the three competencies from the Qualifications Catalog. His self-evaluation is shown in Figure 6.22.

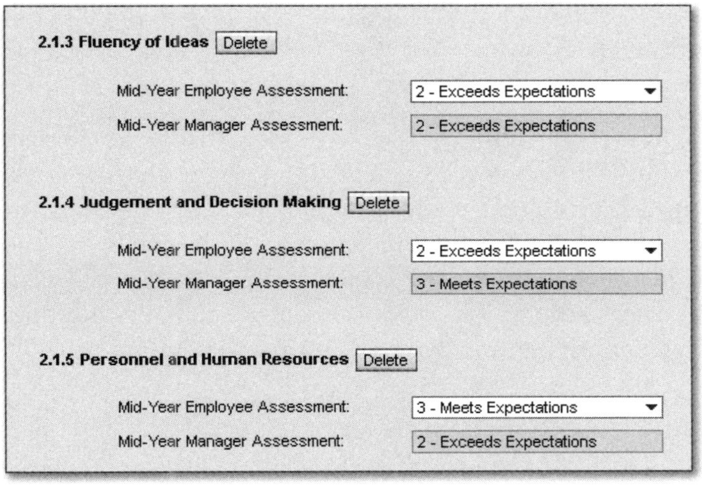

Figure 6.22 Feedback for Competencies

> **Key Point**
>
> Performance Management can be configured to include appraisers other than just the employee and direct supervisor (manager). These "part appraisers" could be subordinates, peers, other managers, or even an external supplier or customer. Organizations should consider their specific requirements when designing their own solution. For the purposes of our discussion, we aren't using part appraisers in the process.

6.4 Summary

One of the most fundamental ways you can retain and develop employees is through a timely performance planning and evaluation process. The assessment phase serves as the foundation for objective setting, talent assessment, and performance measurement. Goals can be set successfully when the employee and manager have a shared understanding of the goals, behaviors, and competencies required for the position, as well as of the measures that assess whether or not the goals were achieved. Corporate goals are created by the Talent Management specialist and can be cascaded throughout the organization. Team goals are created by the manager and can be cascaded to the rest of their team. After the corporate and team goals have been established, individual goals can be set. Goal setting requires specifying the required levels of performance and identifying the objectives to be achieved. It's important that both the employee and manager have a common understanding of what constitutes good performance; this is the foundation upon which the entire Performance Management process is built.

The objective of the talent assessment is to give managers and the Talent Management specialists a snapshot of an employee's potential, risks, core competencies, derailers to progression, and possible talent group nominations. As a result, talent assessment is typically performed without the involvement of the employee. The overall potential rating that is provided is used to calibrate employees in the manager's team, to review performance versus potential in the talent review meeting, and to help identify high-performing employees in the organization.

For individuals who are influential in the success of the organization, their risk of loss and impact of loss ratings can indicate to the Talent Management specialists that action must be taken to retain these individuals within the organization. Employees can also be assessed not only on the competencies that they hold via their position but also on other competencies identified and defined by the organization.

Depending on the organization, the competency groups that are assessed can vary considerably. Managers can also evaluate some attributes (derailers) that could prevent employees from developing or progressing further in the organization. Finally, the manager has the option to assign employees to one or more of the available talent groups in the SAP system.

The objective of the mid-year review is to make sure that performance is on track and to make adjustments to plans that may have changed due to unanticipated events. While it's assumed that feedback is ongoing throughout the performance cycle, the mid-year review is a more formal opportunity to discuss how things are going and to avoid any surprises at year end.

Next we'll look at the development phase, where Frank Jenkins will view his mandated training in the Learner Portal, take and complete web-based training, and book instructor-led courses. This will give Frank the required qualifications for the payroll manager position.

Now that Frank Jenkins has met with his manager regarding the assessment phase, Frank can continue to develop his skills as an employee. The Learning Solution module can help Frank, as well as his manager, continue and manage his training through an integrated system.

7 Competency Phase

This phase of the Talent Management process sees our employee Frank developing his skills for the position of payroll manager. By leveraging integration between Talent Management modules, the *competency phase* seamlessly allows Frank and his manager to act upon established goals and information from previous phases.

7.1 SAP ERP HCM Learning Solution

In Chapter 6, Frank and his manager agreed on three training goals within the appraisal document. These training goals directly correlate to course types within the SAP ERP HCM Learning Solution module, which we'll refer to as the Learning Solution module from now on. In this chapter, we'll explore the steps needed for Frank to achieve these training goals, and we'll walk through the steps (content, catalog, profile, schedule, participation, and close-out) he'll take to complete a course.

7.1.1 Content

As mentioned in Chapter 4, there are two main purposes for the content process:

- Create content
- Upload content

However, this process only applies to web-based training courses because instructor-led training does not involve any content within the Content Management System (CMS) of Learning Solution. This piece of the process is important, so let's look at how to use SAP's own tools to create and upload content.

Content Administrator

Generally, when implementing Learning Solution, you should appoint a content administrator to designate the user who will manage all of the content within the Learning Solution. Let's examine how a content administrator can quickly create and upload a course using SAP's own tools.

The SAP Authoring Environment is a quick and efficient way to produce web-based training. This tool is a separate application from the SAP GUI. So let's quickly create an online course that Frank can search for and enroll in. Figure 7.1 shows the SAP Authoring Environment screen and the PAYROLL ANALYTICS course that we'll use throughout the chapter.

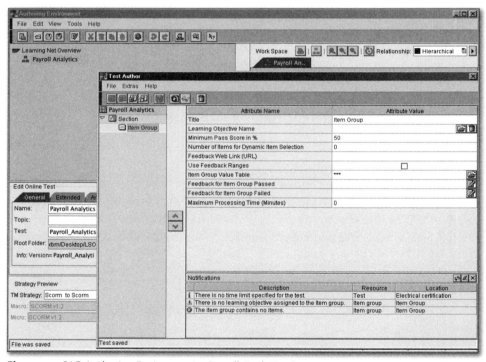

Figure 7.1 SAP Authoring Environment—Payroll Analytics Course

SAP ERP HCM Learning Solution | 7.1

Additional Resources

For the purposes of this book, we won't go into the details of how to create course content. For more information, see *SAP Enterprise Learning* by Prashanth Padmanabhan, Christian Hochwarth, Sharon Wolf Newton, Sankara Narayanan Bharathan, and Manoj Parthasarathy (SAP PRESS, 2009).

After you've finished developing course content, there are a few ways to upload content to the Learning Solution CMS in SAP:

- Directly from the Authoring Environment
- Using the Rapid Content Publishing tool

Because we've already seen the Authoring Environment, let's take a look at the content administrator going through the process of uploading content via the Rapid Content Publishing tool.

First, the content administrator will log in to the Course Administrator Portal, which is shown in Figure 7.2. This user has its own role, which is as the course administrator.

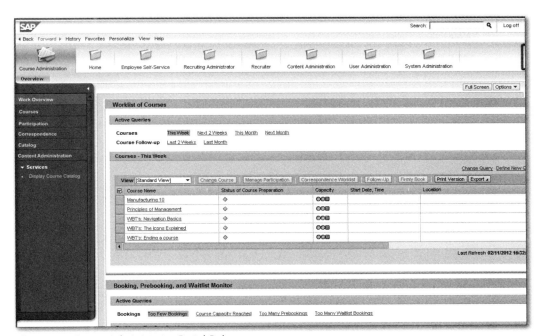

Figure 7.2 Course Administrator Portal Role

Within the Content Administrator Portal, there are other functions besides uploading and managing content:

- Manage course participation
- Correspondence worklist
- Follow-up
- View course capacities, overbookings, and waitlistings

Let's upload some content by following the catalog process. A content administrator navigates to COURSE ADMINISTRATION • CONTENT ADMINISTRATION • PUBLISH COURSE CONTENT. Figure 7.3 shows the Rapid Content Publishing tool that launches after this link clicked.

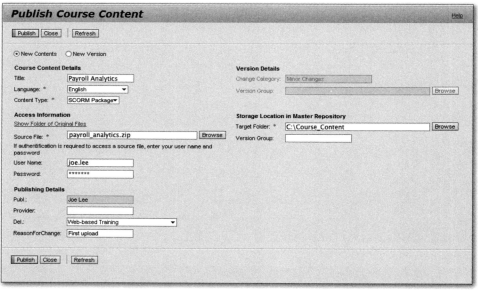

Figure 7.3 Publishing Course Content

The PAYROLL ANALYTICS course that we've developed in the previous step is now uploaded. After the course is published, it becomes part of the CMS and the Learning Solution. This leads us to the next step—the catalog process—in which a content administrator prepares the course for employees.

7.1.2 Catalog

The catalog process is important because it contains some key functions to make the Learning Solution content function properly:

- Assign course content to a course type
- Manage course type to course group relationships
- Manage qualification relationships

Now that the learning content is developed and uploaded, it can be added to a course type object via the SAP backend using Learning Solution transactions. This makes the content available to employees. Transaction LSO_PVCT enables content administrators to view the entire Course Catalog (which contains all courses) and maintain the required technical relationships in the system. Figure 7.4 shows where the PAYROLL ANALYTICS course fits within the HUMAN RESOURCES selection of the Course Catalog.

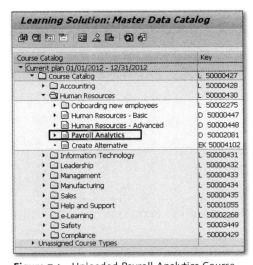

Figure 7.4 Uploaded Payroll Analytics Course

The uploaded content needs to be assigned to a course type (object type D) within the backend SAP system via Transaction LSO_PVCT. The next step in the process is to assign this course type to relationships:

- Course type (D) to a course group (L)
- Course group (L) to the Course Catalog (also object type L)

Course Catalogs, which help organize and categorize your content logically, are the top level of organization for maintaining course types and course groups. For this purpose, Transaction LSO_PVCT allows you to maintain these relationships manually by double-clicking on your course type and then navigating to the RELATIONSHIPS tab. Figure 7.5 shows the RELATIONSHIPS tab, along with some of the relationships it holds.

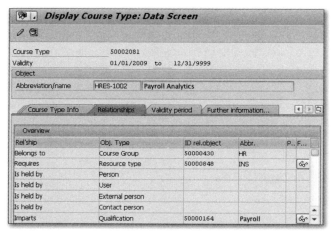

Figure 7.5 Relationships for the Payroll Analytics Course

Figure 7.5 also shows that qualifications can be maintained for these courses as well. As previously stated, when an employee successfully completes a web-based training course, the employee automatically earns the qualification that was imparted on that course.

Now that the course has been set up with the proper relationships, it's time to manage the participation of this course using the profile process.

7.1.3 Profile

The profile process contains a few key features:

- Viewing profile match-ups
- Assigning employees to mandated training

Each learner in the system has what is known as a learner profile. Following the process, let's take a look at Frank's learner profile, which includes all of his qualifications, training, and history. Within Manager Self-Services (MSS), the Personnel Development profile application contains the following information:

- General data (organizational, communication, contract data)
- Appraisals documents (integration from Performance Management)
- Profile matchup (qualifications, recommended training, and mandatory training)
- Training history

Manager

Keeping in line with the process, let's switch roles now to Frank's manager. We first want to take a look at Frank's profile, and what courses he currently has. You can access his profile by navigating to MANAGER SELF SERVICE • TEAM • PERSONNEL DEVELOPMENT. Figure 7.6 shows Frank's personnel development profile.

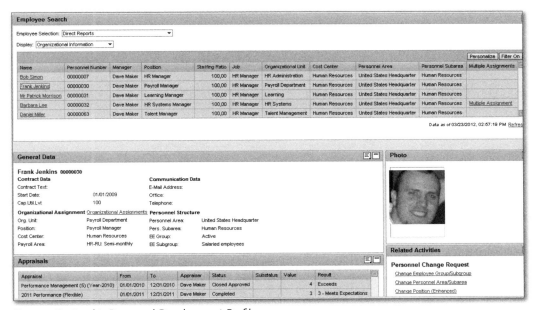

Figure 7.6 Frank's Personnel Development Profile

In relation to the Learning Solution process, let's have a look at the PROFILE MATCHUP area, which contains training-related information. You can see in Figure 7.7 that Frank has been enrolled in the three courses that were assigned to him in Chapter 6 as mandatory courses. Because of the tight integration between modules, these courses not only appear in the appraisal document but also on the learner profile and in the Profile Matchup.

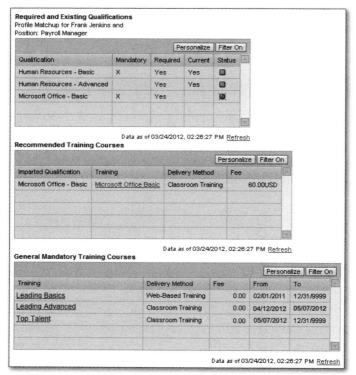

Figure 7.7 Frank's Profile Matchup

Within the profile process, you can also assign more mandatory training to employees. Right now, Frank has three mandatory training courses assigned to him through the Performance Management module. To show the difference between the profile and schedule processes, let's choose a different course other than the Payroll Analytics course. As a manager, let's go through and assign another mandatory training course to Frank's profile: Safety in the Office.

Through the MSS portal, you can navigate to MANAGER SELF SERVICE • TEAM • EMPLOYEE COURSE ASSIGNMENT • MANAGE MANDATORY ASSIGNMENT. This application will walk a manager through the process of assigning mandatory training. Figure 7.8 and Figure 7.9 show how to scroll through the available employees, select FRANK JENKINS, and assign him the SAFETY IN THE OFFICE class.

SAP ERP HCM Learning Solution | 7.1

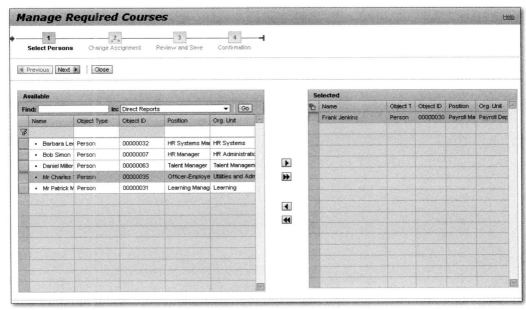

Figure 7.8 Selecting Frank for a New Mandatory Course

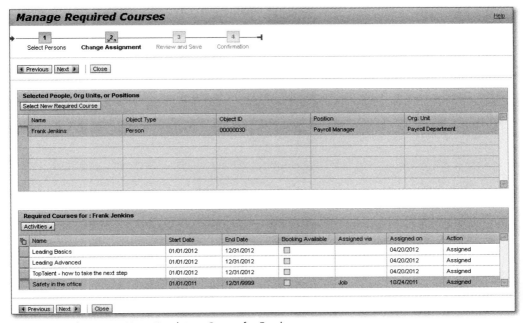

Figure 7.9 Choosing a New Mandatory Course for Frank

257

After this new course is assigned to Frank, it will appear on his profile as REQUIRED TRAINING. However, it will be up to Frank to enroll himself in this course and make sure he completes it.

7.1.4 Schedule

In the schedule process, we'll take a look at a few of the functions necessary to assign employees to a course:

- Selecting participants
- Selecting the appropriate course
- Assigning the participants to that course
- Scheduling a course
- Managing resources

You just saw some, but not all, of these functions when assigning Frank to the Safety in the Office class.

Proceeding with the schedule process, let's add the new Payroll Analytics course to Frank's profile. Still within the manager role, you can manually add a course to Frank's profile through MSS via MANAGER SELF SERVICE • TEAM • EMPLOYEE COURSE ASSIGNMENT • MANAGE PARTICIPATION. Figure 7.10 and Figure 7.11 show the process to assign Frank to this course. You'll notice that it differs from the profile process in that the second step is MANAGE PARTICIPATION, not CHANGE ASSIGNMENT.

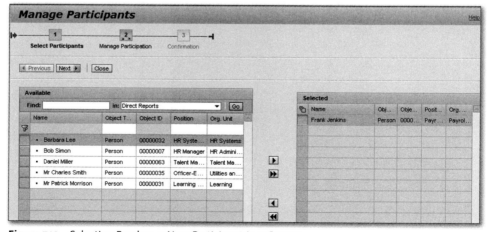

Figure 7.10 Selecting Frank as a New Participant in a Course

SAP ERP HCM Learning Solution | 7.1

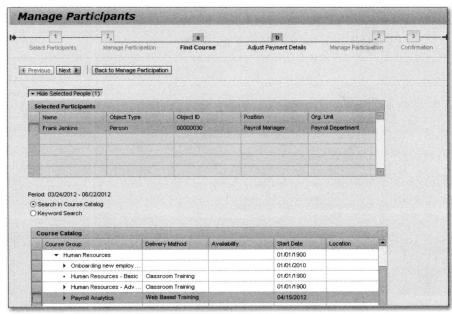

Figure 7.11 Choosing the New Payroll Analytics Course and Assigning Frank

After this is completed, Frank is now enrolled in the Payroll Analytics course. This will automatically place Frank in the course, whether it's web-based training or instructor-led training.

Administrator

For instructor-led training, there is generally some more upfront work required to get a course prepared for learners. The following questions will help you prepare for face-to-face training:

- Where will this training take place?
- When will the training take place?
- Who will be doing the training?

The schedule process allows administrators to launch the Create Course Date application, which will manage these resources in the system. If you log in as an administrator, you can access this application by navigating to COURSE ADMINISTRATION • COURSES • SCHEDULE A COURSE DATE. This application contains many different management tabs, including the following:

- BASIC DATA
- ROOM AND MATERIALS
- INSTRUCTOR
- QUALIFICATIONS AND TARGET GROUPS
- PRICES AND COSTS

For the purposes of this book, we'll look at the BASIC DATA tab, which shows some of this important data. Figure 7.12 shows how you can create a new course name, which will be "Microsoft Office Basic." Some fields, such as SHORT TEXT, LOCATION, and COURSE MIN./OPTMAX (course capacity) are required. Frank will enroll in and participate in this course later in this chapter.

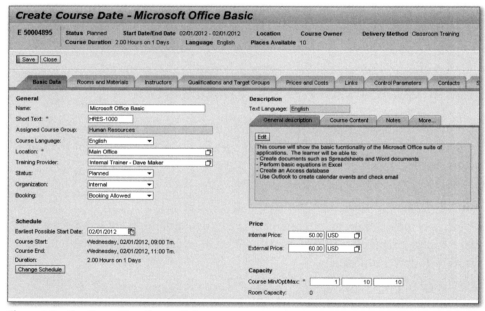

Figure 7.12 Creating a New Course Date

You can see in Figure 7.12 that the TRAINING PROVIDER for Microsoft Office Basic is DAVE MAKER. We'll revisit this later when Dave is assigned as the instructor for this course and becomes involved in the close-out process. Now that you have a new course set up, it's time to have Frank go in to the Learning Solution himself and take some training.

7.1.5 Participation

The participation process contains many functions for learners to use as they seek to continue their training. In this section, we'll explore the following functions:

- Viewing mandatory training
- Searching for a course
- Booking a course

Let's change roles now, and look at training courses through the eyes of an employee. Because all employees in the system can use the Learning Solution module, the process we'll follow isn't just for Frank but for all users of the system.

In Chapter 6, Frank was assigned mandatory training goals by his manager. This integration between Performance Management and the Learning Solution modules allows Frank to see these and execute on these training goals through the Learner Portal. Let's explore how Frank would view and take a mandatory training course, as well as search for other courses to add to his learner profile.

Learner

Frank first needs to log in to the ESS portal to access his training courses. The tabs available to Frank depend on which portal roles have been assigned to him. (See Chapter 9 for more details on portal roles.)

After logging into the portal, he navigates to the MY LEARNING tab. Figure 7.13 shows the My Learning (SAP) application, which has the following features:

- Mandatory courses
- Qualifications
- Quick search
- Top 10 courses
- Training activities and history

As you can see in Figure 7.13, all of the mandatory courses assigned to Frank throughout Chapters 6 and 7—for example, Top Talent and Safety in the Office—appear automatically. Frank can now launch directly into these courses (for web-based training) or see detailed information about a course (both web-based and instructor-led classes).

7 | Competency Phase

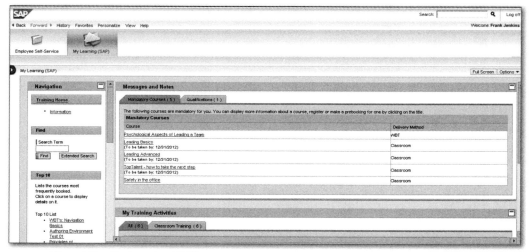

Figure 7.13 My Learning (SAP)

Let's assume that Frank wants to learn more about Microsoft Office. The My Learning (SAP) portal allows Frank to do a number of different actions, including search for a course. Frank can input a course name or a course code in this field to see the specific course he's looking for. Figure 7.13 shows the Navigation panel where Frank will input the search term "Microsoft" and then click the EXTENDED SEARCH button.

Figure 7.14 shows that Frank's search returned two results relating to his search term ("Microsoft").

To see more details on this course, he can click on the course name, and it will show information about the course, such as the following:

- Type (web based, classroom)
- Date
- Cost
- Qualifications

Because this is a classroom instructor-led training course, Frank also needs to choose the dates he would like to attend. By clicking on the dates under the SCHEDULE as shown in Figure 7.15, Frank can view specific information about this date and book the course, as shown in Figure 7.16.

SAP ERP HCM Learning Solution | 7.1

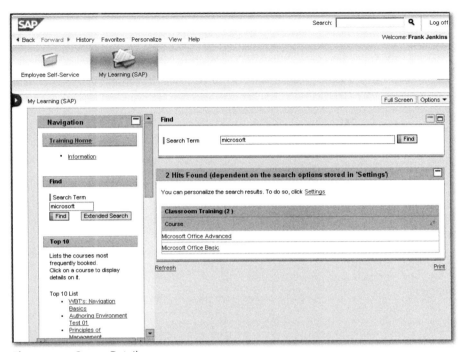

Figure 7.14 Course Details

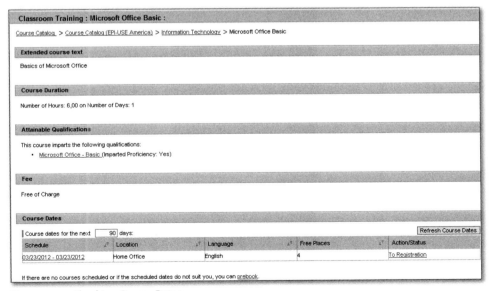

Figure 7.15 Checking Course Dates

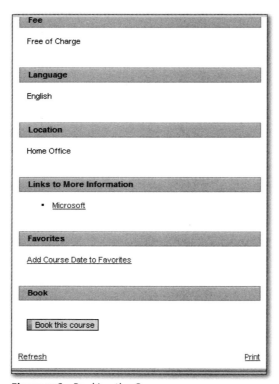

Figure 7.16 Booking the Course

After Frank clicks the BOOK THIS COURSE button, he will be enrolled in the course. Because this is classroom training, Frank will have to make sure he shows up at the right location at the right time. This detail screen shows Frank the location of the course, as well as the date and time.

Continuing with this process, let's shift our attention to what happens on the instructor side of the Learning Solution. Soon we'll assume the role of the instructor of the course that Frank just booked.

7.1.6 Close-Out

The close-out process contains only a few steps, which are performed by both the learner and instructor:

- Perform course appraisal (learner)
- Follow-up steps (instructor)

Before we move on to the instructor entirely, the learner needs to perform a course appraisal. This is an important part of the Learning Solution process because you can leverage the feedback to improve learning throughout your organization.

After Frank has taken the course, he can click on the course detail again within the portal to see the PERFORM COURSE APPRAISAL link (see Figure 7.17). When Frank clicks this link, a course appraisal application opens, allowing him to rate multiple aspects of the course such as the following:

- GENERAL IMPRESSIONS OF THE COURSE
- COURSE CONTENT AND STRUCTURE
- TRAINER
- COURSE LOCATION

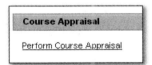

Figure 7.17 Perform Course Appraisal Link

Figure 7.18 shows the course appraisal application.

Now that Frank has completed and rated the course, let's change roles to the instructor and resume the close-out process.

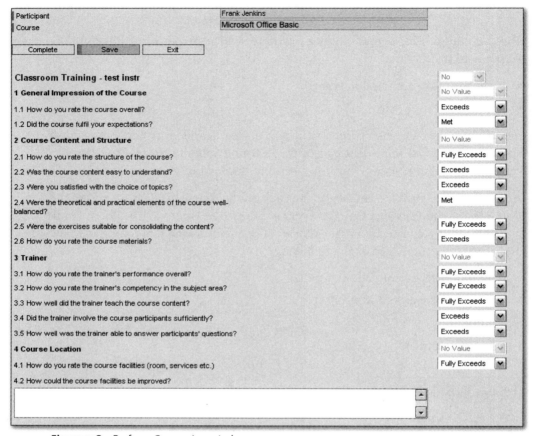

Figure 7.18 Perform Course Appraisal

Instructor

Learning Solution gives instructors their own set of functions within the system. Because they need to determine whether an employee passes or fails a course, the instructor will need to go through the portal to execute these follow-up functions.

To close out a course, instructors can log in to the portal and navigate to INSTRUCTION AND TUTORING • COURSES FOR FOLLOW-UP, and then click on the appropriate course. In Figure 7.19, the instructor selects the MICROSOFT OFFICE BASIC course that Frank has just appraised.

SAP ERP HCM Learning Solution | 7.1

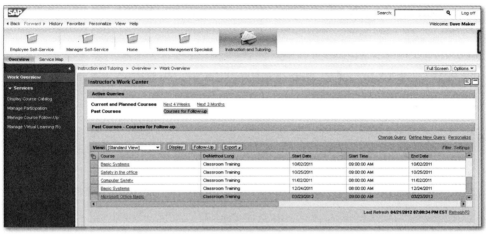

Figure 7.19 Instructor Portal—Selecting Courses for Follow-Up

After the instructor has selected the course, he can click the FOLLOW-UP button to launch the Course Follow-up application. Figure 7.20 shows the Course Follow-Up application that is launched.

There are multiple steps on this application that we'll walk through because they are important to the close-out process:

- CONFIRM ATTENDANCE
- EVALUATE PARTICIPANTS
- TRANSFER QUALIFICATION

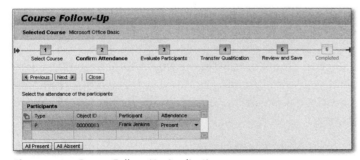

Figure 7.20 Course Follow-Up Application

267

Because we've already selected the course (it appears automatically in the Instructor Portal, or you can select a new course), the application automatically takes you to the next step, which is CONFIRM ATTENDANCE (see Figure 7.20).

In Figure 7.20, you can see that Frank Jenkins was supposed to be an attendee at this course. Let's assume Frank is a great student, and he showed up to the course. This screen simply allows us to confirm Frank's attendance to the course using the ATTENDANCE drop-down.

Next, the instructor evaluates Frank on whether or not he passed the class. This determines whether or not Frank earns credit for the course and earns the qualification that goes along with the course. Figure 7.21 shows the EVALUATE PARTICIPANTS step.

Frank passed this course with flying colors, and the instructor uses the PARTICIPANT ASSESSMENT drop-down box to confirm that Frank has indeed passed this course.

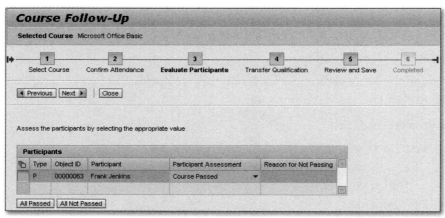

Figure 7.21 Evaluating Frank in the Evaluate Participants Step

The instructor now transfers the qualification earned by completing this course. Again, because this isn't a web-based training, the instructor needs to complete this step manually for participants to earn the qualification. Figure 7.22 shows the TRANSFER QUALIFICATION step.

This creates the technical relationship between Frank and this qualification in the system. After learners have earned a qualification, whether by instructor follow-up or through web-based training, they immediately become eligible for any other course in which this qualification was a prerequisite.

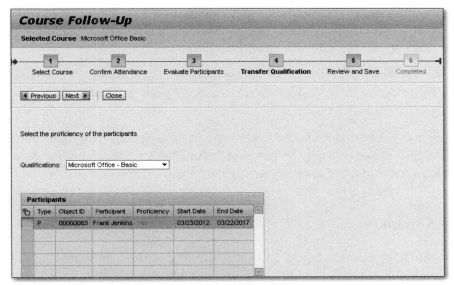

Figure 7.22 Transferring the Qualification to Frank

After the TRANSFER QUALIFICATION step, the instructor is taken to the last step, which is REVIEW AND SAVE, as shown in Figure 7.23.

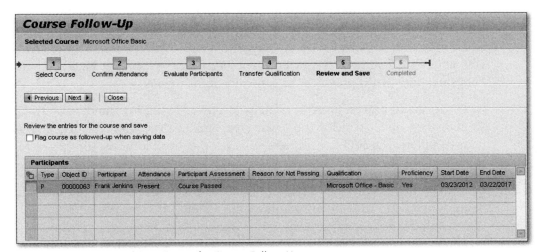

Figure 7.23 Review and Save Screen for Course Follow-Up

This last screen in the Course Follow-Up application allows instructors to review the information they have just entered. This is particularly useful if there are multiple participants because you can view all of the information at a glance.

The instructor clicks NEXT to save the information, and all of the qualifications are transferred to the employees. This step completes the close-out process within the Learning Solution module.

There are many more functions and screens within the Learning Solution module, and we've just walked through a few of them to show the main processes. For more information, refer to *SAP Enterprise Learning* (SAP PRESS, 2009).

7.2 Summary

The Learning Solution module is an incredibly effective tool for managing the ongoing training of employees. With its heavy integration with the other Talent Management modules, you can easily view qualifications that have been earned by your employees, as well as mandate training directly from the Performance Management module.

Starting with the content process, SAP provides the Authoring Environment, which allows you to easily create your own web-based training course. You may also develop your own training course in the authoring tool of your choice, as long as it falls within the AICC and SCORM standards. Within the Authoring Environment, you can upload your newly created content directly, or by using the Rapid Content Publishing tool that is provided for content administrators.

Next, the catalog process links the content developed to the SAP standard Learning Solution data model, which is the course type. Linking the course type to qualifications completes the circle, as learners will earn that qualification upon successful completion of the course.

The profile process assigns mandatory training to employees. This can be done by both managers and administrators in the system. After mandated training is assigned through the Manage Required Courses application, you can see this training in multiple places, one of which is the Personnel Development application in the Learning Portal. The Personnel Development application also displays training history, suggested courses, and qualifications of your employees.

In the schedule process, you can schedule upcoming courses that will be available to learners. By using backend transactions, you can set up multiple learning resources, such as the instructor and classroom availability.

Next comes the participation process. This is the bulk of the functionality for the Learning Solution because this is where learners actually view, manage, and launch their training to earn qualifications and further their careers.

Finally, the close-out phase allows participants in a course to rate the course based on certain criteria and instructors to evaluate and impart qualifications on participants who have completed the course.

This concludes the competency phase. Next, we'll explore the final phase of Talent Management—the progression phase—which encompasses many of the Talent Management modules and contains many features and functions.

The progression phase takes place at the end of Frank's first year at his new company. After his manager completes a year-end review, Frank is then further assessed and reviewed to determine whether he can be classified as a talent.

8 Progression Phase

Now that Frank has been provided with training to help develop his skills for the payroll manager position, the end-of-the-year process begins when Frank's manager completes a year-end review and gives a final rating. This rating is then used to determine Frank's bonus and merit increases.

After the close of the performance review and compensation cycle, respectively, the Talent Management specialist can conduct talent review meetings for high-potential employees like Frank within the organization.

After Frank's talent review meeting is conducted, and he is assigned to a high-potential talent group, he is assigned as a successor to a key position. A talent development plan can also be created and maintained for Frank at this time.

Let's first concentrate on the role of the year-end review.

8.1 SAP ERP HCM Performance Management: Year-End Review

The year-end appraisal is an excellent opportunity for a manager to help coach an employee. When done effectively, this key role in the process offers the following advantages:

- Helps employees set a direction for their careers
- Gives both the employee and the manager time to communicate their expectations and concerns

- Fosters employee motivation and commitment
- Provides opportunities to revise performance development goals

Too often, managers and employees incorrectly believe that coaching and feedback take place only when performance is lagging. Certainly, employees need constructive feedback specific to improving their performance when it doesn't meet expectations. Coaching, however, should support all types of employee performance.

To ensure a productive year-end meeting, both Frank and his manager have each fully prepared themselves prior to the discussion. To be completely organized for the discussion, Frank has prepared himself by doing the following:

- Used the goals established in the objective setting process (see Chapter 6) to guide his performance throughout the year
- Tracked and monitored his performance results
- Collected the appropriate documentation that describes his performance results achieved throughout the entire performance year
- Thought about a preliminary final self-rating for each performance factor and has supporting facts/documentation to help support that rating

Similarly, Frank's manager has prepared for the discussion by doing the following:

- Assembled and reviewed documentation that describe Frank's performance results achieved throughout the entire performance year (not just the few months prior to the review)
- Reflected on each of Frank's areas of responsibilities (What were Frank's achievements? What obstacles may have been present during the course of the year?)
- Obtained feedback from other colleagues as appropriate
- Considered ways that Frank can further improve his performance, develop in his career, or both
- Pulled together a preliminary final rating for each performance factor and assembled supporting facts/documentation to help support the rating (of course, this preliminary rating is subject to changes after hearing and discussing the employee's self-review)

Let's focus on the two steps that comprise the year-end appraisal: complete self-assessment (to be completed by Frank) and complete year-end assessment (to be completed by Frank's manager).

8.1.1 Complete Self-Assessment

Frank will now go into Performance Management to formally document his own performance as part of the year-end review. The first tab is the GOALS tab, in which Frank can evaluate his own performance with regard to corporate, team, individual, and training goals.

The first goal that Frank will evaluate himself against is the corporate goal of "Stewardship," which was created in Chapter 6, Section 6.1.2. You can see Frank's self-assessment in Figure 8.1, which shows the mid-year assessments—and any corresponding comments—made by Frank and his manager.

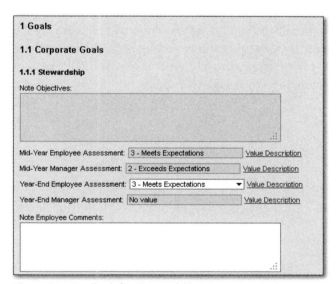

Figure 8.1 Feedback for "Stewardship" Corporate Goal

The next goal that Frank will evaluate himself against is the team goal of "Increase Payroll Accuracy," which was created in Chapter 6, Section 6.1.2. Figure 8.2 shows Frank's team goals and his year-end employee assessment of how he achieved them.

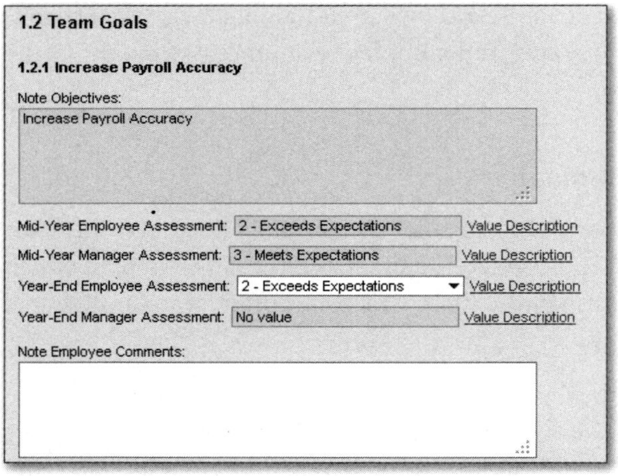

8 | Progression Phase

Figure 8.2 Feedback for "Increase Payroll Accuracy" Team Goal

After Frank provides a year-end assessment and comments on his individual goals, he can review the goals from the Learning Catalog that were recorded during the mid-year review. The LEADING BASICS goal is shown in Figure 8.3. Because these goals were all expected to be completed by the mid-year review, you'll notice that there's no place for Frank to provide a year-end assessment.

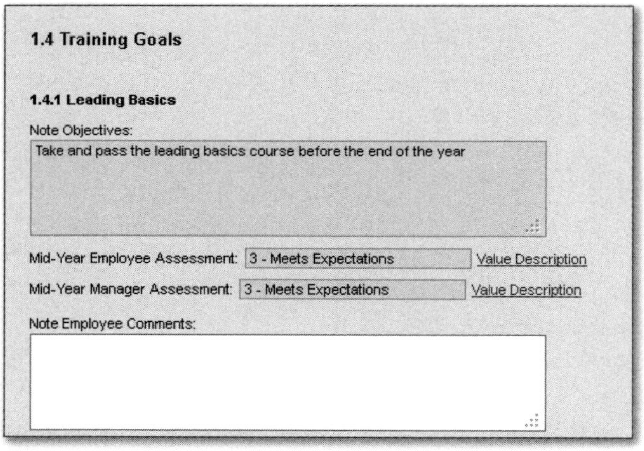

Figure 8.3 Leading Basics Goal from the Learning Catalog

Frank has also taken the initiative of taking another course called Microsoft Office Basic (from Chapter 7). He can now add this new course to his year-end self-assessment document (see Figure 8.4).

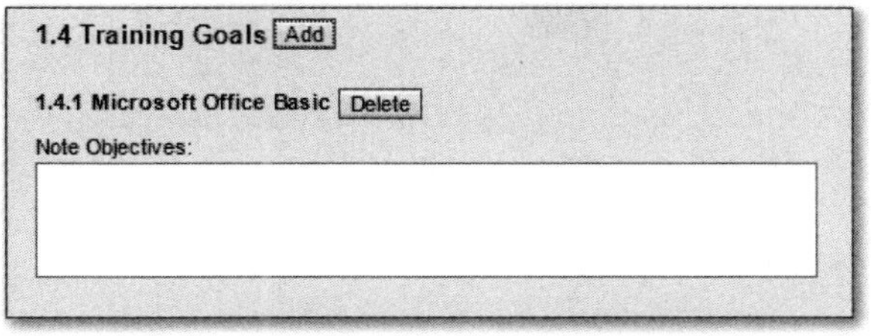

[Figure 8.4 image showing "1.4 Training Goals" section with "1.4.1 Microsoft Office Basic" and Note Objectives text box]

Figure 8.4 Microsoft Office Basic Objective Added from the Learning Catalog

The second tab is the COMPETENCIES tab, which is where Frank will evaluate his performance on the following three competencies from the Qualifications Catalog: fluency of ideas, judgment and decision making, and personnel and human resources. His assessment of these competencies is shown in Figure 8.5.

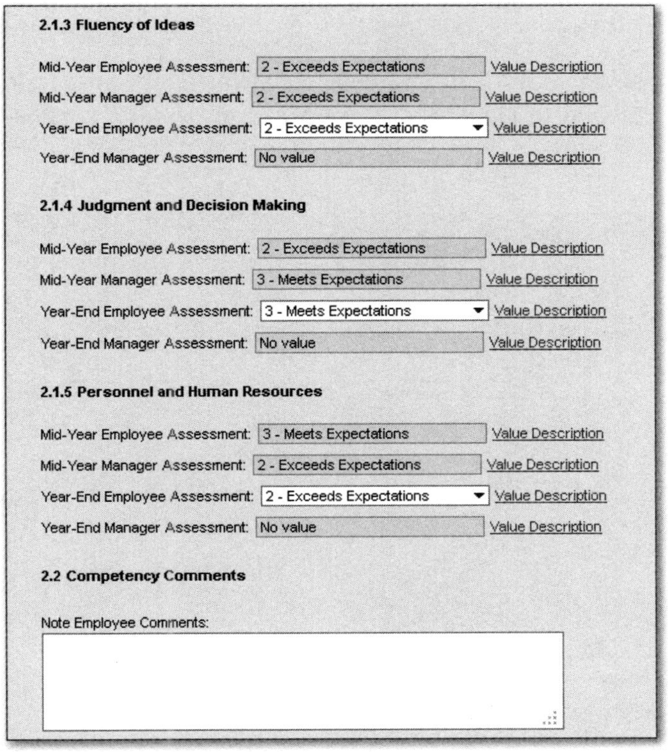

[Figure 8.5 image showing competency assessments for 2.1.3 Fluency of Ideas, 2.1.4 Judgment and Decision Making, 2.1.5 Personnel and Human Resources, and 2.2 Competency Comments]

Figure 8.5 Feedback for Competencies

> **Key Point**
>
> You can determine which tabs show during the mid-year review versus the year-end review through configuration. For more information on configuration in Performance Management, refer to *SAP ERP HCM Performance Management* by Christos Kotsakis and Jeremy Masters (SAP PRESS, 2010).

8.1.2 Complete Year-End Assessment

Now that Frank Jenkins has completed a self-assessment of his performance for the year, his manager, Dave Maker, will now go into Performance Management to formally document Frank's performance as part of the year-end review. Recall from Chapter 6, Section 6.12, that the first tab is the GOALS tab, which allows Dave Maker to evaluate Frank's performance with regard to the corporate, team, individual, and training goals already established.

Just as before, the first goal that Frank will be evaluated against is the corporate goal of "Stewardship." As shown in Figure 8.6, Dave Maker provides an assessment for Frank.

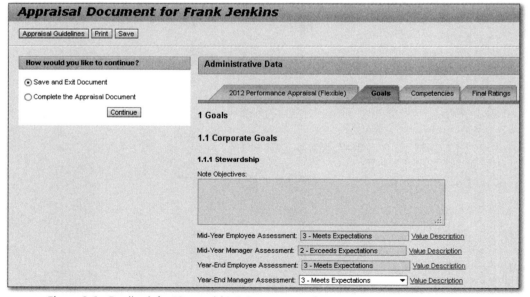

Figure 8.6 Feedback for "Stewardship" Corporate Goal

Next, Dave Maker evaluates Frank on the team goal "Increase Payroll Accuracy" (see Figure 8.7).

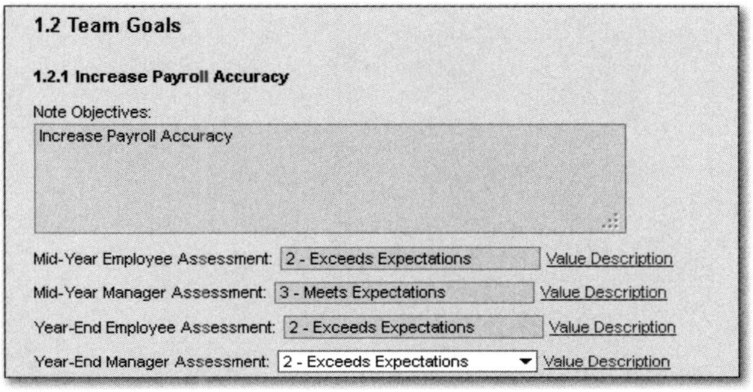

Figure 8.7 Feedback for "Increase Payroll Accuracy" Team Goal

After Dave Maker provides a year-end assessment and comments for Frank's individual goals, he can provide notes on the new objective for Microsoft Office Basic that Frank added during the self-assessment process (see Figure 8.8).

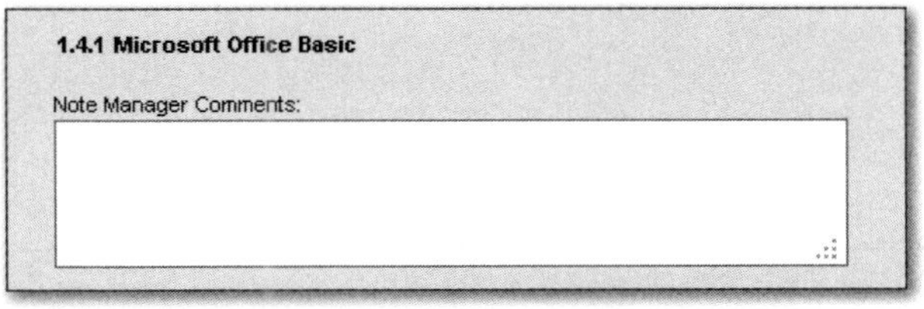

Figure 8.8 Notes for New Microsoft Office Basics Goal

The second tab is the COMPETENCIES tab, which is where Dave Maker will review Frank's performance on FLUENCY OF IDEAS, JUDGMENT AND DECISION MAKING, and PERSONNEL AND HUMAN RESOURCES competencies from the qualifications catalog (see Figure 8.9).

Unlike the mid-year review, there is a new tab called FINAL RATINGS that Dave Maker can now access. It allows him to enter a final rating for Frank's performance for the entire year. Figure 8.10 shows the FINAL RATINGS tab and the year-end rating that Frank's manager has entered.

8 | Progression Phase

2.1.3 Fluency of Ideas

Mid-Year Employee Assessment:	2 - Exceeds Expectations Value Description
Mid-Year Manager Assessment:	2 - Exceeds Expectations Value Description
Year-End Employee Assessment:	2 - Exceeds Expectations Value Description
Year-End Manager Assessment:	2 - Exceeds Expectations ▼ Value Description

2.1.4 Judgment and Decision Making

Mid-Year Employee Assessment:	2 - Exceeds Expectations Value Description
Mid-Year Manager Assessment:	3 - Meets Expectations Value Description
Year-End Employee Assessment:	3 - Meets Expectations Value Description
Year-End Manager Assessment:	2 - Exceeds Expectations ▼ Value Description

2.1.5 Personnel and Human Resources

Mid-Year Employee Assessment:	3 - Meets Expectations Value Description
Mid-Year Manager Assessment:	2 - Exceeds Expectations Value Description
Year-End Employee Assessment:	2 - Exceeds Expectations Value Description
Year-End Manager Assessment:	3 - Meets Expectations ▼ Value Description

Figure 8.9 Feedback for Competencies

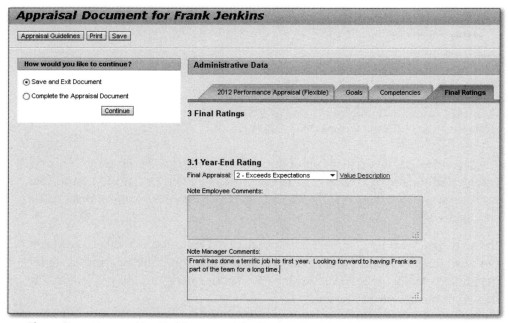

Figure 8.10 Manager Year End Assessment for Frank

Now that the assessment has been completed, let's look at how Frank's final performance rating translates into adjustments to his compensation for the upcoming year.

8.2 SAP ERP HCM Enterprise Compensation Management

Managers play an instrumental role in driving the performance evaluation process. The only way employees will know for sure whether they are meeting certain standards is through specific and timely feedback from their managers. Employees want to know that what they are contributing and what they are being held accountable for have value. By tying short-term bonuses, rewards, and other recognition to performance, employees will be encouraged to achieve optimal performance levels, continue to perform effectively over the long term, and be less likely to seek opportunities outside your organization.

By using SAP ERP HCM Enterprise Compensation Management (ECM), managers can incentivize performance for employees. In this section, we'll simply look at the end-to-end high-level process of ECM, but we won't get into the details of all the features and functionality.

> **Related Resources**
>
> For more detailed information about ECM, refer to *Enterprise Compensation Management with SAP ERP HCM* by Christos Kotsakis and Jeremy Masters (SAP PRESS, 2010).

This section will follow the four-step process that was mentioned previously in Chapter 4 for ECM, which includes the budgeting, reviewing, controlling, and approval processes. Let's take a look at how to use ECM to give Frank a salary increase.

8.2.1 Budgeting Process

There are two main steps within the budgeting process:

- Creating a budget unit
- Assigning a budget

Note that this process is generally done at the beginning of the year. For the purposes of this chapter, we kept all of the ECM functions coupled together for ease of understanding.

Before the organization can give Frank a salary increase, a budget must be planned for Frank's entire organization. This is done by creating a budget unit for the HR organization, and then assigning a fixed budget to Frank's department, which is payroll. As discussed in Chapter 4, this method of starting with the organization's budget is known as top-down budgeting.

Compensation Administrator

The first step in creating a budget for the HR organization is for a compensation specialist to generate a new budget unit (object type BU). This can be done through Transaction PECM_GENERATE_BUDGET or by launching the BSP application Budget Maintenance. Figure 8.11 shows Transaction PECM_GENERATE_BUDGET. After this transaction is executed for the HR organizational unit, Figure 8.12 shows the successful generation of a budget for that organization.

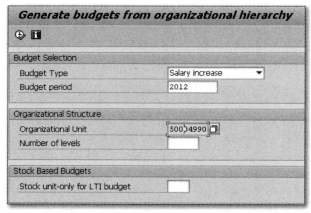

Figure 8.11 Generate Budget

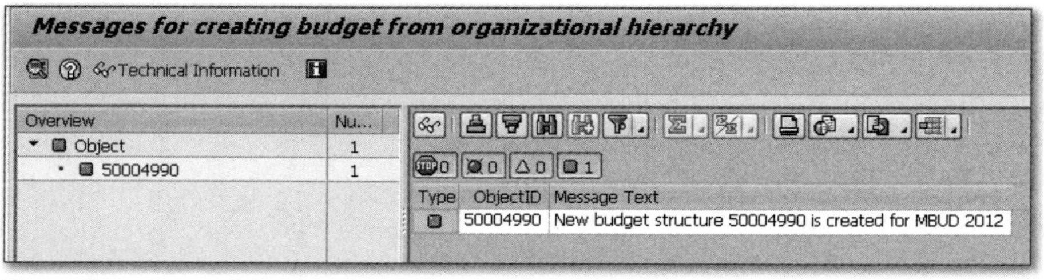

Figure 8.12 Successful Budget Generation

After a budget unit has been created for an organizational unit, the budget can be set and maintained using a frontend BSP interface. (See Chapter 9 for more information on BSP and Web Dynpro.) You can access this interface through Transaction PECM_START_BDG_BSP. Figure 8.13 shows this BSP application.

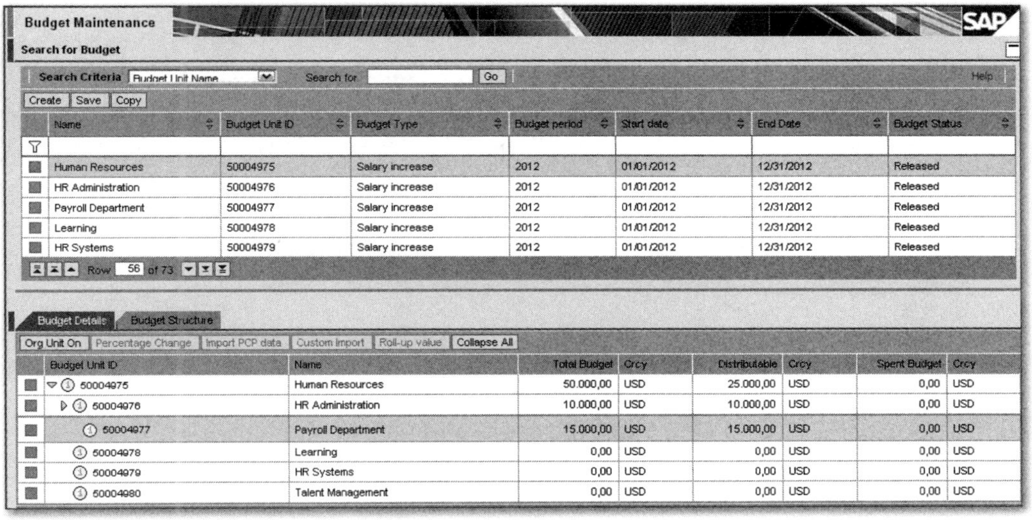

Figure 8.13 Budget Maintenance Application

In the previous figure, you can see that a budget of $50,000 was allocated to the HR organization. Also, Frank's Payroll department has a set budget of $15,000 for managers to distribute among the employees.

After this budget is set, administrators will now check and release the budget. By releasing the budget, Dave Maker can perform salary increases within the allotted budget. Figure 8.14 shows the RELEASE BUDGET button and the success message that appears on the screen.

Checking and releasing the budget is a crucial step in the ECM module because every subsequent step is based on this budget. After the budget is successfully released, it's time to move to the review process.

8 | Progression Phase

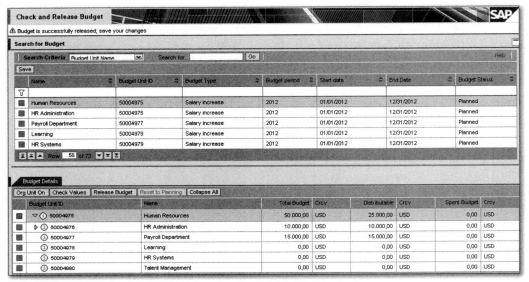

Figure 8.14 Check and Release Budget Screen—Releasing a Budget

8.2.2 Review Process

The review process is fairly straightforward and involves three steps:

1. Choose employees.
2. Perform salary adjustments.
3. Submit.

Now that the budget is in place, let's look at how to distribute the allocated payroll budget to its employees. To do this, let's take the role of Frank's manager, Dave Maker, and use the Compensation Planning tool in the portal.

Manager

Managers can access the Compensation Planning application by navigating to MANAGER SELF-SERVICE • PLANNING • COMPENSATION PLANNING • PLAN COMPENSATION. Once there, Frank's manager can see all of his employees automatically by selecting the proper COMPENSATION REVIEW. Figure 8.15 shows Frank's organization, as well as his coworkers within the Payroll department being selected for planning.

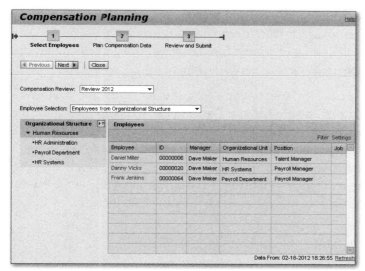

Figure 8.15 Organizational Structure—Choosing Employees for Planning

By clicking the NEXT button, Dave Maker proceeds to the PLAN COMPENSATION DATA step. In Figure 8.16, you can see that Frank's current salary is displayed, along with a new AMOUNT and % fields that let Dave adjust compensation accordingly.

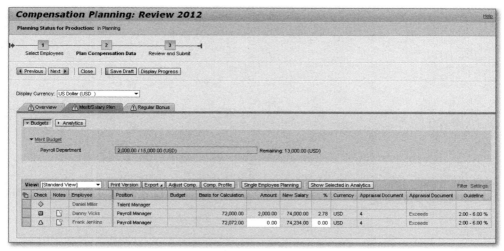

Figure 8.16 Plan Compensation Data Step

Also of note on this screen, Frank's performance appraisal rating appears as a link that lets Dave Maker jump directly into the appraisal document that was finished in the preceding section. This is an easy way for managers to view their employee's performance when it comes time for salary adjustments.

In the PLAN COMPENSATION DATA step, you can manually adjust the compensation number or a fixed percentage. Because Dave Maker wants to give all of the employees in the Payroll department a fixed percentage increase, he enters in the percentage, and the AMOUNT field automatically populates the monetary amount according to that percentage. Because Frank has done exceptionally well this year, Dave gives him a 5% salary increase. Figure 8.17 shows that everyone in the Payroll department gets a 3% salary increase, but Frank receives a 5% increase.

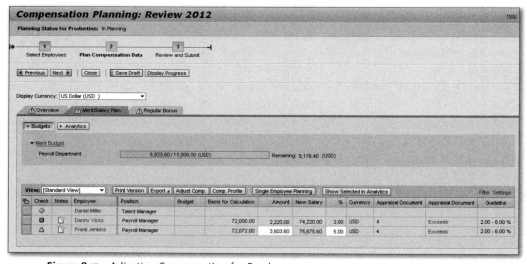

Figure 8.17 Adjusting Compensation for Employees

After these percentages are calculated, the total budget will reflect the amount of money that was used up by the salary increases in the organization. Figure 8.18 gives a graphical representation of the allocated and used budget for the Payroll department.

Figure 8.18 Remaining Budget for the Payroll Department

Frank's manager thinks that the budget looks pretty good for his department, and he'll get a chance to review and submit the proposed salary adjustments. To move from the PLAN COMPENSATION DATA step to the REVIEW AND SUBMIT step shown in Figure 8.19, Dave Maker clicks the NEXT button.

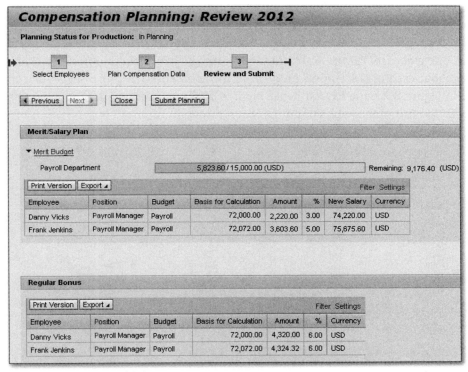

Figure 8.19 Review and Submit

When Dave Maker submits the budget proposal, the review process is completed.

8.2.3 Controlling Process

At this point, the bulk of Dave Maker's work is done. To walk through the controlling process, we'll step into the compensation specialist's role and monitor the progress of budgets and compensation plans.

Compensation Specialist

At any time during the review process, a compensation specialist can monitor the progress of managers and whether they are complying with budget guidelines. Let's take a look at how the Payroll department looks after Dave Maker has increased the department's salaries.

Compensation specialists can launch Transaction PECM_DISP_PROGRESS to view the current progress of all organization's compensation reviews. Figure 8.20 shows the COMPENSATION PLANNING PROGRESS report, which displays important information about each organization's progress in the compensation process. As you can see in Figure 8.20, the Payroll department is displayed along with the processing status that this organizational unit has been through.

Org. Unit for Planning	Pl. Manager	Changed by	First Change On	Last Change On	Process Status	
Payroll Department	Dave Maker	Dave Maker	19.02.2012 13:43:10	19.02.2012 13:43:10	Approved	
	Dave Maker	Dave Maker	19.02.2012 12:28:44	19.02.2012 12:28:44	Requires Approval	
	Dave Maker	Dave Maker	19.01.2012 16:38:32	19.01.2012 16:38:32	In Planning	
	Dave Maker	Dave Maker	10.01.2012 14:14:47	10.01.2012 14:14:47	Requires Approval	
	Dave Maker	Dave Maker	10.01.2012 14:14:39	10.01.2012 14:14:39	In Planning	
	Dave Maker	Dave Maker	09.01.2012 16:48:22	09.01.2012 16:48:22	Approved	
	Dave Maker	Dave Maker	06.01.2012 12:14:51	06.01.2012 12:14:51	Requires Approval	
	Dave Maker	Dave Maker	06.01.2012 11:52:22	06.01.2012 11:52:22	In Planning	
	Dave Maker	Dave Maker	04.01.2012 08:53:58	04.01.2012 08:53:58	In Planning	Prepare process a
CD Production	Norm Lamont	William Right	19.01.2012 16:38:22	19.01.2012 16:38:22	In Planning	
	Norm Lamont	William Right	09.01.2012 16:47:14	09.01.2012 16:47:14	Approved	
	Norm Lamont	William Right	06.01.2012 12:14:50	06.01.2012 12:14:50	Requires Approval	
	Norm Lamont	William Right	06.01.2012 11:52:21	06.01.2012 12:13:21	In Planning	
	Norm Lamont	William Right	06.01.2012 03:38:24	06.01.2012 03:38:24	In Planning	Update process a
	Norm Lamont	William Right	06.01.2012 03:27:09	06.01.2012 03:27:09	In Planning	Update process a

Figure 8.20 Compensation Planning Progress Report with the Payroll Department

Because guidelines haven't been applied to the Payroll department, compliance doesn't need to be ensured at this time. (For more information on guidelines, refer to Chapter 4.)

8.2.4 Approval Process

The Payroll department is part of the HR organization, so the manager of the HR organization will perform the approval process.

High-Level Manager

High-level managers can access the Planning Overview application by navigating to MANAGER SELF-SERVICE • PLANNING • REVIEW PLANNING. Figure 8.21 shows what the manager of the HR organization sees upon logging in to the Planning Overview application.

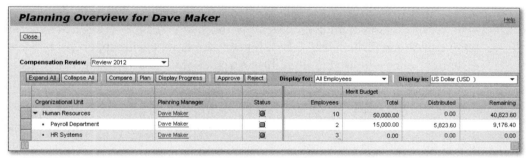

Figure 8.21 Review Planning

The Planning Overview application shows the Payroll department and its budget. The green square icon indicates that the department has completed its review; the red circle icon indicates the opposite. After the manager of the HR organization ensures that the budget for the Payroll department is aligned with the overall budget, he can click the APPROVE button to move forward with the salary adjustments.

> **Key Point**
>
> Because we aren't integrating with the SAP Payroll module in this chapter, we won't cover the next process: the payroll process. Refer to Chapter 4 for more information regarding the payroll process.

8.3 Talent Review Meeting

After the assessment phase is completed and the final performance ratings are confirmed and calibrated (you saw these in Chapter 6 and Chapter 8), the Talent Management specialists and associated business stakeholders can begin reviewing and classifying employees. Conducting a talent review meeting enables the organization to identify its best performing and highest potential employees and to classify them in talent groups for identification in later processes. It also gives organizations an opportunity to discuss the development needs of employees, discuss employee characteristics and behaviors, identify leadership potentials, calibrate employees from different organizational units against each other, ensure that ratings across the organization are consistent and justified, edit talent ratings, and assess employees who, for one reason or another, haven't yet been assessed for performance and/or potential. Although the Talent Review Meeting application will support your review meetings, it doesn't provide all of the answers. Knowing why and how to discuss talents is important, and organizations should set out a clear policy of what needs to be discussed and what methods should be used to discuss them.

The Talent Review Meeting application supports the review process by enabling you to do the following:

- Select the category, level, and support staff
- Create a meeting agenda
- Select participants and distribute agenda handouts
- Display and calibrate employees on performance versus potential grid
- View the long or short talent profile of employees
- Keep a history of all meetings

This functionality allows various talent review meetings to be created and conducted for different levels and parts of the organization. For example, a Talent Management specialist who is responsible for talent management at a global level may create a talent review meeting in category Global Review Meeting for the senior management level, while a Talent Management specialist at a country level might create a talent review meeting in category Local Review Meeting for the senior management level.

This segmentation of reviews is based on the different areas of a business; for global organizations, this means that employees considered for global or central roles can be reviewed separately from those on an individual country or regional basis.

Let's look at how a talent review meeting creates a review meeting (object RM). All talent review meeting data that is created is stored against the RM object in Infotypes 1000 (objects), 7431 (talent review basic data), 7432 (assigned objects), 7433 (participants), 7434 (agenda topics), 7435 (documents), 7436 (deadlines), and 7437 (persons responsible).

8.3.1 Creating, Planning, and Preparing the Talent Review Meeting

A Talent Management specialist must create and prepare a talent review meeting before that meeting can be conducted. We'll walk through the creation and preparation process in this section, in which a talent review meeting is used to look at employees in the United States region. The Talent Management specialist navigates to the TALENT MANAGEMENT SPECIALIST role in the portal and selects the TALENT REVIEW MEETINGS application shown in Figure 8.22.

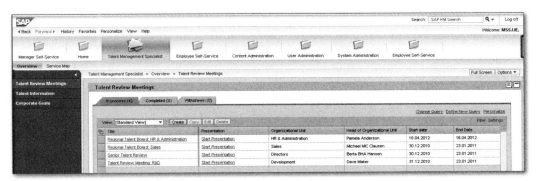

Figure 8.22 Talent Review Meetings Application

Here the Talent Management specialist can view a list of all talent review meetings that have been created but not conducted (IN PROCESS), the meetings that have been conducted (COMPLETED), and the meetings that, for some reason, were created but not conducted (WITHDRAWN). A Talent Management specialist will also see any talent review meetings where an organizational unit within their area of responsibility has been added. Because the current objective is to create a new talent review meeting, the Talent Management Specialist selects the CREATE button.

When a new Talent Review Meeting screen opens, the Talent Management specialist is presented with the first of two tabs. Each of the two tabs—PLANNING and PREPARATION—provides a set of options to classify the talent review meeting and define its content.

Planning

The PLANNING tab is where the Talent Management specialist defines the following details of the talent review meeting:

- Title of the talent review meeting
- The organizational unit(s) that will be the focus of the meeting
- Category (such as global, regional, or local)
- Language
- Level (such as senior management or functional specialists)
- Deadline for meeting completion
- Scheduling (such as over one day or multiple days)
- Meeting date
- Status (such as "In process" or "Complete")
- Support team that will support the conducting of the meeting
- Meeting participants
- Handouts to be distributed

Because this meeting will focus on employees within the United States for senior management positions, the Talent Management specialist enters a suitable title ("US Regional Talent Board"), and selects the key ORGANIZATIONAL UNITS for the meeting, which include FINANCE, HR, and OPERATIONS. The managers of these organizational units and their "children" can be selected directly as meeting participants. Next, the CATEGORY (REGIONAL), LANGUAGE (ENGLISH), and LEVEL (SENIOR MANAGEMENT) are selected.

The level is important because it allows employees to be reviewed in a roll-up. A roll-up means that some employees are reviewed and discussed in multiple meetings that increase in level to build a talent pipeline and to discuss the most talented employees at the top levels of the organization.

> **Key Point**
>
> If an employee is reviewed in more than one talent review meeting, then the performance and potential ratings that are confirmed in the talent review meeting with the highest level will be the ratings stored in Infotype 7408 (potential) and Infotype 7409 (performance); these will be subsequently used by Talent Management.

The DATE and SCHEDULING are selected before the SUPPORT TEAM is chosen and roles are assigned. The support team is made of other Talent Management specialists and managers that assist the organizing Talent Management specialist before or during the meeting, although the exact participants will depend on the level of the meeting and an individual organization's talent strategy. Each support team member can be assigned a meeting role, such as minutes taker or business partner. The support team has the authorization to plan, prepare, and conduct the talent review meeting—if they have the appropriate authorizations for the talent review meeting object (RM) in Infotype 1000 (objects). Because this meeting is for the entire United States region, a global Talent Management specialist is assigned to the support team, along with a colleague of the regional Talent Management specialist to take notes.

After you've assigned the support team, you can select the participants. The managers of the organizational units that will be the focus of the meeting are automatically placed in the PARTICIPANTS list, so the Talent Management specialist selects the HR business partners and the Talent Management specialists that perform talent management on a global level to also attend. These individuals will be able to discuss the reasons for their performance and potential ratings and talent group nominations, whether to accept or reject the ratings and nominations, whether the individuals have other characteristics that align them with the organization's talent strategy, and whether the individuals are suitable for any other talent groups.

Figure 8.23 shows the PLANNING tab of a TALENT REVIEW MEETING that has been recently created.

The final option available to the Talent Management specialist in the planning phase is to prepare the PDF handouts, although this step is done after the preparation stage because that's when the agenda topics are defined. When the handout is created, any of the agenda topics can be included and, beginning with EhP 5, it's possible to insert a calibration grid, list of employees, or Talent Profile for Managers and Talent Management Specialists into a handout (or a combination of all three).

8 | Progression Phase

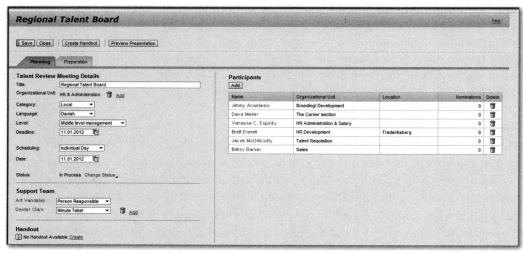

Figure 8.23 Planning Stage of a New Talent Review Meeting

Preparation

In the PREPARATION tab, the Talent Management specialist can assign the filter for the employees that will be the focus of the meeting and create the agenda. The TALENT MONITOR FOR NEW NOMINATIONS displays each of the managers that are assigned as participants in the meeting, and they can be expanded to display their employees that match the filter criteria. By default, SAP delivers two predefined filters, but you can create other compulsory filters in the Implementation Guide (IMG) via Transaction SPRO or the menu path SAP CUSTOMIZING IMPLEMENTATION GUIDE • TALENT MANAGEMENT AND TALENT DEVELOPMENT • TALENT REVIEW MEETING • TALENT MONITOR • DEFINE SEARCH CONFIGURATIONS FOR TALENT MONITOR. The two predefined filters are the Performance and Potential (All Values) filter and the Talent Groups (All Values) filter. The Performance and Potential filter is the default setting.

The Talent Monitor can store notes for employees—either private notes for the Talent Management specialist and support team that can be displayed during the planning and preparation of the meeting, or notes that can be displayed during the meeting. Employees whose talent data has been checked for the meeting can be marked with the CHECKED indicator.

Employees can be added directly to an agenda topic by selecting the COPY icon next to an employee's name or, for all of a manager's direct reports, next to the manager's name. Employees can also be added by dragging and dropping them onto the target agenda topic.

After the Talent Management specialist has reviewed the employees, the next step is to create the agenda for the meeting. When you're creating an agenda, you can add multiple agenda topics of different types. The following are the three types of agenda topic that can be selected:

- **Folder type**
  Used for creating a structure level for the agenda, in which other agenda topics can be added.

- **General type (for discussing non-employee topics)**
  Used for discussing topics not related directly to the review of employees—such as minutes from a previous meeting or key positions that lack adequate bench strength.

- **Talents type (for discussing employees)**
  Used for reviewing and discussing employees.

Figure 8.24 shows a talent review meeting in the preparation stage with two agenda topics added.

Figure 8.24 Preparation Stage of a New Talent Review Meeting

Let's say that the Talent Management specialist first wants to review the minutes from the last talent review meeting for this category and then highlight any key positions without an adequate bench strength that could be filled by employees reviewed during the meeting. To add a new agenda topic to the agenda, the Talent Management specialist selects ADD AGENDA TOPIC • GENERAL, enters the title for the agenda topic, and selects OK. The Talent Management specialist can now attach a PDF copy of the minutes from the previous meeting to the new agenda topic.

For the next agenda topic, the Talent Management specialist wants to review and discuss the employees and adds another agenda topic for talents. He can now add employees to review from the TALENT MONITOR or by using the ADD TALENTS option in the ADD AGENDA TOPIC menu. If he wants to review all employees in the key functions of the United States region, he'll add all of the employees under each of the managers in the TALENT MONITOR section of the screen. As with the Talent Monitor, both private and presentation notes can be stored for employees, and the CHECKED indicator can be used.

After the preparation of the talent review meeting is complete, the Talent Management specialist can preview the talent review meeting using the PREVIEW PRESENTATION button. After the preview is concluded, the handouts can be created to send to the participants, and then the talent review meeting can be saved.

8.3.2 Conducting the Talent Review Meeting

To start the talent review meeting, the Talent Management specialist navigates to the list of talent review meetings and selects the START PRESENTATION hyperlink for the "US REGIONAL TALENT BOARD" TALENT REVIEW MEETING.

The Talent Review Meeting application opens on the agenda. The first agenda topic can be selected from the agenda topics drop-down list or scrolled through using the PREVIOUS AGENDA TOPIC and NEXT AGENDA TOPIC buttons. The Talent Management specialist selects the first agenda topic, and the participants review the meeting minutes from the previous "US Regional Talent Board" meeting. After reviewing the notes, the participants then discuss key positions at a global level that don't have adequate bench strength (e.g., the global payroll manager and global finance manager positions).

After this discussion is concluded, the Talent Management specialist uses the NEXT AGENDA TOPIC button to move to the second agenda topic. The TALENTS agenda type plots all of the employees added during preparation to a nine-box calibration grid, which displays employees using their performance versus potential ratings.

> **Key Point**
>
> From EhP 5 onward, it's also possible to add employees to the calibration grid that are missing either performance ratings, potential ratings, or both. They can be added to the grid square that matches the performance and potential of the employee. During customization, you can choose whether to allow employees to be added that are missing performance ratings, potential ratings, or both.

Talent Management specialists and participants can do the following using the calibration grid:

- Assess potential and performance ratings of employees.
- Edit ratings and calibrate employees from different organizational units against each other.
- View the talent profile of employees, either a short version or the talent profile for managers and Talent Management specialists.
- Compare employees.
- Approve or reject talent group nominations.

Figure 8.25 shows the calibration grid during a talent review meeting, which we'll dissect in this section.

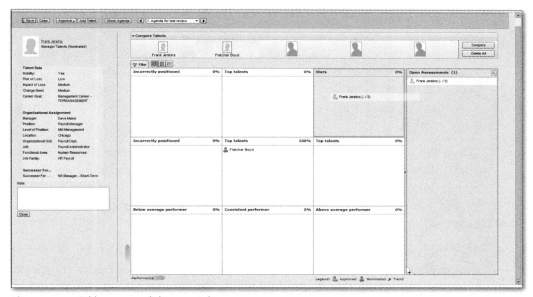

Figure 8.25 Calibration Grid during a Talent Review Meeting

The first focus for the participants is to review the high-performing, high-potential individuals in the top-right quadrant of the calibration grid. The calibration grid can be switched to the business-card view or a list view to display additional employee information. The views can be filtered by one or more criteria (such as talent group or demographic criteria).

The Talent Management specialist drags each of the employees from the quadrant into the COMPARE TALENTS bar above the calibration grid and selects the COMPARE button to bring up a side-by-side comparison of basic talent information for each of the employees. After reviewing this information, the Talent Management specialist can then open the Talent Profile for Managers and Talent Management Specialists for each of the employees to review their talent information, such as competency ratings, mobility, risks and talent group nominations. After reviewing all of the talents and discussing their ratings with the appropriate manager and their peers, they decide that all of the ratings and talent group nominations are correct.

Next the process is repeated for the other quadrants of the calibration grid that are of interest, which are prepared during customizing. The definition of each quadrant is defined in the IMG via Transaction SPRO or the menu path SAP CUSTOMIZING IMPLEMENTATION GUIDE • TALENT MANAGEMENT AND TALENT DEVELOPMENT • CALIBRATION GRID. During the review of the employees in the other quadrants, the Talent Management specialist notices that Frank Jenkins has a good profile and promising ratings. Because two key finance positions have inadequate bench strength and represent a focus for the global Talent Management specialists, the Talent Management specialist decides to increase the Finance department talent pool by assigning Frank Jenkins to the Global Finance talent group. Although this action isn't taken in the meeting, it's noted as a follow-up action by the meeting's minutes taker.

The participants continue to review and discuss the other quadrants of the calibration grid. At some points during this review, the discussions lead to the conclusion that an employee is in the incorrect quadrant based on their performance and potential. The Talent Management specialist can simply drag the employee to a new quadrant to update his or her ratings.

After the meeting is concluded, the Talent Management specialist can initiate the closing process by selecting the APPROVE button to approve all of the ratings and talent group nominations in the whole talent review meeting or just the ratings in the calibration grid. Because reviewing and making assignments to the calibration grid was the last agenda topic, the Talent Management specialist clicks the APPROVE button and selects the option ALL TALENTS OF TALENT REVIEW MEETING. The last steps are to save and close the meeting, which is done by opening the Talent Review Meeting application and changing the status from IN PROCESS to COMPLETE. All decisions made in the meeting are then finalized in the SAP ERP HCM system.

8.3.3 Talent Groups

Recall that talent groups are used by Talent Management specialists to categorize employees into groups based on their performance, potential, or other certain characteristics. During Talent Management processes and activities, such as succession planning and development, these groups can be leveraged to identify specific employees for specific talent needs. Employees can be a member of more than one talent group simultaneously.

Talent Management specialists maintain these groups through the Talent Groups application—found under TALENT INFORMATION in the TALENT MANAGEMENT SPECIALIST portal role—and can create as many groups as are required by the organization to manage its talent pool. Upon creating a talent group, a Talent Management specialist can add a description, set the assignment length of the talent group, add the support team, and upload one or more attachments. As with the talent review meeting, the members of the support team have the same authorizations for the talent group as the Talent Management specialist that created it.

As a follow-up to the "US Regional Talent Board" talent review meeting, the Talent Management specialist navigates to the Talent Groups application in the portal and chooses the Global Finance talent group. Figure 8.26 shows the Talent Management specialist adding Frank Jenkins to that talent group.

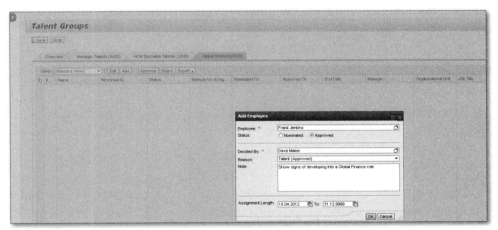

Figure 8.26 Adding an Employee to a Talent Group in the Talent Group Application

Now that all of the employees within the organization have been assessed and reviewed, the Talent Management specialists can begin the process of assigning successors to their key positions. They can also further increase the organization's talent pipeline by making additional talent group nominations and creating successor pools for specific job families.

8.4 Succession Planning

For succession planning, SAP offers SAP Talent Visualization by Nakisa (STVN) SuccessionPlanning, an integrated graphical user interface (GUI) that offers rich functionality for managing the talent identification and succession planning processes in the portal. Although STVN SuccessionPlanning is SAP's solution for succession planning, SAP also offers a basic backend transaction (HRTMC_PPOM) for managing succession planning activities. While this section will focus on the functionality provided by STVN SuccessionPlanning, it will also highlight the equivalent backend functionality where it exists.

> **Key Point**
>
> Nakisa's product release cycle differs from the SAP Enhancement Package release cycle, and the features and functionality in future releases aren't confirmed until the solutions are officially released on SAP Service Marketplace. STVN SuccessionPlanning 3.0 Service Pack 3 (SP3) is the latest release of STVN SuccessionPlanning available at the time of writing, and it's used as the basis for the functionality described in this book. As a result, organizations may find that during an implementation of Talent Management, the functionality and UI in the latest release of STVN SuccessionPlanning differs from what is described in this book.

8.4.1 STVN SuccessionPlanning

STVN SuccessionPlanning is an official SAP-certified Solution Extension, produced by SAP's visualization solutions partner Nakisa. Nakisa is a Tier-1 partner, which means that SAP co-develops, licenses, tests, and supports Nakisa solutions under two solution suites: SAP Organizational Visualization by Nakisa (SOVN) and SAP Talent Visualization by Nakisa (STVN).

Both SOVN and STVN solutions must go through SAP's strict Premium Qualification program before being released on the SAP Service Marketplace. The SAP Premium

Qualification process tests the solutions for security, performance, supportability, accessibility, and documentation. The solutions are supported by SAP for first- and second-level support through the normal OSS channel on SAP Service Marketplace, under Component XX-PART-NKS.

STVN SuccessionPlanning delivers an intuitive, easy-to-use GUI for performing succession planning activities, such assigning key positions, identifying high-performing, high-potential individuals, assigning successors, and reviewing analytics and KPIs. Because STVN SuccessionPlanning is tightly integrated with SAP ERP HCM, it leverages the backend's authorization mechanism and concepts, search functionality, and data model.

> **Key Point**
>
> The search functionality in Talent Management is powered by TREX, so TREX is required because STVN SuccessionPlanning leverages the Talent Management search capabilities, even if the Talent Management searches are only used in STVN SuccessionPlanning. The STVN SuccessionPlanning for Managers application doesn't require TREX for its search capabilities.

Data is read from and written back to the SAP backend system in real time, as if the data was being displayed or maintained directly in the backend system.

STVN SuccessionPlanning's UI is based on the visualization of the organizational units in the Talent Management specialist's area of responsibility. These organizational units are represented in an "orgchart," much like the visualization of the organization structure in SOVN OrgChart. You can easily expand, move, and zoom in or out of this structure.

The reporting structure between positions is also displayed in an orgchart that uses either the standard position to position relationships maintained in SAP or, where these relationships aren't maintained, a reporting structure derived by the SAP system using the organizational assignment of positions within the organization. The choice to use either the standard relationships or derived relationships can be defined in the IMG via Transaction SPRO or the menu path SAP CUSTOMIZING IMPLEMENTATION GUIDE • TALENT MANAGEMENT AND TALENT DEVELOPMENT • BASIC SETTINGS • SPECIFY TYPE OF REPORTING FOR DETERMINING THE MANAGER.

Search listings can be used to search for various data about the objects in the SAP ERP HCM system, such as employee talent data or key position data.

Details about objects can be displayed by selecting an object in the orgchart, from the search listings results, or from another object's details. For example, the *position details panel* displays information that includes the following details:

- The incumbent
- Assigned successors
- Competency requirements
- Career type and level (either directly assigned or inherited from its job)
- Job evaluation (either directly assigned or inherited from its job)
- Key indication (either directly assigned or inherited from its job)

The *employee details panel* displays information that includes the following details:

- Succession plans
- Successor pool assignments
- Talent group assignments
- Competencies held
- Recent performance and potential ratings
- Risk assessment
- Career aspirations, such as preferred jobs, career goals, and mobility preferences

The details panel of an object also allows the Talent Management specialist to perform certain tasks, such as assign, edit or remove key indications, competencies, or successors.

STVN SuccessionPlanning for Managers is a "light" version of the STVN SuccessionPlanning application that is designed for managers. The application contains limited features and functionality that reflect a manager's role in succession planning activities. The manager application displays the positions that are within the organizational unit that the manager manages. For their positions and employees, the manager can view the same data as a Talent Management specialist can. The manager can nominate successors to their positions (which will later be approved or rejected by a Talent Management specialist), set key indications, and perform searches within their area of the organization. No other functionality in STVN SuccessionPlanning is available in STVN SuccessionPlanning for Managers.

8.4.2 Comparing STVN SuccessionPlanning and SAP Functionality

Organizations should implement STVN SuccessionPlanning for their succession planning processes because the STVN solution suite leverages the full functionality and integration provided by SAP. SAP also offers limited succession planning functionality in the SAP backend via Transaction HRTMC_PPOM. Both STVN SuccessionPlanning and the SAP backend enable you to do the following:

- Assign an area of responsibility for a Talent Management specialist
- Navigate through the Talent Management specialist's area of responsibility
- Assign key indications to jobs and/or positions
- Assign career types and evaluation results to jobs and/or positions
- Assign competencies to positions, jobs, job families, and/or functional areas
- Assign employees to successor pools
- Manage successor pools
- Assign employees to talent groups
- Assign successors
- Display the bench strength of a position
- Approve or reject successor nominations
- Display an employee's competencies

Beyond the functionalities just listed, the STVN SuccessionPlanning solution also offers the following functionality, which isn't available via the SAP backend:

- Seamless integration with the portal
- Display of employees on nine-box performance versus potential grid
- Identification of successors for a position using the Profile Match function
- Calibration of successors on ranking versus readiness grid, similar to the calibration grid used in a talent review meeting
- Display of chain of successors
- Display of KPIs in the analytics dashboards
- Bulk approval/nomination of successors and building of successor pools with menu-guided wizards

- Visualization of multiple views of object data in the orgchart, such as position bench strength and employee ratings
- Leverage of numerous reporting capabilities to identify key metrics and quickly search for different information
- Print or export orgcharts and objects details, including multi-paged, tiled printing

Various features in STVN SuccessionPlanning can be configured or customized to support client processes and meet business-specific requirements, such as views, details panels, search listings, and analytics dashboards. We recommend that you use a Nakisa-certified consultant to perform configurations and customizations within SOVN and STVN solutions.

8.4.3 Status Handling

Succession planning uses status handling for assigning employees to talent groups, successor pools, or positions as a successor and for key indication for jobs and positions. These statuses help the Talent Management specialists track whether employees or jobs/positions have been nominated, approved, or rejected for the specific assignment. Employees or positions that have had their nominations approved can have the status of their assignment changed from "Nominated" to "Approved" to reflect this. If an assignment is rejected, then the infotype record in SAP is delimited at the date of rejection. No infotype records exist for rejected status.

It's worth noting that in Transaction HRTMC_PPOM, if the status is changed without changing the date period, then the existing record will be changed, and the history is lost.

8.4.4 Successor Pools

Like talent groups, succession planning also uses successor pools to classify employees. However, a successor pool is specific to a job family and indicates that the assigned employee is suitable for one or more jobs in the job family. When performing a successor profile match for a position, a successor pool can be selected as the source for the employees to match to the position.

Succession Planning | 8.4

> **Key Point**
> Prior to the release of SAP Note 1632504, it was possible to maintain readiness and ranking when assigning an employee to a successor pool. Because this has no meaning in the context of this form of assignment, SAP removed these attributes. However, it can't be guaranteed that this SAP note has been implemented, so STVN SuccessionPlanning still requires that these attributes are maintained upon assignment of an employee to a successor pool.

In STVN SuccessionPlanning, a profile match exists at the job family level to find employees for the successor pool. It works in much the same way as the position profile match.

A position can also be assigned to a job family, although functionality is historical and remains in place for organizations that used the pre-EhP 4 data model for succession planning.

8.4.5 Bench Strength

Bench strength is a risk-based measurement of the approved successors assigned to a position. It creates a score based on each successor, which takes into account any other successor assignments each successor may have. This is to ensure that accurate risk value is assigned to the overall value of the succession plans because if an employee is assigned to multiple positions as a successor, there is a higher risk that the employee will be appointed to another of the positions for which they are a successor.

In the bench strength calculation, each approved successor is worth a score of 1, minus 0.25 for every other successor assignment the successor has. A successor can't contribute less than 0.25 to a bench strength score.

For example, a position has two successors: Successor A is only a successor for this position, but Successor B is a successor for this position and two other positions. Successor A contributes 1 to the bench strength, while successor B contributes 0.5 (1 minus 0.25 for each of the other successor positions held). Therefore, the bench strength for the position is 1.5.

In a best practice scenario, the ideal bench strength is 3 for each key position. However, the BAdI `HRTMC_SUCCESSOR_BENCH_STR` can be enhanced to provide a customer-specific bench strength calculation.

8.4.6 Talent Identification

Although the Talent Management specialist has already identified some high-performing, high-potential individuals in the talent review meetings, STVN SuccessionPlanning offers a nine-box grid called the Grid, to easily identify individuals that may not have been included in the talent review meeting process for one reason or another. The Grid offers similar functionality to the calibration grid in the talent review meetings, but in STVN SuccessionPlanning, it can be accessed on an ad hoc basis by the Talent Management specialist and isn't restricted by the mandatory filter criteria like the calibration grid is.

The Talent Management specialist accesses the Grid from the EMPLOYEES menu in STVN SuccessionPlanning. Because Talent Management specialists have a wide number of fields to choose from, they can cover a wider number of employees:

- Organizational unit name or ID
- Central person ID
- Personnel number
- First or last name
- Position name or ID
- Job name or ID
- Job family name or ID
- Talent group
- Personnel area

As with all search listings in STVN SuccessionPlanning, the Talent Management specialist can also filter the search results using the ADVANCED SEARCH feature.

Because the Talent Management specialist is looking for high-performing, high-potential employees in the finance area, he searches by organizational units containing "Finance." This search yields a large number of results, so the Talent Management specialist uses the ADVANCED SEARCH feature to filter results down by the PERSONNEL AREA of the HEAD OFFICE. Like with the calibration grid in a talent review meeting, the Talent Management specialist can view the details of each selected employee in the details panel alongside the Grid. Suitable employees can be added to a successor pool or talent group with just a few clicks, directly from their details.

The Talent Management specialist reviews the details of some of the high-performing, high-potential individuals and assigns them to various talent groups and successor pools, depending on their competencies, attributes, and career aspirations. For example, Jayne Pearson is the deputy financial controller and has an excellent record of high performance and potential over the past three years. She also displays aspirations to progress into a management career and is at risk of leaving in the future. The Talent Management specialist assigns Jayne to the Global Finance talent group.

Figure 8.27 shows the Grid with an employee's details displayed in the details panel.

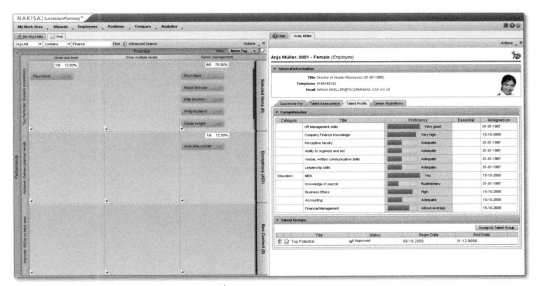

Figure 8.27 The Grid in STVN SuccessionPlanning

Now that the Talent Management specialist has increased the company's talent pipeline, the specialist can begin to exploit this talent pipeline when searching for and assigning successors to key positions.

8.4.7 Assigning Successors

It's now time to assign successors to the global finance manager position to increase the bench strength and reduce risk should the incumbent of the position leave.

The Talent Management specialist first reviews the position details to get an idea of the competencies, career path, and other attributes that are required. Although the Talent Management specialist can use the Assign Successor function to assign a known individual as a successor, if he doesn't have a specific individual in mind, he can opt to use the Profile Match function.

The Profile Match function matches employees to the position based on the competencies held by the employee versus the competencies required by the position. The Profile Match ranks the matched employees by a suitability percentage and gives the Talent Management specialist the opportunity to view a gap analysis of the employee's competencies against the position competencies. This information can be used to judge the suitability of the employees and also provide a basis for creating a development plan for the employees that are assigned as successors.

To open the Profile Match function, the Talent Management specialist navigates to the SUCCESSION tab of the position details and selects the PROFILE MATCH button, which is located next to the ASSIGN SUCCESSOR button. The Profile Match function opens in a new window and immediately displays employees that match the position based on the default criteria. If there are no matches, then the Search Panel automatically opens so that the Talent Management specialist can select alternative criteria. The Talent Management specialist can search for employees from the following sources:

- The successor pool of the job family that the positions is assigned to
- The successor pool of another job family
- A talent group
- An organizational unit
- Across all employees in the organization

In addition to the sources for employees, the Talent Management specialist can also select which of the position competency requirements he wants to search by. The competencies of the position are displayed in two sections, CORE COMPETENCIES and NON-CORE COMPETENCIES, so that the Talent Management specialist can see the important competencies that are required for the position. If a competency is marked with the ESSENTIAL flag, then only employees with this competency will be matched.

When the Talent Management specialist wants to use the Global Finance talent group, he selects the TALENT GROUP option and searches for the "Global Finance

Succession Planning | **8.4**

talent group". The Talent Management specialist decides to begin the search with all of the position competencies selected because the optimal successors will have most or all of the position competencies. After the Talent Management specialist selects the FIND MATCH button, the match employees are displayed in the left panel.

Several employees are listed in the results list, but the Talent Management specialist is particularly interested in the two individuals that are at the top of list: Frank Jenkins and Jayne Pearson. Figure 8.28 shows the results list of the Profile Match function.

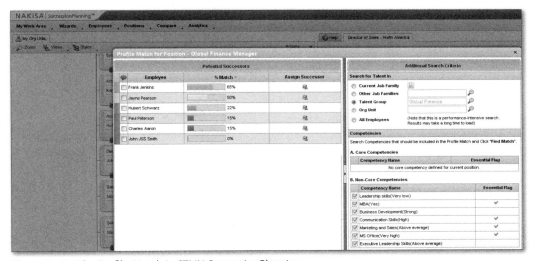

Figure 8.28 The Profile Match in STVN SuccessionPlanning

The Talent Management specialist selects the checkbox next to both employees and, in the SELECTED ITEMS box at the bottom of the Profile Match window, selects VIEW COMPETENCY MATCH-UP VS. POSITION to launch the gap analysis. The COMPARE COMPETENCIES window opens and displays a column for the position and columns for each of the selected employees. The performance, potential, and risk of loss values for each employee are displayed along with the employee's photo. The position column displays the competency proficiency for each of the position competencies. Each of the employee columns displays the competency proficiency that the employee holds and an icon to specify the position requirement proficiency. Below the list of position requirement competencies is a list of all of the competencies held by the employees that aren't required by the position and their proficiency. This

309

information can provide additional value in determining whether the employee is a suitable candidate to be a successor for the position.

Figure 8.29 shows the COMPARE COMPETENCIES window for the GLOBAL FINANCE MANAGER position with FRANK JENKINS and JAYNE PEARSON.

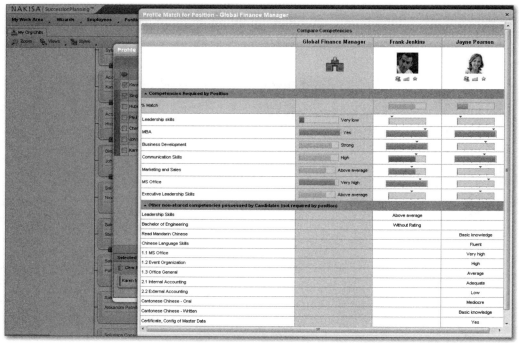

Figure 8.29 The Compare Competencies Gap Analysis in STVN SuccessionPlanning

The Talent Management specialist reviews the competency matches, decides that both employees are good candidates as successors of the position and closes the COMPARE COMPETENCIES window to return to the Profile Match window and assign the individuals as successors. However, the Talent Management specialist wants to review other attributes of the employees before making a final decision. In the SELECTED ITEMS box, the Talent Management specialist selects VIEW PROFILES to open the employee details for each employee alongside each other to check the career goals, mobility, and risks of the employees and make a decision about their ranking and readiness for the position. This enables the Talent Management specialist to ensure that the career aspirations of the employee match that of the position.

After the review is complete, the Talent Management specialist decides that both Frank Jenkins and Jayne Pearson are suitable successors. The Talent Management specialist closes the Compare Competencies window and selects the ASSIGN SUCCESSOR button next to Frank Jenkins. This opens the Assign Successor window, which is also used when the ASSIGN SUCCESSOR function is selected in the position details.

Figure 8.30 shows Frank Jenkins being assigned as a successor.

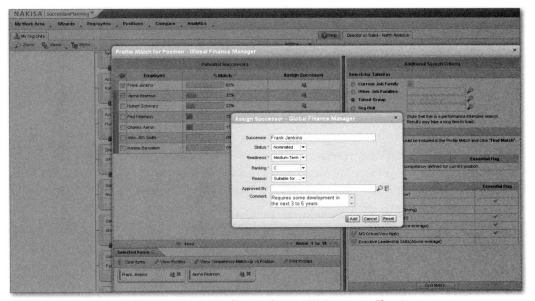

Figure 8.30 Assigning a Successor in the Profile Match in STVN SuccessionPlanning

In this window, the Talent Management specialist enters the STATUS (NOMINATED or APPROVED), the READINESS, and the RANKING. A reason, alternative assigned by user, and comment can also be selected or entered optionally if applicable. Readiness specifies how ready the individual is to assume the position. For example, the candidate is ready in the short term (1-2 years), medium term (2-3 years), or long term (3+ years). Ranking, on the other hand, is often used differently from organization to organization, but it typically specifies the value of the employee to the position. The values used for these are defined in the IMG via Transaction SPRO or the menu path SAP CUSTOMIZING IMPLEMENTATION GUIDE • TALENT MANAGEMENT AND TALENT DEVELOPMENT • SUCCESSION PLANNING.

The Talent Management specialist selects NOMINATED status because the decision should be reviewed in a talent review meeting. Also, because Frank Jenkins requires some development of his competencies, his READINESS is set to MEDIUM-TERM and his RANKING to C. The Talent Management specialist also selects a REASON and enters a comment about Frank Jenkins' required development before selecting ADD. The Talent Management specialist repeats the same assignment process for Jayne Pearson.

Now that Frank Jenkins and Jayne Pearson have been added as successors, the Talent Management specialist closes the Profile Match window and sees the successor assignments in the position details. Because some new successors have been assigned to the position, the Talent Management specialist opens the Successor Calibration grid by selecting the SHOW GRID button. This plots all of the successors of the position onto a grid based on their ranking and readiness attributes in a similar way to the Grid. Like the calibration grid in the talent review meeting, the individuals on the Successor Calibration grid can be dragged and dropped to other quadrants to change their ranking, readiness, or both. Using the Successor Calibration grid can ensure that successors are aligned, particularly because successors may have been assigned at different times and over a long period, the readiness and ranking of successors should change as development increases competency proficiency and, therefore, suitability as a successor. It's also worth noting that as positions can change their requirements over time, successors must be calibrated accordingly to ensure that the most capable candidates are identified.

Figure 8.31 shows the Successor Calibration grid of the GLOBAL FINANCE MANAGER position. Here Frank Jenkins and Jayne Pearson can be seen visually ranked against the other successor, Patsy Coffmann. Patsy Coffman is both the most ready and most highly ranked of all of the successors.

For organizations that choose not to leverage STVN SuccessionPlanning, Transaction HRTMC_PPOM can be used to assign successors to positions, as shown in Figure 8.32. Via this transaction, the Talent Management specialist navigates to the position, selects the SUCCESSOR tab, and clicks the INSERT ROW button ( ). The Talent Management specialist then selects the successor and enters the same information as is entered in STVN SuccessionPlanning.

Succession Planning | 8.4

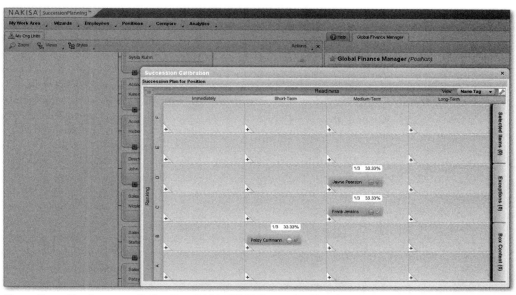

Figure 8.31 The Successor Calibration Grid in STVN SuccessionPlanning

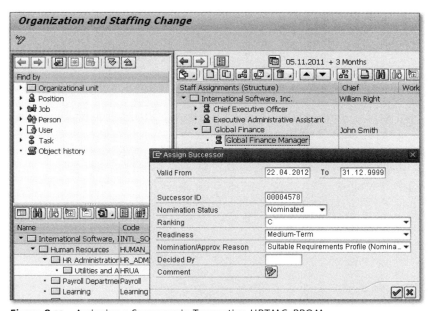

Figure 8.32 Assigning a Successor in Transaction HRTMC_PPOM

8.4.8 Wizards and Comparison

STVN SuccessionPlanning also has two features that may be useful to Talent Management specialists: wizards and comparison. Wizards let the Talent Management specialist perform bulk processing tasks in simple, guided, step-by-step wizards. The comparison feature allows two objects to be compared side by side.

Three wizards are available for the Talent Management specialist; all are accessible from the WIZARDS menu in the module menu:

- NOMINATE SUCCESSORS
- APPROVE SUCCESSORS
- BUILD SUCCESSOR POOLS

Figure 8.33 shows the APPROVE SUCCESSOR wizard being used to approve two successors to the CHIEF FINANCIAL OFFICER position.

Figure 8.33 Step 3 of the Approve Successors Wizard in STVN SuccessionPlanning

In the comparison module, a Talent Management specialist can compare two objects (e.g., organizational units, positions, or employees) against each other. There is no restriction on comparing objects of the same type, so, for example, a position can be compared to an employee side-by-side to review competency and career aspiration suitability. Like the wizards, the comparison module is accessed from the module menu. Figure 8.34 shows Frank Jenkins and Jayne Pearson being compared in the Compare module.

Succession Planning | 8.4

Figure 8.34 Comparing Two Employees in the Compare Module of STVN SuccessionPlanning

8.4.9 Reporting and Analytics

STVN SuccessionPlanning contains three main areas that can provide reporting:

- Analytics dashboards
- Search listings
- Views

Let's explore each of these further.

Analytics Dashboards

The main source of reporting information in STVN SuccessionPlanning is the analytic dashboards, which are generated by Nakisa function modules and don't require additional software, such as SAP NetWeaver Business Warehouse or SAP BusinessObjects. The five available dashboards each deliver a number of key performance indicators (KPIs) to provide the Talent Management specialist with an overview of the situation in their area of responsibility:

- **Overview dashboard**
  Provides an overview of KPIs from the other four dashboards.
- **Succession Planning dashboard**
  Contains a plethora of important information for a Talent Management specialist and includes the following KPIs, among others:
  - Total number of positions
  - Total number of key positions
  - Key positions with successors
  - Key positions with no successors
  - Key positions with 1 successor
  - Key positions with 2 successors
  - Key positions with 3 successors
  - Key positions with 4 successors
  - Key positions with successors ready now
  - Key positions with successor readiness
  - Successors planned for more than one position
  - Average successor bench strength
- **Competency dashboard**
  Provides an overview of the competency distribution of core competencies, languages, and basic competencies within the Talent Management specialist's area of responsibility.
- **Holder/Successor dashboard**
  Covers KPIs around gender, average age, average tenure, and nationality of both holders and successors.
- **Potential/Performance dashboard**
  Gives a breakdown of the performance and potential ratings in the past five years.

Each of the dashboards can be segmented using any of the following criteria:

- Personnel area
- Personnel subarea
- Employee group

- Employee subgroup
- Company code
- Nationality code
- Gender

Figure 8.35 shows the Succession Planning dashboard.

Figure 8.35 Analytics Dashboard in STVN SuccessionPlanning

As a complement to the analytics dashboards, the search listings also provide a source of information.

Search Listings

The search listings provide a powerful method for the Talent Management specialist to search through SAP ERP HCM data. There are 13 predelivered search listings, split into the Talent Management specialist's work area search listings (located in the My Work Area module), employee search listings (located in the Employee module), and position search listings (located in the Position module). The following are search listings for the Talent Management specialist's area of responsibility:

- My Org Units
- My Positions
- My Employees

The employee search listings return results not just exclusively to the Talent Management specialist's area of responsibility. Following are the employee search listings:

- Employees
- Talent in talent groups
- Employees assigned to job families
- Talent groups

The position search listings, like the employee listings, also return results that are outside of the Talent Management specialist's area of responsibility, including the following:

- All positions
- Positions with successors
- Key positions
- Key positions with successors
- Positions with career types
- Job families with successors

The employee search listings and positions search listings aren't restricted by area of responsibility, like those in the My Work Area module. Each of the search listings has a vast range of search criteria available.

The final source for reporting information is from views.

Views

While views aren't specifically reports, they can provide a quick overview of information across a number of objects in the orgchart. Each object type has a number of views that can be selected from the VIEWS menu when displaying the orgchart.

One particular example is the position succession status view, which provides the successor bench strength and number of successors that are ready immediately. When this view is selected, all positions that are expanded in the orgchart will display this information.

Other information that can be displayed includes talent ratings and succession status, both for positions and for the employees. By default, all positions will display the key indication icon. If the position is a chief position, it will display the chief position icon shown in Transaction PPOME; otherwise, it will display the standard position icon shown in Transaction PPOME.

8.5 Talent Development

Now that the talent review meetings and succession planning has taken place, the Talent Management specialists can create individual development plans for the employees identified in these processes. SAP provides the Development Plan application for this process.

Unlike a development plan in the performance appraisal, the development plan used in Talent Management can be created to monitor development activities over a long period. It offers greater benefits when developing successors or potential leaders for whom the required skills can take a number of years to develop.

8.5.1 Creating the Development Plan

Because Frank Jenkins has been assigned as a successor to the Global Finance Manager position, he needs a development plan to set and monitor the development of his competencies, skills, and behaviors that will prepare him for his future role. After the Talent Management specialist creates the development plan, it will be displayed in the DEVELOPMENT PLAN tab in the employee's Talent Profile for Managers and Talent Management Specialists and by the employee's manager in the Assessment application in MSS.

The Talent Management specialist navigates to TALENT INFORMATION in the TALENT MANAGEMENT SPECIALIST portal role and then searches for "Frank Jenkins." He selects FRANK JENKINS from the generated list and then clicks the DEVELOPMENT PLAN button.

The development plan has a number of predefined development areas in which development goals can be created. These development areas are defined during the creation of the development plan form in the IMG. To add a development goal, the Talent Management specialist selects ADD DEVELOPMENT PLAN STEP and then chooses either ADD CUSTOM DEVELOPMENT GOAL or ADD DEVELOPMENT GOAL USING QUALIFICATION.

A custom development goal is a freely definable development goal; in contrast, the development goal using qualification creates the development goal based on a qualification from the Qualifications Catalog. The functionality available for both development goals is the same.

Let's say the Talent Management specialist wants to add a development plan step for Frank Jenkins to develop his leadership skills, so he selects ADD DEVELOPMENT PLAN STEP and chooses ADD CUSTOM DEVELOPMENT GOAL. The Talent Management specialist enters a title for the goal ("Management Practices") and inputs a date period from today until the end of the fourth calendar year from now. Because the organization will consider Frank Jenkins to be ready for the Global Finance Manager position in three to five years, the development goal is aligned to complete his development within this period.

The percentage progress of the development goal can be maintained along with the ranking, which is measured on a predefined scale. That scale is selected during the creation of the development plan form in the IMG. Because this is a new development plan, the PROGRESS % and RANKING are left as blank values.

Development measures can be added to help the employee follow the development goal and to provide a benchmark for measuring the progress and ranking of the development goal. Two options are available.

The first option, ADD ACTION THAT CAN BE FREELY DEFINED, allows the Talent Management specialist to define any measure he chooses. A title, type, status, and description can be maintained for the action.

The second option, ADD TRAINING, allows the Talent Management specialist to select a course from the Course Catalog as the development goal. In addition to these options, the specialist can add a note to the development goal.

The Talent Management specialist wants to set a development measure for Frank Jenkins, so he selects ADD ACTION THAT CAN BE FREELY DEFINED. The development goal is called "Increase payments accuracy and efficiency" and is given the TYPE "Mentoring" and the STATUS "New". A description about how Frank Jenkins will mentor and motivate his staff to increase their work ethic and efficiency is entered into the development measure, as shown in Figure 8.36.

Figure 8.36 Adding a Development Goal to a Development Plan

The Talent Management specialist also wants Frank Jenkins to take a management training course. The specialist uses the ADD TRAINING action to open the Course Catalog, navigating through the Course Catalog structure to add the course "Management Techniques & Practices." Figure 8.37 shows the COURSE CATALOG navigation tree.

After all of the development goals have been added to the development plan, the Talent Management specialist can save it in the Development Plan application.

8 | Progression Phase

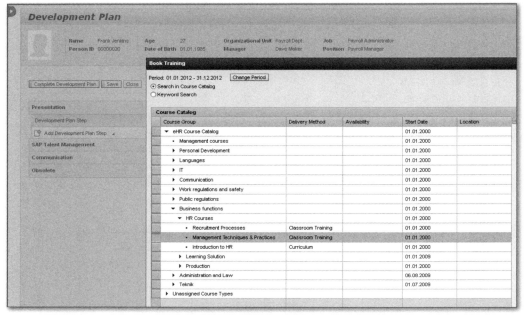

Figure 8.37 Selecting a Course from the Course Catalog

8.5.2 Tracking and Maintaining the Development Plan

After the development plan is saved, it will be displayed in the DEVELOPMENT PLAN tab in the employee's talent profile for managers and Talent Management specialists. In MSS, the manager can access the development plans for their employees by navigating to TALENT MANAGEMENT, opening the ASSESSMENT application, and selecting the DEVELOPMENT PLAN tab. The manager can also make changes to the development plan here, adding new development goals or updating the status of the existing goals on an ongoing basis. The Talent Management specialist can maintain the development plan in the Talent Information application, where it was created.

Figure 8.38 shows the DEVELOPMENT PLAN tab in the talent profile for managers and Talent Management specialists.

Although the development plan is a long-term, evolving document, it can be irrevocably set to complete when all goals are met using the COMPLETE DEVELOPMENT PLAN button.

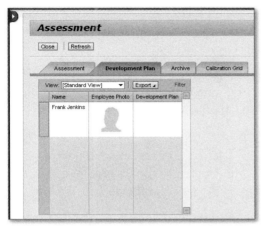

Figure 8.38 Displaying the Development Plans in MSS

8.6 Summary

The progression phase has now come to an end, and the review, identification, and development planning of employees has been completed. The organization is now performing end-to-end talent management and has already planned coverage for its key positions and development of its key employees—its talent.

The year-end appraisal is an excellent opportunity for the manager to help coach the employee. Coaching, however, should support all types of employee performance. Both managers and employees should prepare for the year-end performance meetings. In fact, the only way your employees can confirm that they are meeting certain standards is through specific and timely feedback from their managers. Employees want to know that what they are contributing and what they are being held accountable for have value.

If you tie short-term bonuses, rewards, and other recognition to performance, employees will feel encouraged to achieve optimal performance levels, perform effectively over the long term, and be content to develop their careers inside your organization.

Managers can incentivize performance for employees by using Enterprise Compensation Management (ECM). By following the ECM process, your organization can effectively create, distribute, monitor, and control employee compensation throughout your company. ECM comes with a variety of tools to easily and efficiently create compensation plans for your employees. With the new graphical features in EhP 5, distributing budgets has never been easier.

The talent review meeting allows organizations to review and classify their employees. This process enables the organization to understand who its best performing and highest potential employees are and to classify them in talent groups for identification in later processes.

For succession planning, SAP offers SAP Talent Visualization by Nakisa (STVN) SuccessionPlanning. This integrated GUI offers rich functionality for managing the talent identification and succession planning processes in the portal.

Unlike a development plan in the performance appraisal, the development plan can be created to monitor development activities over a long period. This offers greater benefits when developing successors or potential leaders where the required skills can take a number of years to develop.

Following the progression phase, the organization can prepare for the next yearly cycle, starting at the assessment phase. The induction phase will occur as new employees are sought and hired into the organization, or as organizational changes occur.

Next we'll review the underlying technologies and frameworks used by the Talent Management applications.

We recommend that you give due diligence to some technical considerations when implementing Talent Management. Use this chapter as reference guide about the underlying technologies and frameworks used by the various Talent Management applications.

9   Technical Considerations

SAP ERP HCM Talent Management uses a variety of technologies across its various modules. When implementing Talent Management, it's important to understand the different technologies that are used and how they interact with one other from both a software and hardware perspective. You also need to have the correct hardware and software components to support the applications. Having an understanding of these technologies will ensure a solid foundation for your implementation and will enable both a smooth implementation and a stable system landscape capable of use by the organization.

9.1   Technical Architecture

When discussing and analyzing architecture as it relates to technology, we have an opportunity to cover everything from the detailed components of each technology layer, to the entire network, which could include the Internet, intranet, and local area network. For the purposes of this book, we'll keep the analysis at a high level and just cover the most important technical components needed for each Talent Management application.

Because of the wide variety of technical components to consider, depending on which Talent Management application is being implemented, this section has been divided up by individual applications to discuss the main differences.

9.1.1 SAP E-Recruiting

SAP E-Recruiting (again, just E-Recruiting from here on) typically has one of the more complex architectures of all of the Talent Management applications. For instance, the solution can be installed in many different ways, with the following options covering the most common environments:

- **Stand-alone with integration into backend systems**
  E-Recruiting is installed on a separate SAP instance.

- **SAP ERP installation**
  E-Recruiting is installed as an integral part of the SAP ERP solution as an add-on.

- **SAP ERP installation with external user interface (UI)**
  E-Recruiting is installed on the SAP ERP instance as an add-on, and a separate, stand-alone web application server is established in the DMZ to host the external candidate UI. The stand-alone web application server doesn't store any relevant data in the database but instead integrates with the core E-Recruiting system via an RFC connection.

In addition, as we'll soon detail, you can use many optional components as bolt-ons, add-ons, or integration points to enhance the user experience. The following is an incomplete list of such components:

- **Adobe Document Server**
  An Adobe Document Server must be properly configured for a hiring manager to use form-based requisition requests as part of the standard Manager Self-Service (MSS) offering.

- **Search components**
  As of the SAP E-Recruiting Search Functions 1 (HCM_ERC_SES_1) business function, E-Recruiting uses the Search Engine Service (SES) as an interface between E-Recruiting and the Search and Classification search engine (TREX) for indexing and searching structured data. Alternatively, the unstructured data is managed by Knowledge Provider (KPro), which is a service of the Web Application Server (Web AS) that provides a similar type of interface for accessing the search engine.

- **Web proxy**
  E-Recruiting is no different from many other applications that are exposed to the Internet, where companies want to protect their data as best as possible. One option for doing this is to use a proxy server to receive requests from the

Internet and forward them to the E-Recruiting system. Aside from URL naming conventions, the users don't notice a difference. SAP typically recommends using their proprietary solution (SAP Web Dispatcher), but it's also possible to use other third-party software. Aside from adding an additional layer of protection, this type of software also provides load balancing, URL filtering, and web caching functionality.

- **SAP NetWeaver Process Integration (SAP NetWeaver PI)**
  This optional component can be used as an open integration and application platform to enable service-oriented architecture for business applications. SAP NetWeaver PI is typically used to interface E-Recruiting with SAP HCM for new hire integration or with third-party vendors for background checking, job boards, assessments, and résumé parsing. As an alternative, options such as remote function calls, HTTP/S calls, and batch files can also be used to achieve very similar results.

- **Résumé parsing**
  This is another set of functionalities that is optional to implement. In general, a service extracts information from an electronic document (such as a résumé) and sends it to a server. The data is then structured so that it can be automatically transferred into the profile of a candidate, where he can quickly confirm his contact information, education background, and work experience. Although E-Recruiting is delivered with an interface that enables the processing of data from vendor services, it requires customers to commission the vendor to perform the required business process externally.

Even though this isn't an all-inclusive list of components, you can clearly see that the E-Recruiting technical landscape can become very overwhelming. Therefore, we recommend that you do plenty of upfront technical research and analysis prior to starting the project to avoid delays in the middle (or end) of the project.

9.1.2 Performance Management

After you choose which Performance Management solution best meets your needs (as described in Chapter 4), the technical architecture is relatively straightforward. Regardless of which solution you select, the Performance Management functionality is delivered as part of SAP ECC 6.0 and can be presented to the users via the SAP NetWeaver Portal or SAP NetWeaver Business Client (as of EhP 5).

9.1.3 Learning Solution

Depending on which functionality is implemented, the SAP Learning Solution can require the most complex architecture of all of the Talent Management applications. As described throughout Chapter 7, the five main areas of the SAP Learning Solution are as follows:

- **Learning Management System**
  Used to control learning processes and manage the course offering (such as cancellations, registrations, waitlists, and overall scheduling).

- **Learner Portal**
  Web-based UI that allows learners to manage their training needs.

- **Instructor Portal**
  Web-based UI that instructors use to manage the participants and activities of their courses.

- **Learning Content Management System**
  Used to store and manage learning content. Although you can use non-SAP content management systems, you need to plan for some security and firewall considerations.

- **Authoring Environment**
  Supports the creation of tests and structuring of eLearning content via the Repository Explorer.

Each of these areas may require its own technical components, or a shared variation of them, that will require support and maintenance. For example, both the Learner Portal and Learning Management System require a TREX server to support searching functionality, while the Authoring Environment is the only area that requires the Content Player, which uses the SAP J2EE Engine. In any case, we recommend that you first determine which business functionality is desired and then research which supporting technical components are required.

9.1.4 Enterprise Compensation Management

Similar to Performance Management, the technical architecture required to use the standard Enterprise Compensation Management (ECM) functionality is very simple. It, too, is delivered as part of SAP ECC 6.0 as either one or many business functions, and it can be presented to the users via the SAP NetWeaver Portal or SAP NetWeaver Business Client (as of EhP 5) by using the appropriate business packages.

9.1.5 Talent Development

The standard Talent Development functionalities (such as development plans, talent profiles, talent assessments, and talent reviews) are all delivered as part of SAP ECC 6.0 as business functions and require the applicable SAP NetWeaver Portal business packages. Additionally, Enterprise Search 7.02 (Embedded Search using TREX 7.10) and Adobe Document Services 7.02 are required to support the talent review meeting functionality. Finally, SAP NetWeaver Graphics Service 1.0 is needed to store attachments and notes for talent profiles, talent review meetings, and talent groups.

9.1.6 Succession Management

The standard Succession Management functionalities—such as determining and setting key positions, and creating and maintaining succession plans—can be supported by functionality that is delivered as part of SAP ECC 6.0 as a business function and, therefore, doesn't require a complex technical infrastructure. However, for a more robust solution, SAP highly recommends using SAP Talent Visualization by Nakisa (STVN), which requires a slightly more sophisticated architecture (described in more detail in Section 9.5).

9.2 User Interfaces

As of EhP 5, SAP ERP HCM—and, more specifically, Talent Management—offers customers two options for displaying/accessing their business applications: the SAP NetWeaver Portal and the SAP NetWeaver Business Client (NWBC). This section will highlight the similarities and differences of each option, as they relate to the Talent Management applications discussed in this book.

First, each interface offers users a single point of entry into the various applications they need to use on a daily basis. Aside from some minor aesthetic differences, the average user won't notice many variances between the two options. For example, Figure 9.1 and Figure 9.2 show the minor differences between the standard RECRUITER start page in the portal and the NWBC for HTML.

9 | Technical Considerations

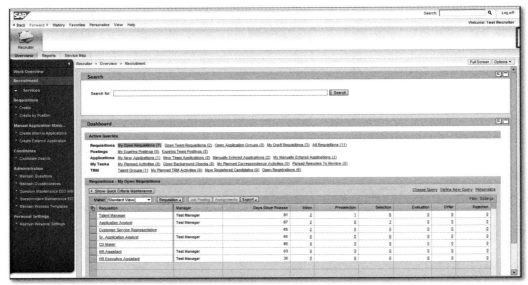

Figure 9.1 Recruiter Role Displayed in SAP NetWeaver Portal

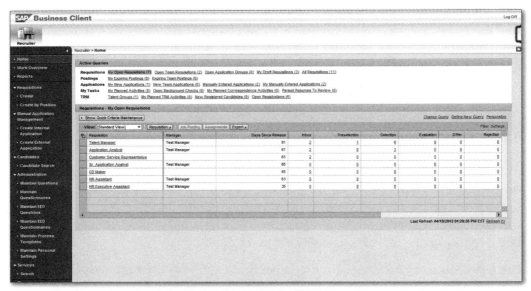

Figure 9.2 Recruiter Role Displayed in NWBC for HTML

9.2.1 SAP NetWeaver Portal

The SAP NetWeaver Portal offers a zero-footprint, multi-platform solution that provides customers with a single point of entry for all of their SAP solutions, third-party applications, legacy systems, internal and external web content, and collaboration tools. It offers a robust role-based architecture that uses a combination of roles, worksets, pages, and iViews to manage and integrate business content in one central location.

> **Related Resources**
>
> More information about roles, worksets, pages, and iViews can be found in *The Complete Guide to SAP NetWeaver Portal* by Manish Chaitanya (SAP PRESS, 2012).

Although this isn't as much of an issue as it was years ago, it's still important to remember that any portal solution is typically shared across an entire organization and not just within HR. This was an issue in the past because before many organizations developed an overall portal strategy, their HR teams often found themselves leading the "charge" and consequently designing an overall portal strategy for the entire organization, rather than just for HR. Recently, it has become more common for HR teams to determine how to integrate into an existing (SAP or non-SAP) portal. Although integrating with a non-SAP portal is typically not an issue, the overall architecture can become cumbersome from a technical perspective, especially as it relates to user authentication and role maintenance. This is why, as of EhP 5, organizations are excited to take advantage of the new HCM NWBC roles that can eliminate the need of the SAP NetWeaver Portal.

9.2.2 SAP NetWeaver Business Client

Looking at the NWBC in a bit more detail, you'll see that there are actually two available options: the NWBC for HTML and the NWBC for Desktop.

NWBC for HTML

This lightweight, browser-based solution is for casual users of NWBC. It offers a subset of functionality of the NWBC for Desktop with a zero footprint and is only available for ABAP systems. This solution can be easily integrated into an existing SAP or non-SAP portal environment without a significant amount of effort.

NWBC for Desktop

This is a .NET-based application that targets power users and can also run against single ABAP systems or against an SAP NetWeaver Portal using the Portal Content Directory as role repository. However, as mentioned previously, managing roles and authorizations within SAP GUI (i.e., via Transaction PFCG) is actually preferred by most organizations because it can save a significant amount of maintenance time and effort. So aside from the installation differences between the two NWBC options, the NWBC for Desktop also includes menu functionality, search capabilities, and various navigation options.

The following standard NWBC roles are available with EhP 5:

- Manager Self-Service (MSS)
- Employee Self-Service (ESS)
- Recruiter
- Recruiting administrator
- HR administrator
- Talent Management specialist
- Training administrator
- Instructor and tutor

The actual Talent Management modules themselves contain their own technology in addition to integrating with other software. This technology is Web Dynpro for ABAP, which is standard across all Talent Management modules.

9.3 Web Dynpro for ABAP

Web Dynpro for ABAP (hereafter, Web Dynpro) is a cutting-edge UI technology that is standard across the Talent Management suite. With EhP 5, Web Dynpro has officially replaced Business Server Pages (BSP) technology from previous versions of Talent Management. There are a few applications that still use BSP technology in Learning Solution and ECM, but Web Dynpro is used the most throughout these applications.

The following are the many advantages of Web Dynpro over the previous BSP technology:

- Structured design process
- Based on Model-View-Controller (strict separation between layout elements and business logic)
- Components and applications that can be enhanced, configured, and reused
- Standard tools to easily change the layout and navigation

> **Related Resources**
>
> For more detailed information about Web Dynpro for ABAP, refer to *Getting Started with Web Dynpro ABAP* by Dominik Ofenloch and Roland Schwaiger (SAP PRESS, 2010).

This section will explore many areas of Web Dynpro, including features, functions, and development tips and tricks.

9.3.1 Architecture

Web Dynpro uses a different concept than traditional development. Instead of programming graphical elements, Web Dynpro lets you drag and drop graphical elements on the screen and "bind" them to data objects. This allows for rapid development and configuration.

Web Dynpro uses the same basic elements for each application. These elements can be declared using the ABAP Workbench (Transaction SE80) or the SAP NetWeaver Developer Studio (NWDS). Using either of these tools, you can generate a large portion of your application without having to implement your own code.

A Web Dynpro component is a stand-alone entity that contains all of the parts necessary to execute a Web Dynpro application. These parts include windows, views, and controllers. Figure 9.3 shows the high-level structure of a Web Dynpro component.

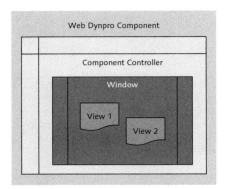

Figure 9.3 Architecture of a Web Dynpro Component

Let's take a look at each piece of a component, as they are required for a Web Dynpro application to launch.

View

The view is the main section of a Web Dynpro component that houses and organizes UI elements. These interface elements can be arranged and positioned using structured layout variants that are delivered with the standard Web Dynpro development tools.

Some examples of these elements include buttons, drop-down lists, text boxes, roadmap navigation, pictures, and Adobe Flash Islands. Figure 9.4 shows a few of these standard elements within a LAYOUT view, and how they appear within Transaction SE80.

Another important feature of the Web Dynpro view is a plug. Plugs are navigation channels that allow for information to flow from one view to another. Depending on which direction data is flowing from view to view, this can either be an inbound plug or an outbound plug.

Figure 9.5 shows two different views passing information back and forth using inbound and outbound plugs. Also, each view has various graphical elements that are part of the UI.

9.3 Web Dynpro for ABAP

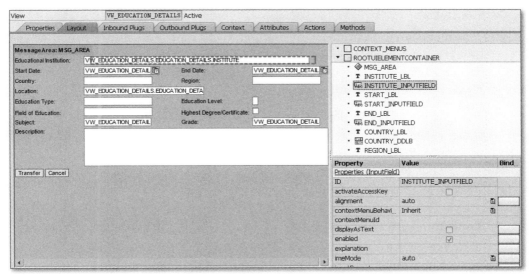

Figure 9.4 Web Dynpro Screen Elements in Layout View

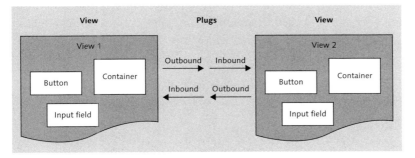

Figure 9.5 Data Flow between Views Using Plugs

Window

A window in the context of Web Dynpro is used to combine many views and allow them to easily communicate and pass data to one another. A window is required to display views within a browser. Like views, windows also contain plugs, and these plugs can pass data to and from other windows, allowing for easy, structured navigation in your application.

Controllers

Controllers are one of the most important and functional pieces within a Web Dynpro component. Data that is displayed onscreen is accessed using a view controller. Each and every view has its own controller, allowing for ABAP code to be executed on an individual view basis.

Along with view controllers, a global controller exists within a Web Dynpro component. This component controller supplies all of the information needed to run the entire Web Dynpro component. The data gathered by the component controller extends to all controllers within the component and is valid for the runtime lifecycle of that component.

Context

Now that you have an understanding of views, windows, and controllers, let's explore how this data is structured and shared between these pieces of a component. By using the context model, data integrity is maintained throughout the component.

The structure of context is similar to that of Extensible Markup Language (XML), in which nodes and attributes are used to organize data. Figure 9.6 shows the logical structure of how Web Dynpro uses context, and Figure 9.7 shows how the context appears within Transaction SE80.

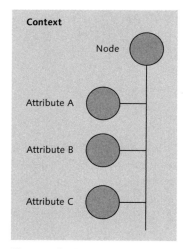

Figure 9.6 Context Structure

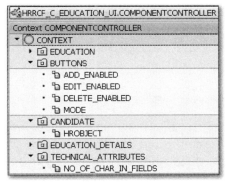

Figure 9.7 Context Structure in Transaction SE80

When creating and using context, cardinality must be enforced. This means that structural integrity relationships need to be maintained between the data and the element that will use the data. An example of this is a drop-down list. Because a drop-down list contains many data elements, cardinality is 1:n (one to many), meaning the node can contain many element instances (each drop-down entry). Table 9.1 shows the various cardinalities for any given node.

Cardinality	Description
0:1	The node can contain a maximum of one element, which doesn't have to be instantiated.
0:n	The node can contain multiple elements but allows for none to be instantiated.
1:1	The node must contain one element, and it must always be instantiated.
1:n	The node can be multiple elements, but at least one must be instantiated.

Table 9.1 Cardinality

9.3.2 Configuration

Web Dynpro leaves room for the customer to manipulate screen elements to fit their business need through configuration. Each component can contain its own configuration, letting you essentially create your own custom components and applications with very little effort.

9 | Technical Considerations

Configuration is different from developing and customizing Web Dynpro in the sense that you aren't directly manipulating the data on the screen, but rather simply rearranging the screen to suite your needs. This is done by using two different types of configurations: component configurations and applications configurations.

Component Configuration

As discussed in the previous section, Web Dynpro compartmentalizes similar functions in components. These components can be configured on an individual basis, allowing for elements to be moved, hidden, or disabled on the screen. Figure 9.8 shows a component configuration for a given Web Dynpro component.

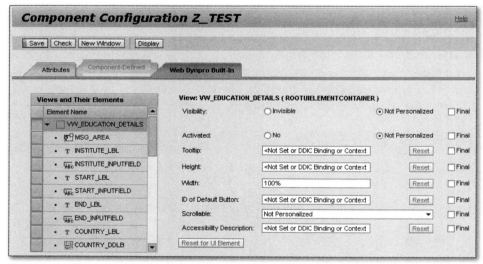

Figure 9.8 Component Configuration

Application Configuration

A Web Dynpro application essentially consists of many components working together to achieve a certain goal. An example of this is the Requisition Create program in E-Recruiting. When creating a requisition, a sequence of screens appears that constitutes the application.

Application configuration lets you enable custom component configurations in your application so that after you've created a component configuration, you can put that configuration in the overall application. Figure 9.9 shows an application configuration, and Figure 9.10 shows a custom component configuration within it.

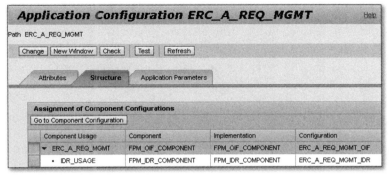

Figure 9.9 Application Configuration

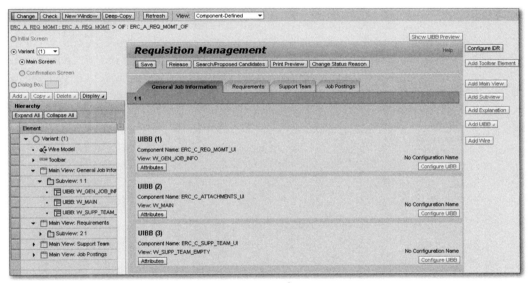

Figure 9.10 Application Configuration—Component Configuration

9.3.3 Developing with Web Dynpro for ABAP

Configuration in Web Dynpro is very powerful, but you may need to develop your own Web Dynpro application or enhance the standard SAP applications. This includes anything from creating a new field on the screen, to adding functionality, to creating custom screens. We recommend using the enhancement framework to accomplish this easily.

9 | Technical Considerations

Enhancement Framework

Changes to any standard delivered code from SAP are generally known as modifications. Modifications can be dangerous because your own code can corrupt standard functionality, essentially breaking the application. We don't recommend modifications because any upgrade or OSS note could overwrite your modification, disabling any custom functionality.

To help customers implement their own code safely, SAP has implemented the enhancement framework. In the context of Web Dynpro, the enhancement framework allows you to put in custom screen elements, code, and navigation with any given Web Dynpro component.

Enhancements can be implemented either directly on the view or within a controller. By clicking the ENHANCE button (⊚), you can create an enhancement implementation. Within the view, you can add or suppress any given screen element. Figure 9.11 shows the suppressing of a screen field, which shows a red "X" next to the field name on the right side of the screen. Although the screen field is still within the component, it won't appear onscreen at runtime.

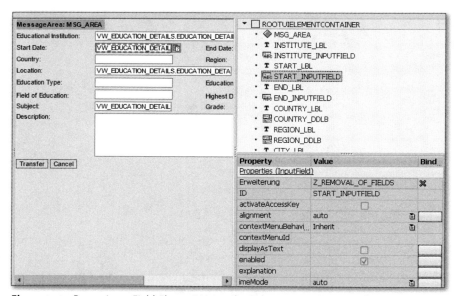

Figure 9.11 Removing a Field Element Using the Enhancement Framework

You can also enhance controllers in the same way. However, because controllers contain code, the enhancement framework allows code to be placed in three areas: pre-exit, post-exit, and overwrite exit. Pre-exit enhancements allow for your custom code to be executed before the standard SAP code, while post-exit enhancements execute code after the standard processing. Overwrite exits allow for none of the SAP standard code to execute, but instead use customer code for processing. Figure 9.12 shows how you can access these three types of enhancements within Transaction SE80.

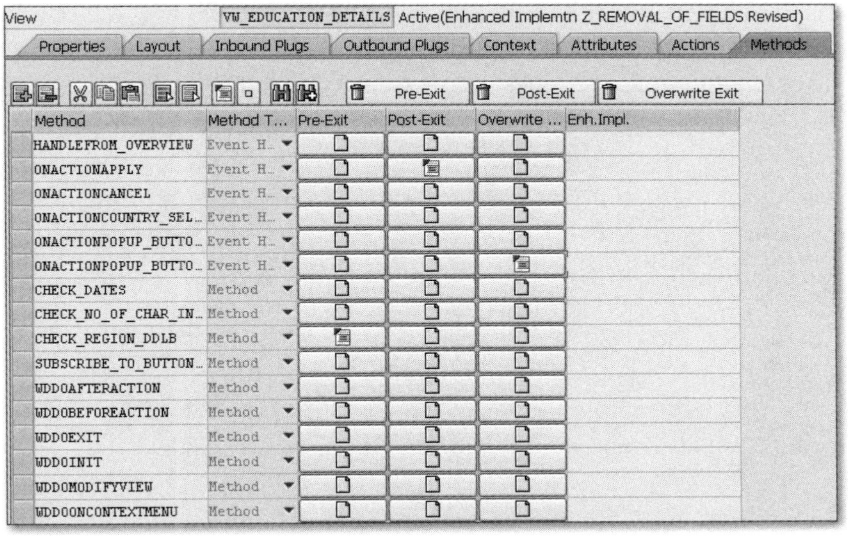

Figure 9.12 Pre-Exit, Post-Exit, and Overwrite Exit Enhancements

All of these enhancements are known as implicit enhancements, meaning the customer enhancements are directly within the Web Dynpro components. However, you can execute and manage explicit enhancements—otherwise known as Business Add-Ins (BAdIs)—outside of Web Dynpro components and can use them for many other core functions of your application.

9 | Technical Considerations

9.4 Business Add-Ins

BAdIs are enhancement spots that SAP provides to customers to insert their own code. They are basically user exits at strategic points of functionality within all Talent Management modules.

To properly use BAdIs, you must create what is known as an implementation. This implementation will be automatically called after the BAdI is activated, meaning that your code will be executed

Each module has a wide range of BAdIs that can be used. Most of these can be found in Transaction SPRO under the respective module tree. Figure 9.13 shows an example of what BAdI access looks like in Transaction SPRO for ECM.

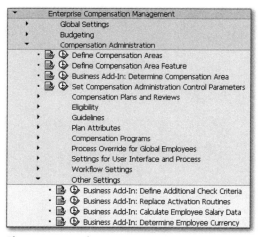

Figure 9.13 BAdIs in Transaction SPRO

Because there are many BAdIs per module, let's take a look at just some of the BAdIs available for each of the modules.

E-Recruiting Sample BAdIs

The following are just some of the BAdIs that are specific to the E-Recruiting module. Their functionality ranges anywhere from background checks, to attachment types, to candidacy searches.

- `HRRCF_BGC_DUPL_CHECK`: Enhancement for BGC duplicate check
- `HRRCF_BGCORDER_RP`: Enhancement for background check order response
- `HRRCF_GET_AD_HOC_ACT`: Parameter for activities in Application Wizard
- `HRRCF_POWL_REFRESH`: Refresh of POWL queries
- `HRRCF_PRE_POSTING`: Preliminary posting (Career Portal)
- `HRRCF_RESPARSE_RELID`: Enhancement for related ID of bulk résumé parsing
- `HRRCF00_CDCYLIST_LANG`: BAdI definition for languages available in `T77RCF_CDCYLIST`
- `HRRCF00_DATAOVR_ATTACHMENTS`: BAdI filter for attachments for data overview
- `HRRCF00_GET_DEFAULT_TEXTS`: BAdI to determine proposal texts for posting
- `HRRCF00_GET_DUPL_EXT_CAND`: BAdI to determine external candidates that match a search pattern
- `HRALX_HRALXSYNC_BADI`: BAdI to determine the data synchronized in Report HRALXSYNC

Performance Management Sample BAdIs

These sample BAdIs for the Performance Management module may be especially useful, as Performance Management has many exits to customize this module to fit your business:

- `HRALX_HRALXSYNC_BADI`: BAdI to determine the data synchronized in Report HRALXSYNC
- `HRHAP00_ACC_HEADER`: Appraisal document—header data access
- `HRHAP00_ACTION_LOG`: Appraisal document—action log
- `HRHAP00_ADD_HEADER`: Appraisal document—additional header data
- `HRHAP00_ADD_ON_APPL`: Development: add-on application
- `HRHAP00_ADMIN`: Appraisal document—admin. functions
- `HRHAP00_AUTHORITY`: Appraisal document—authorization check
- `HRHAP00_BC_ELEMENT`: Business Check Elements
- `HRHAP00_BUT_ACCESS`: Appraisal document—pushbutton access

- `HRHAP00_CATEG_CREATE`: Development: catalog—category creation
- `HRHAP00_CATEG_EXMPLE`: Catalog—create example category
- `HRHAP00_CHECK_CUSTOM`: Development: customizing—check tables and settings
- `HRHAP00_DOC_DEF_D1`: Appraisal document—default appraiser
- `HRHAP00_DOC_DEF_D2`: Appraisal document—default appraisee
- `HRHAP00_DOC_DEF_DE`: Appraisal document—default completion period
- `HRHAP00_DOC_DEF_DN`: Appraisal document—default appraisal Document Name
- `HRHAP00_DOC_DEF_DP`: Appraisal document—default part appraisers
- `HRHAP00GOAL_PERIOD_PMP`: Predefined performance appraisal process
- `HRHAP00_FOLLOW_UP`: Follow-up processing for appraisal form enhancements

Enterprise Compensation Management Sample BAdIs

Like Performance Management, ECM has many BAdIs that can enhance your implementation of this module at key areas of the process. Consider implementing some of these sample BAdIs:

- `HRECM00_ACTIVATION`: Replace activation procedure/new Infotype 0008
- `HRECM00_AGEDATA`: Aging of survey market data
- `HRECM00_BDG_EE`: Calculation of budgets amounts per employee
- `HRECM00_BDG0001`: Compensation budgeting: User-exit
- `HRECM00_CALCBASE`: Replace determination of calculation base salary
- `HRECM00_EFFDATE`: Replace determination of effective date
- `HRECM00_ELIGIBILITY`: Replace or extend eligibility check
- `HRECM00_ELIGP`: Replace evaluation of feature ELIGP
- `HRECM00_EMAIL_ADDRESS`: Set up email addresses
- `HRECM00_GUIDELINE`: Replace or extend guideline evaluation
- `HRECM00_MATRIX_SEGM`: Methods for compensation matrix dimension
- `HRECM00_NOTIF_AGENT`: Set up agents for the tasks
- `HRECM00_PARTICIPANT`: Extract participant info for outbound IDoc
- `HRECM00_PLANNING_UNIT_SERVICES`: Planning unit services

- `HRECM00_SALARY`: Replace evaluation of salary and salary-related quantities
- `HRECM00_STATSTYPE`: Get value for a statistical paygroup of an employee
- `HRECM00_STKUN`: Replace determination of stock unit for a review item

Learning Solution Sample BAdIs

Learning Solution BAdIs can extend the standard functionality of the module in many ways. These sample BAdIs are available for Learning Solution:

- `LSO_CANCELREASONS_C`: Determine cancellation reasons when learner cancels in web
- `LSO_CE_PERNR_ASSGMT`: BAdI for generating personnel assignment description
- `LSO_CHECK_BOOKING`: Customer Enhancement for Additional Checks for Booking
- `LSO_COLLABORATION`: Integration SAP Learning Solution—Collaboration Room
- `LSO_CORRESPONDENCE01`: LSO: Rules for course-related correspondence
- `LSO_CORRESPONDENCE11`: LSO correspondence: BAdI for mail output
- `LSO_CORRESPONDENCE12`: LSO correspondence: BAdI for additional information in mails
- `LSO_CORRESPONDENCE41`: Correspondence control options
- `LSO_CORRESPONDENCE43`: LSO correspondence: Change output control options
- `LSO_FOLLOWUP`: Set qualification proficiencies at follow-up
- `LSO_LEARNER`: Customer enhancement for learner
- `LSO_LEARNER_SET`: Reverse user mapping for `LSO_LEARNER`

Talent Development Sample BAdIs

Talent Development, like the rest of the Talent Management modules, also contains many useful BAdIs to enhance functionality. Consider these sample BAdIs that are available for the Talent Development module:

- `BADI_ESH_IF_OBJECT_DATA`: BAdI for TREX data extraction for indexing
- `BADI_HRTMC_DR_FIELDS`: BAdI to evaluate fields for data retrieval

9 | Technical Considerations

- `HRTMC_ASSESSMENT_AVERAGE`: Enhancement to calculate average performance and potential assessment scores when assessed by more than one manager
- `HRTMC_SUCCESSOR_BENCH_STR`: Calculation of successor bench strength

9.5 STVN Technical Requirements

Recall that SAP Talent Visualization by Nakisa (STVN) is a composite application that is deployed on SAP NetWeaver Composition Environment (SAP NetWeaver CE). SAP NetWeaver CE used to be a standalone environment, but now it's included as a component of SAP NetWeaver Enterprise Portal 7.3.

STVN SuccessionPlanning is delivered as a Software Component Archive (SCA) file to deploy into SAP NetWeaver CE. The SCA file contains an Enterprise Archive (EAR) file, used by Java EE for packaging one or more modules into a single archive for easy and robust deployment. After the application is deployed, it can be accessed via a web browser using a URL.

> **Key Point**
>
> Before the application can be configured, a serial file must be requested from SAP Support. This is done in SAP Service Marketplace by raising an OSS support message under Component XX-PART-NKS-LKY, including licensing and contact information. Nakisa will dispatch the serial file via email shortly after receiving the OSS support ticket from SAP Support.

In addition to deploying the application in the SAP NetWeaver CE component, an ABAP Add-on and Transport Package must be imported into the target SAP system that STVN SuccessionPlanning will connect to. The ABAP add-on contains the function modules, programs, and data structures required for data communication between STVN SuccessionPlanning and SAP and for support of versions of SAP prior to ECC 6.0 EhP 4. The Nakisa Transport Package contains the evaluation paths and HR Organizational Charting Interface (HR_OCI) configurations required for reading structure data in SAP.

Additionally, you can store user preference data in a database (either standalone or one used by the SAP NetWeaver CE component), although this is an optional component. User preference data doesn't require a significant amount of disk space.

> **Key Point**
>
> We recommend that you consult the latest versions of the Master Guide, Compatibility Matrix, and Nakisa Capacity Planning Guide before planning and implementing any STVN software so that you meet the correct requirements. You should especially look into the deployment guide, ABAP add-on guide, and Nakisa Transport Package guide before deploying any of these components into the SAP NetWeaver CE component or SAP. All of these guides are available in the application package that is downloaded from SAP Service Marketplace.

STVN SuccessionPlanning runs using the Java Virtual Machine (JVM) installed as part of the SAP NetWeaver CE installation. It connects to SAP using the SAP Java Connector, which is distributed with the application. Data retrieval and writeback is done using remote-enabled function modules in SAP. Some of these function modules are contained in the ABAP add-on package, although a number of standard SAP function modules are also used.

Basic configuration can be performed using the AdminConsole. The AdminConsole is a GUI frontend for performing the following tasks, among others:

- Configuring SAP connections
- Setting up authentication
- Setting user preferences
- Setting print and export preferences
- Configuring available analytics and set Alerts
- Editing captions
- Setting variables, such as performance scale and risk criteria object ID via log information, and maintaining log settings
- Creating new data access functions or integrating an SAP function module
- Performing an RFC trace
- Retrieving system information

All of these tasks are documented in the Administrative Guide, which we recommend that you consult before beginning any configuration activities.

Any other type of configurations must be performed outside of the AdminConsole. Configuration activities that are performed directly in the application configuration files are called customizations. The configuration files are XML files that control application behavior. We recommend that you use only Nakisa-certified consultants or experienced professionals to perform customizations.

9.6 Summary

SAP ERP HCM Talent Management contains many different technologies that work together to provide a cutting-edge, stable environment for customers. In this chapter, we explored some of the underlying technical architecture that supports Talent Management, including some key pieces that make up each of the Talent Management modules.

We then took at a look at some of the variations of Talent Management UIs, including SAP NetWeaver Business Client and SAP NetWeaver Portal. These interfaces showed how Talent Management modules are delivered to an end user.

Recall that all Talent Management modules themselves are based on Web Dynpro for ABAP technology. This technology is SAP standard-delivered and presents a unique and powerful way to develop and deploy solutions. We also covered how to enhance SAP code using the Enhancement Framework.

Another way to enhance standard SAP functionality is to implement BAdIs. BAdIs are a great way to strategically tweak functions within Talent Management modules. We also explored some of the technical considerations and requirements for SVTN.

Let's switch our attention from technical considerations to best practices. Chapter 10 focuses on capitalizing past experiences and lessons learned to minimize obstacles during implementation.

Your organization can benefit from implementing a talent management solution in many ways. Making these projects successful requires an awareness of the unique challenges related to each initiative. Consequently, we recommend you absorb the lessons learned and best practices of successful Talent Management implementations before you begin.

10 Best Practices and Lessons Learned

If you've ever been involved in a technology implementation, then you've probably heard the phrase, "If we knew then what we know now, we probably would have done things very differently." That is usually because events occurred during the course of the project that were unforeseen or baffling at the time. What seemed challenging then, however, can often be used as an advantage both now and in the future. We call these *lessons learned*.

Lessons learned are the retrospection that we frequently develop after completing a project. If we take advantage of what these lessons learned can offer us, they can be priceless tools instead of frustrating memories. When identifying lessons learned, the short-term goal should be to recognize and then document what went well, what didn't go well, and why; the ultimate goal is to encounter fewer problems and setbacks and to pave the way for future projects.

The practice of documenting a string of lessons learned eventually leads to the development of best practices—those guidelines, ideas, procedures, or methods that have proven to reliably lead to a desired result. Simply put, best practices are the very best ways that you, your team, or your organization has found to do something. As invaluable intellectual assets, best practices help organizations remain highly competitive, so they should be standardized so that an entire team or organization can follow them. To that end, the following sections represent best practices that should be reviewed when implementing a Talent Management project.

10 Best Practices and Lessons Learned

10.1 Implementation Considerations

Overall, implementing a talent management solution is not very different from implementing any other system-related project. Most importantly, we recommend that you establish your core processes prior to starting the technical implementation. Don't use the technical implementation as your approach — or excuse — for organizational change or process implementation. These core processes should be fully engaged, if not completed, prior to commencement of the implementation project.

Whether you're part of a global or small- or medium-sized enterprise, your goal should be to simplify your business rules and segmentations as much as possible. Let business flow in the system and avoid legacy-based restrictions and exceptions that don't add value or maintain core company values and strategies.

You should plan on achieving full and active participation in the project by the most senior levels of management. To do this, establish an executive sponsor who can not only help promote the specific modules being implemented but also champion the overall talent strategy. This executive sponsor can formulate a steering committee that is responsible for guiding the project and serving as a final line of escalation. Other employees will more easily grasp the importance of your project if they see the executive sponsor using and becoming knowledgeable about the vocabulary of the system and processes of the company.

One of the most critical success factors is to engage the end users as early and as often as possible throughout the project's lifecycle. If your end-user community is exceptionally large, then you should consider nominating a small group of employees as subject matter experts (SMEs) to represent the larger population. For starters, invite them to your blueprint workshops, where they'll have the opportunity to become engaged with the project and see how the standard system works. Invite them to actively participate in a fit gap analysis, and challenge them to envision using the standard system as much as possible. You can use their feedback to design solutions that meet their needs and present workarounds where applicable.

At the end of the design (or blueprinting) phase, use playback sessions or conference room pilots to simulate the to-be system. The conference room pilots should include a combination of screen captures, mockups, and, where possible, demonstrations that confirm the solution that will be delivered after the project is complete. By doing this, users can gain a sense of ownership and you eliminate the chance of surprises during the testing and go-live phases.

Finally, when contemplating the scope of your implementation, give special consideration to modularity or a phased approach. Rarely will you need to implement everything at once, so it's possible to implement pieces of functionality at a time — even within a module. For example, within SAP E-Recruiting, consider going live without electronically interfacing with a third-party assessor or integrating résumé parsing. Alternatively, another option is to use prototypes or pilots, which can help you get an understanding of your company or organization's unique process and UI requirements.

10.2 Staffing

Staffing a talent management project is very similar to staffing any other type of project, but there are a few key lessons learned that you can apply.

One of the most important things to do is to figure out what types of skills will be needed from both a technical and business perspective. You'll need to use these as requirements and assess whether there are gaps from a capacity or knowledge standpoint (or both!) in relation to your internal talent pool. If time allows, which it often doesn't, you have to choose whether to send a select number of employees for training, hire new employees, supplement the implementation team with consultants, or, as in most cases, choose a blended approach of all three.

Talent management skills tend to be scarce, and projects often require the use of consultants. Regardless of whether they are consultants from SAP, a consulting partner, or an independent contractor, you should use them efficiently and effectively by aligning them with internal team members so that they can share as much knowledge as possible. We recommend that you use functional consultants that have experience with the specific modules that are in scope and not just Talent Management experience in general. This book has emphasized that each area is unique in many different ways; just because someone has experience with E-Recruiting doesn't mean that that person will be as proficient in the Learning Solution. (This isn't as important when it comes to developers because, for the most part, each area now uses the same basic foundation and principles.)

> **Key Point**
>
> If money is no object, or your business environment leaves you no choice but to staff a majority of the implementation team with consultants, then be sure to properly plan for a significant amount of knowledge transfer to an appropriately sized support structure in anticipation of their departure. You want to avoid watching the implementation team walk out the door before sharing any of their expertise with internal users.

Other areas where projects typically need support from an expert are on the Basis and security teams. Organizations that have used SAP for an extended period of time often have internal teams that are dedicated to these areas and so assume that they can easily support the Talent Management projects. Although the teams may be very competent and experienced, you shouldn't underestimate the many new concepts and components that the Talent Management areas introduce. Consequently, we strongly recommend that you determine whether expert advice will be needed as early as possible.

Team members that often get overlooked, or improperly planned for, are SMEs and specialists from the business community. These individuals are typically in high demand and have a limited amount of time to dedicate to your project. So rather than burning out some of your best employees, be cognizant of their time, and try to only use them for short-term, specialized tasks, rather than using them as full-time team members. The result will be a group of much happier team members that are more willing to share critical information.

10.3 Change Management

Change management is a chameleon-like term whose meaning seems to shift depending on who you're talking to. In a general sense, change management is a structured approach for ensuring that changes are thoroughly and smoothly implemented and that the lasting benefits of change are achieved. The focus should be on the wider impacts of change, particularly on how individuals and teams transition from their current situation to the new one. The underlying principle is that change doesn't happen in isolation; instead, it impacts the whole organization, affecting everyone it touches.

One big way companies risk the success of an SAP implementation is by underestimating the impact that change management can have on the success of the project. Neglecting the change management piece of an SAP implementation can be a very costly mistake, and better use of change management strategies can help companies avoid failure. To this end, we'll now look at how change management is defined in a more specific context.

10.3.1 Change Management on Closer Inspection

Change management is a structured approach to transitioning teams and organizations from a current state to a desired state. It's an organizational process directed at helping employees accept and embrace the changes to their current business environment.

There are four important pieces of change management: thoughtful planning, sensitive implementation, consultation with the employees affected by the change, and involvement of the employees affected by the change.

In order to work, change must be realistic, achievable, and measurable. Organizations should ask the following questions when contemplating any technology implementation:

- What do we want to achieve with this change?
- Why are we making this change?
- How will we know that the change has been successful?
- Who is affected by this change?
- How will those affected react to the change?
- How much of this change can we manage as an organization?
- What parts of the change do we need help with as an organization?

Change management approaches vary considerably from organization to organization and from project to project. The first question to consider when tasked to manage change within the organization is what change management means for the specific situation. Many organizations and consultants use formal change management toolkits and methodologies. To this end, the activities involved in managing change include (but aren't limited to) the following:

- Ensuring the reasons for the change are clearly expressed and understood
- Identifying "change agents" who can help play the role of ambassadors for change
- Assessing all of the stakeholders and defining the nature of sponsorship

- Planning the involvement of the change sponsors
- Scheduling how and when changes will be communicated
- Organizing the delivery of the communications messages
- Assessing the impact of the changes on all stakeholders, and providing support for those impacted
- Assessing the training needs driven by the change
- Scheduling when and how training will be implemented
- Agreeing upon success indicators and regularly measuring and reporting on them

To successfully manage change, it's therefore necessary to manage the larger impacts of the change, but first you must plan for them.

10.3.2 Change Management Strategy

The first thing that an organization needs to do when beginning a technology implementation is to build a change management plan that identifies how the business processes are going to change with the new SAP system and which employees are affected. Change management begins long before end-user training, but training remains an important facet of the change management strategy.

Training

The change management plan should also include a training plan, which defines (among other things) the who, what, where, when, and how of training delivery. By the time users get to the training stage of the project, there should be few surprises, if any. Training should show the end users how to use the new system and should crystallize what they already know about the organizational changes.

Just as you did with an executive sponsor, you should consider handpicking a few key users to show the application to after it's stable. Those users can play a key role in getting others excited about the new application and its benefits. Consider these training-related key points:

- At the start of each training session, remind the employees of what they are expected to be able to do at the completion of the course.
- Base the training content on what the employees will be required to do differently after the implementation.
- Because there will be employees who may have spent years working in the old system, make the training extremely practical and easy to understand.
- Develop on-the-job aids (such as checklists, flow charts, and templates) that can be brought into the workplace after training has been completed.
- Ensure that the managers of the employees being trained are actively supporting the program by attending the training themselves and introducing the trainer at the start of each session.

Now let's look at how communications fits into the overall change management strategy.

Communications

Communications are at the heart of any successful change management strategy. Your change management plan should also include a comprehensive, written communication plan that addresses all of the following items:

- Rationale for change
- Clearly outlined vision, mission, and objectives of the implementation
- How the change fits in with the strategic objectives and values of the organization
- The implications of the change for the employees
- Consistent and frequent communications about the change using multiple channels (verbal, written, bulletin boards, intranet, etc.)
- Availability and accessibility of new information
- Schedule and channels for employees to request clarifications and ask questions
- Treatment of sensitive aspects of organizational change management (face-to-face communications are preferable to email and written notices, which can oftentimes be weak at conveying and developing understanding)
- Opportunities for employees to spend time with the change leaders and sponsors in small groups

- Schedules for interactive workshops and forums in which all employees can explore the changes together
- Opportunities for employees to network with each other, both formally and informally, to share ideas about change and change management
- Measurements used to chart progress publicly
- Public recognition and awards for each positive approach and accomplishment

Communicating to end users the benefits of the new system and why the application is being deployed is just as important as the training. When asking your organization to change, you can't over-communicate. In fact, it seems that regardless of how frequently organizations communicate change, employees are never satisfied. Too frequently, organizations don't effectively communicate these important facets. As a result, employees don't take the initiative seriously and will often not perceive the software being implemented to be the important change that the organization does. Effective communication typically requires the following components to be working together seamlessly:

- **Scope**
  The message should be presented clearly and in detail.

- **Source**
  The employee receiving the message should be able to trust the sender of the message.

- **Delivery**
  The delivery method must meet the needs of both the sender and the receiver.

- **Content**
  The content of the message has to resonate with the employee on a level that is meaningful to the employee.

Change brings with it challenges. Coping with change involves the understanding and use of effective communication. Success in accomplishing improved productivity, greater efficiency, or better service depends on how well all parties communicate the change.

> **Key Point**
>
> For more information on managing change, refer to *Managing Organizational Change during SAP Implementations* by Luc Galoppin and Siegfried Caems (SAP PRESS, 2007).

10.4 Summary

By documenting lessons learned from challenging or successful implementations, you can develop best practices that guide future efforts and reliably lead to a desired result. These best practices are invaluable because, as collective intellectual assets, they can help organizations remain highly competitive.

There are three important areas to consider when developing best practices: implementation, staffing, and change management. All of these facets demand effective planning ahead of time.

The next and final chapter of this book will explore the future of Talent Management, as well as exciting new offerings and resources from SAP.

Talent Management is a growing strategy from SAP, so it's prudent to explore some of the available solutions, as well as the future, of Talent Management. Being resourceful and knowing where to look for solutions during a Talent Management initiative is one of the most important aspects of the project.

11 Talent Management Resources

Like other SAP areas of business, SAP ERP HCM Talent Management is an ever-changing technology. From a technological perspective, the Talent Management modules have grown leaps and bounds in the past few years. This includes a heavy concentration on providing the best, most high-demand functionality and timely updates to the user interface (UI).

These changes aren't restricted to the modules themselves but apply to the entire roadmap for all of Talent Management solutions. Becoming more and more popular is the need for rapid-deployment solutions, or solutions that can be installed and go live in a very short time frame. The software-as-a-service model is also a very popular concept. SAP has many competitors that use the software-as-a-service model and recently entered this space themselves.

At the time of this writing, SAP has completed the purchase of a company called SuccessFactors. This exciting acquisition greatly expands SAP's offerings for Talent Management solutions. Let's explore the difference between on-premise solutions (which were covered in this entire book) and the new cloud-based solutions.

11.1 On-Premise and Cloud-Based Talent Management Solutions from SAP

SAP offers both on-premise and cloud Talent Management solutions with its Talent Management and SuccessFactors solutions, respectively. Like Talent Management, SuccessFactors offers a number of modules to cover the end-to-end Talent Management processes, including the following:

- SuccessFactors Performance & Goals
- SuccessFactors Compensation
- SuccessFactors Succession & Development
- SuccessFactors Recruiting
- SuccessFactors Learning
- SuccessFactors Premier Jam

Most organizations who have invested in core SAP and want to begin using Talent Management find themselves asking the question "Should we go for an on-premise or a cloud solution?" Although SuccessFactors is SAP's "go-forward" solution for Talent Management, the cloud solution doesn't suit all organizations and all business strategies. There are often a number of data, legal, and security implications to consider when moving data and processes into the cloud. For some organizations—typically government organizations or organizations with complex business processes—making the move to the cloud simply isn't possible. On the other hand, other organizations benefit greatly from using a "one size fits all" solution that requires minimal in-house maintenance or support.

You should evaluate the options available to you while taking into consideration the factors and impacts of using both on-premise and cloud technology. SAP, analysts, and your implementation partner can provide you with the latest information available to enable you to properly analyze and determine which solution is the best fit for your organization.

Let's shift our attention to SAP's roadmap, and the advantages and disadvantages of both approaches, based on the information available at the time of writing (spring of 2012).

> **Note**
>
> The information used here is subject to change at any time; it's possible that when your organization needs to make an evaluation, the information available may differ from what has been described in this chapter.

11.1.1 SAP Roadmap

In early 2012, SAP announced the completion of its $3.4B acquisition of SuccessFactors and that it now offered customers a choice of whether to use SAP on-premise or cloud solutions. Following the acquisition, SAP announced that the SuccessFactors BizX Suite would be its go-forward solution for talent management, recruiting, compensation, and learning for new customers. At the same time, the company announced that it would remain committed to SAP ERP HCM Talent Management, but that from here on, it would only deliver "selected innovations" in the suite. Additionally, SAP announced that it had extended its maintenance of SAP ERP HCM until at least 2020 and that it would not force any customers to migrate to SuccessFactors.

In the Statement of Direction released by SAP and Nakisa in 2012, SAP emphasized its continued commitment to STVN as its on-premise solution extension of choice for Talent Management. SAP also re-affirmed that Nakisa will continue to deliver on the strategic roadmap created jointly with SAP. Due to SAP's commitment to only deliver "selected innovations," Nakisa is now likely to lead innovation in the SAP HCM ERP Talent Management area. Between late 2012 and 2013, SAP and Nakisa are expected to deliver improvements that focus on the following:

- Integration of talent profile, talent analytics, and job architecture
- Development Planning, integrated with STVN Career Planning and STVN SuccessionPlanning
- Mobility capabilities for executives and key business stakeholders

As with previous releases, Nakisa will continue to deliver innovations in stability, performance, quality, and functionality for SAP customers during and after this period.

11.1.2 Advantages and Disadvantages

At the time of publication, both on-premise and cloud solutions offer different benefits, advantages, and disadvantages, and they will satisfy different types of organizations. At a glance, Talent Management is a more mature, flexible, and integrated solution, while the SuccessFactors BizX Suite offers a rapid, best practice implementation, with a user-friendly UI and minimal in-house system management.

On-Premise

Talent Management currently allows a greater degree of flexibility and customization, providing strategic talent management and business-specific requirements to organizations using SAP ERP HCM. The ability to customize the system to a large extent means that organizations can realize most, if not all, of their business requirements in Talent Management. The high level of integration means that master data and functionality in other modules can be leveraged in Talent Management by standard. SAP's strong authorization concept means that data can be protected from unauthorized access exactly as the business desires.

Although there are a number of benefits to using Talent Management over SuccessFactors BizX Suite, there are also some advantages to using SuccessFactors BizX Suite that need to be considered. Talent Management can have a lengthy implementation if complex business processes need to be mapped and documented. Customization of the SAP ERP HCM system isn't a lengthy process, but additional development can add significant time and cost to an implementation. Inexperienced implementation partners can also extend the length of an implementation project, and, although fairly uncommon, there is a risk that selecting the wrong partner can create unnecessary delays in the design and realization of a project.

For organizations with a very specific talent management strategy that want to leverage an existing investment in SAP ERP HCM and the SAP NetWeaver Enterprise Portal, Talent Management is likely to be the solution of choice for the time being.

Cloud

At the time of writing, the SuccessFactors BizX Suite is a best practice solution that offers some amount of customizable features but not to the same extent as Talent Management. The suite can be implemented rapidly and efficiently and quickly provides organizations without complex requirements the ability to realize talent management benefits.

For customers who don't currently leverage SAP ERP HCM, don't have the required master data for Talent Management, or use SuccessFactors Employee Central, then an implementation of SuccessFactors BizX can be more favorable. As mentioned in Chapter 3, Talent Management requires a well-designed Jobs Catalog and Qualifications Catalog, in addition to SAP NetWeaver Enterprise Portal or SAP NetWeaver Business Client. Additional hardware can also be required for TREX, STVN SuccessionPlanning, and E-Recruiting.

Because the SuccessFactors BizX Suite is hosted in the cloud, SuccessFactors customers don't need to own or maintain their own hardware. This can significantly reduce ongoing costs for hosting and maintenance, as well as upgrades and support package installations.

For organizations that want to quickly deploy a simple best practice solution that requires little to no maintenance, then SuccessFactors BizX is likely to be the solution of choice.

Hybrid

For some organizations it makes more sense to go with a hybrid approach. This is where part of the core HR system is on-premise, and part of the system is using a cloud solution. A common scenario might be where an organization uses SAP ERP HCM for its core HR system while leveraging SuccessFactors for its Talent Management processes.

This type of approach can combine the best of both worlds for particular processes. For example, customers can leverage the powerful SAP ERP HCM system for master data and payroll for their HR team and then provide managers and other business users with the easy-to-use interface for performing such processes as performance reviews and compensation budget activities. Because a number of customers won't replace their core HR system, this approach is likely to become popular for those that want to move part of their business processes into the cloud.

11.1.3 The Future

SAP is planning to invest heavily in the SuccessFactors BizX Suite over the coming years, and as a result, a number of the mentioned points may become redundant in the years following publication. Although Talent Management is tightly integrated and highly customizable, it's possible that SuccessFactors BizX will become a more integrated, flexible, and customizable solution over time.

We recommend that you seek out the latest information from SAP, well-regarded analysts, or your implementation partner to determine what type of solution is best for your organization.

11.2 Mobile Solutions

Along with the new cloud solutions, SAP has recently offered some great mobile solutions for businesses. Let's take a look at some of the HR-specific mobile solutions available from SAP:

- **SAP Employee Lookup mobile app**
  Your staff can search a directory of managers and coworkers, as well as access organizational information about other employees.
- **SAP Leave Request mobile app**
  With this application, employees can easily submit a request for leave. This includes all types of requests, such as sick leave, vacation time, or otherwise.
- **SAP Timesheet mobile app**
  Now employees can save countless hours by managing their time entry via a mobile device. This application lets your company create, submit, manage, and review working time.
- **SAP HR Approvals mobile app**
  HR approvals just got much more efficient; now managers can administer approvals such as employee requests on their mobile devices.
- **SAP Interview Assistant mobile app**
  This Talent Management-specific application helps hiring managers interview candidates by letting them see candidate information, create notes, and submit interview results and feedback—all through their mobile devices.
- **SAP Manager Insight mobile app**
  Managers can now view important employee information (profiles, KPI reports, diversity, etc.) from their iPads.
- **SAP Travel Receipt Capture mobile app**
  Your traveling employees will now have a much easier time capturing their receipts on the go. With this application, they can efficiently organize, submit, and track all of their expense receipts all from their mobile device.
- **SAP Travel Expense Approval mobile app**
  Managers also now have an easy way to manage their employees' travel expenses by viewing, approving, or rejecting expense reports from a mobile device.
- **SAP Learning Assistant mobile app**
  Your employees can now utilize training on the go. The SAP Learning Assistant Mobile App lets them find and access learning content.

The playing field for talent management is expected to evolve in the next few years, so let's shift our focus to reliable sources of information about SAP's projects.

11.3 SAP Resources

This section details information sources that may help you gain a better understanding of the SAP Talent Management applications. These resources can be used on an ongoing basis.

SAP offers several places to find answers to commonly asked questions. Two of the most commonly used sources are the SAP Service Marketplace and SAP Online Help. We'll now look at each of these in more detail.

11.3.1 SAP Service Marketplace

Solution documentation is available for registered users on the SAP Service Marketplace website. For those who don't have a Service Marketplace username and password, we recommend that you speak to one of your project leaders or Basis resources about how to obtain one. A lot of good documentation is available in the Media Library sections of the Service Marketplace.

To download Talent Management product documentation from the Media Library, go to *http://service.sap.com/erp-hcm*, and log in with your Service Marketplace username and password. Figure 11.1 shows the page after authentication.

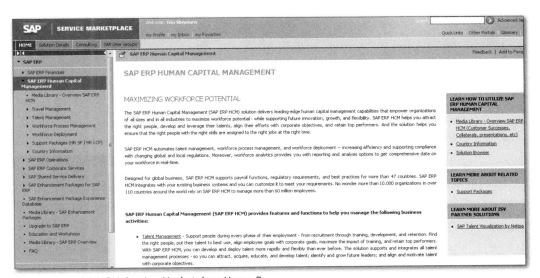

Figure 11.1 SAP HCM Service Marketplace Home Page

11 | Talent Management Resources

On the left-hand navigation panel, follow the path SAP ERP • SAP ERP HUMAN CAPITAL MANAGEMENT • TALENT MANAGEMENT. You'll be able to access the Media Library of any of the Talent Management applications by selecting one of them. Once in the Media Library, you can access collateral, detailed documentation, and overview presentations on functionality.

The SAP Notes section of the Service Marketplace (previously called Online Service System, or OSS) is where SAP customers can go when they are looking to troubleshoot an issue. Given that SAP has aggressively upgraded the Talent Management applications over the past few years, you should refer to this site frequently to research software fixes and workarounds for known product bugs.

The SAP Notes section of the Service Marketplace can be accessed directly by going to *http://service.sap.com/notes*, as shown in Figure 11.2.

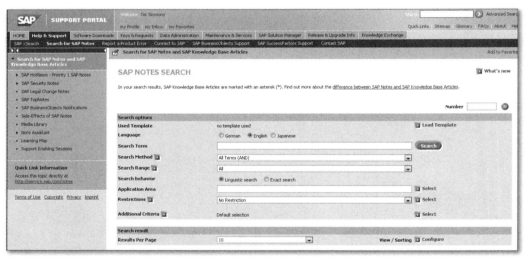

Figure 11.2 SAP Notes Main Search Page

The notes for the Talent Management applications are categorized within the Personnel Administration and Training and Event Management (Learning Solution) application areas, as shown in Figure 11.3.

⊟ PA		Personnel Management
	PA-AS	HR Processes&Forms
	⊞ PA-BC	Basis
	⊞ PA-BN	Benefits
	PA-CE	Concurrent Employment - Personnel Management
	⊞ PA-CM	Compensation Management
	PA-CP	Personnel Cost Planning and Simulation
	⊞ PA-EC	Enterprise Compensation Management
	PA-EIC	Employee Interaction Center
	⊞ PA-ER	E-Recruiting
	⊞ PA-ESS	Personal Information ESS scenarios
	PA-GE	Management of Global Employees
	PA-IS	Personnel Information Systems
	PA-MA	HR Manager's Desktop
	⊞ PA-OS	Organizational Plan
	⊞ PA-PA	Personnel Administration
	PA-PAO	Personnel & Organization
	⊟ PA-PD	Personnel Development
		PA-PD-AP	Appraisal Systems
		PA-PD-DP	Development Plans
		PA-PD-PM	Objective Setting and Appraisals
		PA-PD-QR	Qualifications and Requirements
		PA-PD-SP	Career and Succession Planning
	⊞ PA-PF	Pension Schemes
	⊞ PA-PM	Funds and Position Management
	⊞ PA-RC	Recruitment
	PA-TM	Talent Management
	⊞ PA-XF	Expert Finder
⊟ PE		Training and Event Management
	⊞ PE-DA	Day-to-Day Activities
	⊞ PE-IN	Integration
	⊞ PE-LSO	SAP Learning Solution
	⊞ PE-LSX	External Learning Solution
	PE-OF	Business Event Catalog
	⊞ PE-PR	Training and Event Preparation
	PE-RA	Recurring Activities
	PE-RE	Information Menu
	PE-RPL	Room Reservations Management

Figure 11.3 PA Application Area and All Subsidiary Application Areas

We highly recommend that you use this site as a primary resource. Often by visiting SAP Notes first, you'll save yourself the trouble of having to do research elsewhere.

11.3.2 SAP Community Network

The SAP Community Network (SCN) is an online community of developers, configurators, and other project team members. SCN, which is shown in Figure 11.4, can be accessed directly by going to *http://scn.sap.com*.

11 | Talent Management Resources

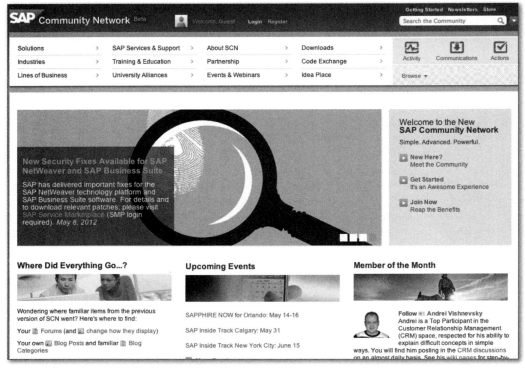

Figure 11.4 SCN Community Home Page

After users register for free, they can access forums, eLearning classes, blogs, wikis, and downloads.

11.4 HR Expert

In contrast to SCN, which is a free site, HR Expert is a subscription-based online magazine that focuses on tips, case studies, and best practices. Authors of the articles are usually seasoned SAP practitioners who have been through several SAP implementations.

HR Expert, which is shown in Figure 11.5, can be accessed directly by going to *www.hrexpertonline.com*.

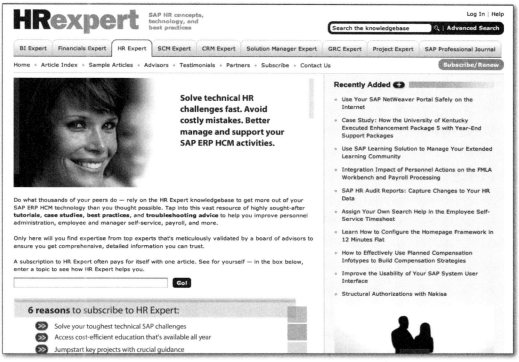

Figure 11.5 HR Expert Online Home Page

HR Expert is an excellent resource because it focuses on real-world experiences. Because it's a subscription-based resource, the magazine has less of a popular following than its free peers. Check with your own organization to see if it already has an account established. If you're able to get access, exploring the site is well worth your time.

11.5 Conferences

Two annual conferences continue to be the most popular and cover topics that include talent management: the SAP HR Conference and SAPPHIRE. Various other SAP User Group conferences are held in many regions locally.

11.5.1 SAP HR Conference

The SAP HR Conference (sponsored by Wellesley Information Services) brings together SAP Partners, exhibitors, and customers in an effort to share best practices and to see the new SAP functionality. Consequently, the SAP HR show is a great networking event and learning opportunity for those who attend.

The event is hosted yearly in both the United States and Europe. You can access information about HR 2013 at *www.hr2013.com*.

11.5.2 SAPPHIRE

Every year SAP hosts a combined ASUG/SAPPHIRE event (*www.sapandasug.com*) to show off its most recent solutions to both current and prospective clients. The SAP SAPPHIRE show includes speaker presentations, demos, and an exhibitor area, and it is another great networking event and learning opportunity for attendees.

Let's examine the role that SAP User Groups play in the SAP community.

11.6 SAP User Groups

SAP User Groups are country-based organizations made up of partners and SAP professionals. The groups provide a valuable channel for information for SAP customers and partners, and they also help to provide SAP with feedback to help improve products and services.

SAP User Groups run conferences on a yearly basis; these conferences are a good place to get information more specific to local markets, rather than the more high-level information found at the global SAP conferences. Generally these conferences are visited by SAP User Group members and, depending on the interest of the user group members, may cover talent management and related topics. SAP works closely with many of its user groups worldwide and runs its annual SAPPHIRE conference in conjunction with the annual ASUG conference.

There are currently 32 SAP User Groups operating in various territories, such as the United States (ASUG) or Germany (DSAG); they are listed on the SAP User Groups website (*www.sapusergroups.com*).

The Americas' SAP Users' Group, which is one of the largest, is made up of SAP partners and professionals based in the Unites States. It includes more than 2,000 companies to date. Figure 11.6 shows its web page (*www.asug.com*).

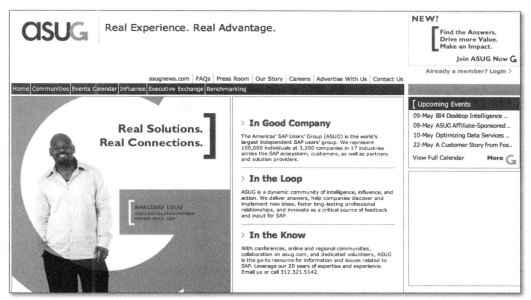

Figure 11.6 ASUG Home Page

11.7 Social Media

Social media is a popular resource for connecting in the SAP ERP HCM community and keeping up to date on its developments. Let's examine five of the most common platforms.

11.7.1 LinkedIn

LinkedIn is a social networking website launched in May 2003 that is geared toward business professionals. You can register for free at *www.linkedin.com*.

LinkedIn gives you access to several groups relating to SAP Talent Management trends and best practices:

- SAP HCM Talent Management (*www.linkedin.com/groups?gid=152688*)
- SAP HCM Professionals (*www.linkedin.com/groups?gid=162292*)
- SAP and SuccessFactors (*www.linkedin.com/groups?gid=4278743*)
- Visualization Solutions by Nakisa (STVN & SOVN) (*www.linkedin.com/groups?gid=1834360*)
- SAP E-Recruiting (*www.linkedin.com/groups?gid=2536748*)
- SAP LSO Enterprise Learning (*www.linkedin.com/groups?gid=163511*)

11.7.2 XING

Similar to LinkedIn, XING (*www.xing.com*) is another social networking site aimed at professionals. Unlike LinkedIn, XING is largely popular within Germany and central Europe but isn't generally used globally.

11.7.3 Facebook, Google+, and Twitter

These three social media sites have been tapped by both businesses to reach their users and users to reach each other. For example, Facebook (*www.facebook.com*) is geared toward individuals and was launched in February 2004. After you've registered (free), you can "friend" other users or "like" an SAP HCM group to access posts from users of the group. It's a great way to network with other individuals who have similar interests.

In 2011, Google (*http://plus.google.com*) launched its own social networking site to rival Facebook. Google+ is used by a number of SAP professionals due to its less personal nature. Many well-regarded analysts post on Google+ and can be include in your circles without the "friend" designation you must use in Facebook.

Twitter (*www.twitter.com*) users create free accounts, which they use to "follow" other organizational and personal accounts to share information and network. Like Facebook, after you "follow" someone, you can view their tweet posts. Twitter is used by many SAP professionals and is a great way to network with other individuals who have similar interests and keep up to date with the latest news, blogs, and opinions of well-regarded industry analysts.

11.8 Summary

As with most technology, the SAP Talent Management landscape will inevitably change with the growth of cloud technology; consequently, it's wise to ensure that you have the latest information not just from SAP, but also from well-regarded analysts and your implementation partner. SAP, SuccessFactors, and Nakisa will continue to innovate, so you should evaluate all of the available solutions for SAP Talent Management for on-premise, cloud, and mobile.

You can leverage many resources to find solutions to your Talent Management challenges, whether this is analyzing the technology options or planning an implementation. You certainly won't be the first person to encounter issues during an SAP Talent Management implementation, so be sure to take advantage of the resources listed in this chapter. Whether the next Talent Management implementation is your first, your tenth, or your twentieth, we hope the information in this chapter and throughout this entire book has been helpful to you. Best of luck to you as you journey through SAP Talent Management!

A   Bibliography

"Building Successful Organizations: Workforce Planning in HHS." United States Department of Health and Human Services, 1999. Print.

"Change Management: Making Organization Change Happen Effectively." Mind Tools. Web. 26 June 2012. <http://www.mindtools.com/pages/article/newPPM_87.htm>.

"Change Management: Organizational and Personal Change Management, Process, Plans, Change Management, and Business Development Tips." Ethical Work and Life Learning. Business Balls. Web. 26 June 2012. <http://www.businessballs.com/changemanagement.htm>.

"Departmental Regulation: Position Management and Vacancy Control." Publication no. DR 4020-250-002. United States Department of Agriculture, 2010. Print.

Effron, Marc. "2011 State of Talent Management." New Talent Management Network, 2011. Print.

Heathfield, Susan. "Communication in the Workplace." About.com. Web. 26 June 2012. <http://humanresources.about.com/od/glossaryc/qt/communication-in-the-workplace.htm>.

"Impacting Business Results Through Effective Human Capital Management: Leading Practices in Workforce Planning." Accenture, 2005. Print.

Lockwood, Nancy R. "Talent Management: Driver for Organizational Success." *2006 SHRM Research Quarterly*. Society for Human Resource Management, 2006. Print.

O'Leonard, Karen, and Stacey Harris. "Bersin & Associates Talent Management Maturity Model." *Bersin & Associates Research Bulletin* 5.34 (2010). Print.

"Position Management Handbook for Supervisors/Managers." Arizona National Guard Human Resources Office. Web. 26 June 2012. <http://www.azguard.gov/hro/documents/posmgmt.pdf>.

Schooley, Claire, and Chris Tratar. "A New Wave in Talent Management: Integrated Performance & Learning." 18 Aug. 2011. Talent Management webinar.

Simmons, Tim. "Leading Practices in Workforce Planning." EPI-USE, 2012. Print.

"Strategic Workforce Planning." County of Fairfax, Virginia, 2003.

Sullivan, John. "Calculating the Cost of a Vacant 'COV' Position: A List of the Possible 'COV' Factors." Rep. *The Fordyce Letter*. Print.

"Tracking Global Trends: How Six Key Developments are Shaping the Business World." Publication. Ernst & Young, 2011. Print.

"Training for Change: Change Program Training Plan." Training for Change. Business Performance. Web. 26 June 2012. *<http://www.businessperform.com/change-management/training_for_change.html>*.

Wellins, Richard S., Audrey B. Smith, and Scott Erker. "Nine Best Practices for Effective Talent Management." Development Dimensions International. Print.

"When Workforce Goals Meet Corporate Strategy: Six Tips for Getting the Greatest Value from Alignment." Gainesville: SumTotal Systems, 2011. Print.

Working Girl: Exploring the Lighter Side of Human Capital Management. Web. 14 June 2012. *<http://ls-workgirl.blogspot.com/>*.

"Workforce Cost Planning with mySAP ERP: Maintain a Competitive Edge with Workforce Cost Planning." SAP AG, 2004. Print.

"Workforce Planning Instruction Manual." United States Department of the Interior, 2001. Print.

B   The Authors

Joe Lee is a Talent Management consultant and has more than seven years of technical and functional SAP experience in a variety of modules, including Talent Management, SD, MM, WM, FI/CO, and SAP NetWeaver Portal. Originally an ABAP developer, he has experience in functional, technical, testing, and team lead roles. Joe is a contributing speaker at ASUG conferences, as well as a featured Talent Management expert on SAPinsider. He has deployed Talent Management software to private, public sector, and global clients, specializing in third-party integration architecture, Web Dynpro for ABAP, and UI branding.

Tim Simmons has more than seven years of experience as an SAP consultant working with SAP Talent Management applications within the SAP ERP HCM module, including E-Recruiting, Performance Management, and Enterprise Compensation Management. Originally introduced to the SAP HCM product as a functional/business process subject matter expert, Tim has since transitioned into application consulting, where he balances functional and technical responsibilities with project management tasks. Tim actively participates in various phases of the business development and delivery cycle, including pre-sales, implementation, and support.

Contributors

Jon Jenkins is a solution architect with an M.B.A. in business management. He has been working with SAP software since 1998 and currently balances functional, technical, and project management responsibilities on a daily basis. His areas of focus and interest continue to be in Talent Management, which include SAP's on-premise and cloud-based (SuccessFactors) solutions. Jon remains active in the SAP community by contributing to the SAP Insider Learning Network, as well as frequently speaking at the annual SAPinsider conference.

Luke Marson is an SAP Mentor and senior solution architect for SAP ERP HCM Talent Management, SAP Organizational Visualization by Nakisa (SOVN), and SAP Talent Visualization by Nakisa (STVN) solutions. He has significant experience in these areas, having delivered more than 25 projects in territories across Europe, the Middle East, and Asia to organizations of various sizes and types in different industries and sectors. He is an active contributor to the SAP Community Network forums and a regular blogger on SAP ERP HCM Talent Management, SOVN, STVN, and SuccessFactors topics. He has also contributed to numerous articles and podcasts for SAPinsider and other publications.

Index

2010 Talent Management Factbook, 30

A

AAP report, 75
Accomplishments tab, 219
Activities, 112, 113
Administrator Portal, 139, 142, 145, 152
Adobe Connect, 136
Adobe Document Server, 326
Adobe Flash Islands, 118, 122, 130
AICC, 270
Americas SAP Users Group (ASUG), 371
Analytics, 161
Application, 109, 204
Application configuration, 338
Application Link Enabling (ALE), 115
Appraisal, 20
    Document, 18, 62, 117, 118, 123, 124, 125, 127, 128, 130, 132, 133, 152, 159, 167, 169, 178, 228, 232, 234, 235, 255, 256
    Template, 18, 117, 118, 121
Appraisals Catalog, 85
Appraise, 123, 129, 178
Appraiser, 247
Approval, 154, 164
Architecture, 21
Area, 43
Assessment, 236, 240
Assessment form, 236
Assessment phase, 22, 227, 236, 247
Audit Report, 163
Authoring Environment, 135, 138, 250, 270, 328
Authorization, 174
Authorization concept, 362

B

Background check, 214
Base pay, 153
Basic competencies, 238
Basic pay, 58
Behaviors, 247
Bench strength, 174, 305
Benefits, 43
Best practices, 23, 349
Blueprint workshop, 350
Booking, 18
Book participants, 145
Bottom-up budgeting, 155, 156, 157
Budget, 281
    Approval process, 289
    Controlling process, 287
    Review process, 284
Budgeting, 153, 154
Budget maintenance, 154, 155, 156, 157
Budget plan, 155, 157, 162, 165, 179
Budget unit, 154
Business Add-In (BAdI), 122, 244, 342
    Enterprise Compensation Management, 344
    E-Recruiting, 342
    Learning Solution, 345
    Performance Management, 343
    Talent Development, 345
Business area, 43
Business functions, 103
Business partner, 48, 53, 55
Business processes, 105
Business Server Page (BSP), 154, 332
Business unit, 43

C

Calibration, 123, 130, 172, 173, 177
Calibration grid, 173

Index

Candidate, 17, 19, 178, 203
   Profile, 109, 110
   Registration, 204
   Shortlist, 111
Cardinality, 337
Career goal tab, 220
Cascade goals, 126, 132, 220
Cascading, 168
Catalog, 137, 252, 253, 270
Central person, 48, 53, 55
CEO involvement, 26
Change assignment, 144
Change management, 352, 353
Change management plan, 354
Check and release budget, 158
Chief position, 41, 53, 54, 55, 166, 231
   Direct report, 53
Child organization, 47
Classroom training, 264
Close-out, 137, 149, 150, 249, 260, 265, 270, 271
Cloud, 362
Cloud-based solutions, 359
Communications, 355
Company, 43
Company code, 58, 60
Company goals, 133
Company strategy, 133
Compensation, 15, 17, 20
Compensation analytics, 161
Compensation Management, 57, 153
   Budget unit object, 282
Compensation plan guidelines, 159
Compensation planning, 152, 153, 158, 160, 161, 163, 179
Compensation process, 166
Compensation review, 158
Compensation specialist, 154, 155, 156, 162
Competencies, 66, 82, 126, 129, 133, 172, 227, 233, 234, 236, 238, 239, 244, 247
Competency assessment, 172
Competency group, 238, 248
Competency phase, 22, 249, 271
Competitive advantage, 82, 102
Compliance, 162
Component configuration, 338

Conclusion, 23
Conference room pilot, 350
Confirm attendance, 150, 268
Consultant, 351
Content, 137, 270
Content administrator, 139, 250, 251, 252, 270
Content Administrator Portal, 140
Content Management System, 135, 140, 149, 249, 251, 252
Context, 336
Control data, 58
Controllers, 336, 341
Controlling process, 154, 162, 164
Core competencies, 82, 102, 169, 177, 223, 235, 238, 241, 248
Corporate goals, 18, 126, 168, 170, 228, 229, 231, 232, 233, 242, 245, 247
Correspondence, 114
Correspondence worklist, 252
Cost center, 64
Cost plan, 156
Course Administrator Portal, 251
Course appraisal, 265
Course Appraisal application, 150
Course capacity, 260
Course Catalog, 127, 132, 133, 140, 152, 253
Course creation, 18
Course group, 140, 253
Course history, 147
Course type, 140, 144, 253, 270
Create Course Date application, 259
Critical success factor, 350
Crystal Reports, 177
Currency key, 58

D

Dashboard, 124
Data transfer, 115, 215
Delivery method, 133, 178
Department, 43, 46, 47
Depreciation meter, 84, 96
Derailer, 169, 172, 223, 235, 236, 239, 241, 248
Design phase, 350

Development phase, 248
Development plan, 168, 169, 174, 175, 176, 225, 308, 319, 322, 361
Disposition, 216
Division, 43, 46, 55

E

Education, 116, 219
Education information, 205
Education tab, 218
EEO report, 75
Effective communication, 356
Eligibility, 153, 159
Employee engagement
　Bottom line, 31
Employee performance
　Rewards and recognition, 31
Employees, 43, 48, 57, 58, 59, 61
　Data, 57
　Details panel, 302
　Development, 16
　Group, 60, 61, 62
　Structure, 54, 232, 261
　Subgroup, 60, 61, 62
Employee Self-Service (ESS), 153, 332, 261
Enhancement, 340
Enterprise Compensation Management (ECM), 83, 281, 323
Enterprise Services, 136
Enterprise structure, 40, 48, 58, 60, 62, 101
E-Recruiting, 104, 177, 181, 193, 362
　Application, 110
　Administrator, 198
Evaluate Participants screen, 150
Evaluation process, 247
Executive sponsor, 350
Extend offer, 213
Extensible Markup Language (XML), 336
External learning services, 134
External user interface, 326
External work experience, 218

F

Feedback, 248
Final appraisal, 129, 132
Final rating, 159, 167
Financial Accounting, 57
Fit gap analysis, 350
Flexible solution, 118, 120, 122, 129, 132, 178, 235
FLSA status, 73, 75
Follow-up, 150, 252, 265, 266, 267, 270
Formal evaluation session, 241
Functional area, 63, 64, 65, 67, 101
　Description, 66
　Object, 66
Future development, 223

G

Generating the documents, 228
Global implementations, 113
Goal, 117, 129, 227, 231, 232, 234, 243, 245
　Goal setting, 248
Google recruiting strategies, 31
Guidelines, 153, 161, 179
　Defined, 167
　In compliance, 162

H

Handout, 173
Hierarchy structure, 40
High-performing employees, 237
High-potential employees, 237
Hire, 105, 113, 114, 115, 213
Hiring manager, 112, 210
Holder, 56
Holder relationship, 55
HR administrator, 16, 17
HR Expert, 368
HR manager, 16, 17
HR Processes and Forms, 194
Hybrid, 363

Index

I

Identifying the participants, 228
Impact of loss ratings, 248
Implementation considerations, 350, 365, 368, 369
Implementation lead, 16, 20
Incumbent, 174
Individual booking, 145
Individual goals, 126, 127, 170, 233, 245, 248
Induction phase, 22
Ineligible, 163
Ineligible for review, 159
Infotype 0001 (organization assignment), 75
Infotype 0008 (basic pay), 75
Infotype 1001 (relationships, 68
Infotype 1002 (description), 68
Infotype 1005 (planned compensation), 75
Infotype 1610 (EEO/AAP), 75
Infotype 5070 (job family), 68
Inheritance principle, 100
Instructor, 141, 266, 268
Instructor-led training, 22, 134, 249, 259, 261
Instructor Portal, 23, 134, 149, 150, 268, 328
Integration, 22, 115
   ALE, 115
   Analytics& Reports, 177
   ECM, 127, 133
   Enterprise Compensation module, 129
   Jobs Catalog, 116, 133, 152, 177
   Learning Solution, 132
   Organizational Management, 116, 132, 151, 166, 176
   Payroll, 167
   Performance Management, 152, 159, 167, 177, 270
   Personnel Administration, 116, 132, 167, 176
   Qualifications Catalog, 116, 133, 152, 177
   Talent Development, 132, 152
Internal work experience, 217, 223
Internet Communication Framework, 105
Interview, 105, 112
Interview process, 211
Invite to apply, 207, 208
IT manager, 16, 19

J

Java Virtual Machine (JVM), 347
Job, 45, 49, 63, 65, 67, 73, 75, 80, 82, 83, 92, 98, 115, 144, 152, 166, 232
   Job creation, 18
   Job description, 73
   Job level, 64
   Job object, 101
   Job performance, 82
   Job posting, 106, 197, 201
   Job pricing, 153, 166, 179
   Job search, 108
   Job title, 73
   Task, 73
Job board distributor, 202
Job family, 63, 65, 67, 68, 70, 73, 80, 83, 92, 98, 101, 300
   Hierarchy, 70
   Job family object, 68
Jobs Catalog, 106, 152, 177

K

Key indication, 192
Key position, 192
KPI measurement, 229, 230

L

Leadership competencies, 238
Leadership potential, 237
Lead recruiter, 198
Learner, 261
Learner Portal, 22, 134, 146, 147, 148, 248, 328
Learner profile, 254, 256
Learning, 83
   Catalog, 234, 243, 245
   Courses, 133
   Development, 133
Learning Content Management System, 328
Learning Management System, 133, 328
Learning Solution, 178, 249
   Training goal, 233

Legal entity, 58
Lessons learned, 23, 349
LinkedIn, 371
Live-in code, 73
Long-term incentive (LTI), 152, 159, 166, 179

M

Manage course participation, 252
Manage Participants application, 145, 147, 258
Manage Required Courses application, 142, 145, 270
Manager Self-Service (MSS), 158, 165, 221, 255, 256, 258, 326, 332
Mandatory course, 142, 144, 255, 261
Mandatory training, 147, 255, 261
Mass-adjust, 164
Mass booking, 145
Materials Management, 57
Merit, 179
Merit/Salary tab, 159
Mid-year assessment, 243
Mid-year review, 128, 234, 241, 244, 248
Mobile solutions, 363
Mobility, 220, 221, 223
My Learning, 261

N

Nakisa, 174
Nakisa Transport Package, 346
New hire administration, 18
New Talent Management Network, 26
Nine-box calibration grid, 174, 296
NWBC for Desktop, 332
NWBC for HTML, 329, 331

O

Object, 56
Object characteristic, 83
Objective setting, 227, 228, 232, 235, 247, 248

Object-oriented design, 41
Object type, 80
 Object type FN, 64
 Object type JF, 67
 Object type O, 43, 44
 Object type P, 54
OFCCP, 207
Offer, 114
 Offer letter, 114
Offline content player, 135
Offline distribution, 135
Onboarding, 114, 115
Online content player, 135
On-premise solution, 359, 361
Organization, 48, 53
Organization job code, 73
Organizational assignment, 75, 169
Organizational competencies, 81
Organizational Management, 17, 18, 39, 40, 41, 46, 48, 53, 56, 80, 81, 106, 116, 151, 176, 231
 Benefits, 40
 Object types, 41
Organizational Management structure, 101
Organizational performance, 82
Organizational plan, 41, 42, 50, 53, 54, 55, 73, 101, 126
Organizational planning, 48
Organizational structure, 45, 51, 52, 55, 64, 83, 115, 116, 124, 159
Organizational trends
 Engagement, 33
 Harmonizing HR practices, 32
 Integrated processes and systems, 33
 Offshoring, 33
Organizational unit, 41, 45, 46, 47, 48, 49, 50, 51, 52, 55, 58, 101, 116, 132, 144, 154, 155, 156, 158, 159, 163, 166, 170, 173, 228, 229, 231
 Object, 101
 Structure, 232
Orgchart, 301
Overbookings, 252

P

Parent organization, 44
Part appraiser, 247
Participant assessment, 268
Participation, 137, 271
Pay grade type, 75
Payroll, 43, 57, 60, 62, 154, 165, 166, 179
Payroll manager position, 229, 231, 235, 238
Percentage change, 157
Performance, 18, 222, 244, 247
    Appraisal, 168, 169, 173
    Cycle, 241
    Objectives, 241
    Planning, 247
    Review, 227
Performance Distribution Models, 130
Performance Management, 57, 62, 83, 117, 178, 235, 244
    Competencies, 277, 279
    Final ratings, 279
    Goals, 275, 278
    Self-assessment, 275
    Year-end assessment, 278
    Year-end review, 273
Performance Management documents, 229, 230, 231
Performance Management process, 232, 248
Performance Measurement, 227, 247
Performance versus potential, 248
Perform course appraisal, 265
Periodic feedback, 241
Person, 42, 45, 48, 55, 69, 98, 101, 144, 156
Personal data, 176
Personal development, 17
Personnel, 58
Personnel Administration, 18, 39, 54, 56, 57, 58, 62, 80, 101, 116
Personnel area, 58, 60, 62
Personnel Cost Planning, 156, 157
Personnel Development application, 255, 270
Personnel structure, 62
Personnel subarea, 58, 59, 60
Person object, 53, 54, 56, 58, 60, 83
Phased approach, 351

Plan, 123, 126
Plan compensation, 159
Planning overview, 164
Planning process, 228
Plugs, 334
Portal Content Directory, 332
Position, 41, 42, 45, 48, 49, 52, 53, 54, 55, 56, 63, 65, 67, 70, 73, 75, 80, 83, 92, 98, 101, 115, 116, 156, 166, 227, 233, 238, 241, 247, 248
    Create, 51
    Object type, 50, 54
    Object type S, 50
    Status, 50
Position details panel, 302
Position management, 184, 185, 186, 187
Potential, 222
    Assessment, 169, 172
    Form, 237
    Grid, 174
    Rating, 237, 248
Power Object Work List (POWL), 111, 125, 150
Prebooking, 145
Predefined scale, 237
Predefined solution, 118, 129, 132, 133, 178
Prepare process, 123, 124, 228
Process configuration, 118
Process template, 19, 104, 112, 113
Productive feedback, 241
Proficiency, 82, 84, 85, 86, 88, 89, 91, 92, 94, 99, 116
    Assign, 70
    Description, 89, 94, 96
    Name, 89
    Rating, 239
    Scale, 83, 84, 88, 90, 102, 133
    Text, 83
Profile, 137, 254, 256, 258, 270
Profile Match function, 174, 177, 255, 309
Progression phase, 23, 271, 273, 323
Publication, 106
Publication channel, 107
Publish course content, 252

Q

Qualifications, 17, 18, 20, 23, 63, 66, 68, 81, 83, 86, 90, 94, 95, 96, 98, 100, 102, 106, 116, 127, 133, 141, 146, 149, 152, 177, 191, 197, 205, 223, 224, 234, 253, 261, 268, 270
  Alternative qualifications, 83
  Block, 98
  Desired qualifications, 110
  Essential qualifications, 99
  Group, 83, 90, 94
  Subgroup, 90
Qualifications Catalog, 39, 80, 81, 82, 83, 85, 86, 90, 101, 102, 116, 152, 177, 244, 247
Qualitative scale, 84, 85, 86, 88
Quantitative scale, 84, 88, 90
Questionnaire, 110, 112, 211

R

Ranking, 175
Rapid Content Publisher, 140, 251, 252, 270
Rapid-deployment solution, 359
Recruiter, 19, 111, 112, 114, 199, 206
Recruiting, 15, 19, 178
Recruiting profile, 108
Rejecting candidates, 114
Rejection of Application activity, 211, 212
Relationship, 45, 47, 48, 54, 65, 189
  B|007, 190
Report RHTM_T77TM_JF_Level, 71
Reports-to hierarchy, 64
Required training, 258
Requirement, 83
Requisition, 17, 19, 106, 111, 116, 181, 198, 199
  Education requirements, 201
  Form, 195
  General job information, 199
  Qualifications, 201
  Questionnaires, 201
  Requirements, 199

Restricted recruiter, 199
Résumé parsing, 205, 327
Review, 123, 127, 154, 158
Review and Save, 269
Rewards program, 31

S

Salary adjustment, 18, 286
Salary grade/broad band, 73
Salary survey, 153
Sales and Distribution, 57
SAP Best Practices for HCM (USA), 64, 67, 68, 73, 75
SAP BusinessObjects, 177
SAP Community Network (SCN), 367
SAP Corporate Goals and Values, 170
SAP Enterprise Learning, 136
SAP E-Recruiting, 83
SAP ERP HCM Performance Management, 228, 241
SAP ERP HCM Talent Management, 48, 171
  Foundational components, 42
  Foundations, 39
  Resources, 365
SAP HR Conference, 370
SAP Job Architecture, 39, 63, 67, 80, 81, 101, 361
SAP NetWeaver Business Client, 104, 327, 329, 331
SAP NetWeaver Business Warehouse, 104, 177
SAP NetWeaver Composition Environment, 346
SAP NetWeaver Portal, 104, 139, 169, 171, 174, 327, 329, 331
SAP NetWeaver Process Integration, 105, 117, 327
SAP Notes, 366
SAP Organizational Visualization by Nakisa (SOVN), 300
SAP roadmap, 360
SAP SAPPHIRE, 370
SAP Service Marketplace, 365

SAP Talent Visualization by Nakisa (STVN)
  SuccessionPlanning, 63, 174, 175, 179, 300, 346, 361, 362
  Analytics, 315
  Career Planning, 361
  Compare, 314
  Grid, 306
  Profile Match, 308
  Search listings, 315, 317
  Wizards, 314
SAP User Groups, 370
SAP Web Dispatcher, 327
Save Search Query, 109
Scales, 85, 102, 116
Schedule, 137, 144, 145, 147, 256, 259, 271
Scheduling a course, 258
SCORM, 138, 149, 270
Screen process, 105, 111, 208
Search criteria, 207
Self-assessment, 245
Side-by-side comparison, 208
Skills profile, 223, 224, 239
Social media, 371
Software-as-a-service model, 359
Software Component Archive (SCA), 346
Software Deployment Archive (SDA), 346
Source process, 105, 108, 203
Span of control, 241
Specialist competencies, 238
Staff assignment, 42, 48, 50
Staffing, 351
Static web-based course, 147, 149
Status handling, 304
Subject matter expert, 350, 352
Subprofile, 83
SuccessFactors, 359
  SuccessFactors BizX Suite, 361, 362
  SuccessFactors Employee Central, 362
Succession, 15, 18, 20
Succession Management, 167
Succession planning, 168, 169, 174, 177, 179, 300
Successor, 174, 177
Successor Calibration grid, 312
Successor pools, 304
Suitability check, 208, 209

Support group, 198, 201
Support structure, 352
Support team, 201

T

Talent analytics, 361
Talent and engagement lifecycle, 24
Talent assessment, 168, 171, 173, 223, 224, 227, 235, 236, 247, 248
  Potential, 236
  Risks, 236, 238
Talent Development application, 152, 167, 176, 179
Talent Development/Succession Planning, 20, 57, 83
Talent-driven organization, 26, 27
Talent group, 168, 169, 172, 177, 222, 236, 248, 299
  Nomination, 235, 241, 248, 300
Talent management, 25
  Communications, 29
  Decisions, 27
  Definition, 15
  Drivers, 35, 36
  Evolution of HR, 28
  High visibility, 26
  Initiative, 26
  Integration, 29
  Organizational success, 29
  Philosophy, 29
  Primary owner, 29
  Responsibility, 28
  Strategies, 26
  Support, 28
  Trends, 32
Talent Management Maturity Model
  Level 1, 30
  Level 2, 30
  Level 3, 30
  Level 4, 30
Talent Management specialist, 19, 63, 168, 169, 170, 171, 172, 174, 175, 176, 179, 217, 221, 228, 229, 235, 238, 241, 247, 248, 332

Talent personnel, 16, 19
Talent pipeline, 300, 307
Talent pool, 206
Talent profile, 115, 116, 152, 168, 169, 173, 175, 176, 178, 181, 216, 219, 221, 223, 225, 239, 361
Talent-related attributes, 240
Talent review meeting, 168, 172, 173, 237, 248, 290
  Application, 290
  Conducting, 296
  Infotype, 291
  Planning, 291, 292
  Preparation, 294
  Review meeting object, 291
Target audience, 16
Task area, 64
Tasks, 48, 101
Team goals, 126, 168, 228, 232, 233, 242, 245, 248
Technical architecture, 325
  Enterprise Compensation Management, 328
  Learning Solution, 328
  Performance Management, 327
  SAP E-Recruiting, 326
  Succession Management, 329
  Talent Development, 329
Technological trends
  Confidentiality and security issues, 34
  Data privacy, 34
  Facebook, 34
  Generation Y, 34
  LinkedIn, 34
  Smartphone, 34
  Twitter, 34
Tell a Friend, 109
Third-party authoring tools, 138
Time Management, 57, 62
Top-down budgeting, 155
Training, 18, 19, 134, 354
Training Administrator Portal, 135
Training and Event Management, 135
Training goals, 126, 152, 233, 234, 243
Transaction HRTMC_PPOC, 63, 102
Transaction HRTMC_PPOM, 63, 102, 174, 191

Transaction HRTMC_PPOS, 63, 102
Transaction LSO_PVCT, 140, 253
Transaction OOSC, 70, 85, 87
Transaction PA48, 216
Transaction PECM_CHANGE_STATUS, 165
Transaction PECM_EVALUATE_GRANT, 162
Transaction PP01, 58, 60, 62, 63, 65, 98, 102, 188
Transaction PPOME, 42, 46, 47, 52, 53, 54, 63, 102
Transaction PPPM, 98, 191
Transaction S_AHR_61016497, 65, 68, 73
Transaction SPRO, 59, 60, 62
Transfer qualification, 267, 268, 269
TREX, 301, 326, 328, 362

U

Uploading content, 136
User, 48, 53, 55, 65
User interface, 329

V

Validity dates, 229
Validity period, 84, 96
View, 334, 340
Virtual Learning Room, 136

W

Wage type, 61
Waitlisting, 145, 252
Web-based training, 22, 134, 141, 152, 248, 249, 254, 259, 261, 268
Web Dynpro for ABAP, 118, 122, 153, 179, 332, 333, 336, 337, 339
Window, 335
Work experience, 116, 168
Workflow, 244
Workforce planning, 182
Workplace planning programs, 32
Work schedule, 61

X

Xcelsius, 177
XING, 372

Y

Year-end rating, 129
Year-end review, 130

- A complete guide to the tax structures, schemas, and rules that drive US Payroll processing logic

- Integrate your organization's payroll with benefits, taxes, and accounting

- Master advanced topics, such as overpayments, accruals, payroll interfaces, garnishments, and more

Satish Badgi

Practical SAP US Payroll

If you're responsible for setting up, configuring, or using SAP US Payroll, you know that even its minor idiosyncrasies can cause headaches and holdups in your HR processes. This book gives you the tools you need to get up to speed on payroll implementation and cutover, time management, and payroll troubleshooting. This new edition includes updated information for SAP ERP 6.0 and EHPs 5 and 6. Balanced coverage of payroll processes, configuration, and real-life scenarios helps you develop applicable skills.

464 pp., 2. edition 2012, 69,95 Euro / US$ 69.95
ISBN 978-1-59229-421-3

www.sap-press.com

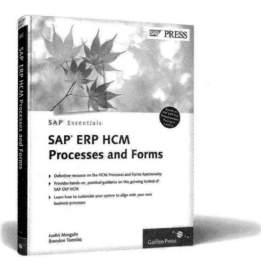

- Adapt business processes and configure SAP ERP HCM Processes and Forms, with practical, real-world examples, tips, and tricks

- Improve the accuracy of your HR master data with greater flexibility and increased process efficiency

- Learn how to customize your system to align with your unique business processes

Justin Morgalis, Brandon Toombs

SAP ERP HCM Processes and Forms

Cut through the HR red tape with this comprehensive guide to customizing and implementing ERP HCM P&F. Streamline your most common organizational data processes into one discrete process for optimal HR workflows. Configure and optimize HCM with ease through real-world examples, step-by-step instructions and tips and tricks. This title will teach you to maximize the powerful combination of web based forms, online document storage, and support structural based decision making. Perfect for busy consultants, managers and super users, this is an end-to-end solution that includes configuration steps, overall business scenarios, and the dos and donts of mapping business processes.

approx. 300 pp., 69,95 Euro / US$ 84.95
ISBN 978-1-59229-425-1, Oct 2012

www.sap-press.com

- Little-known tips and tricks from the SAP experts

Ajay Jain Bhutoria, Cameron Lewis

100 Things You Should Know About HR Management with SAP

Have you ever spent days trying to figure out how to generate a personnel report in SAP ERP HCM only to find out you just needed to click a few buttons. If so, you'll be delighted with this book — it unlocks the secrets of SAP ERP HCM. It provides users and super-users with 100 tips and workarounds you can use to increase productivity, save time, and improve the overall ease-of-use of SAP ERP HCM. The tips have been carefully selected to provide a collection of the best, most useful, and rarest information.

298 pp., 2011, 49,95 Euro / US$ 49.95
ISBN 978-1-59229-361-2

www.sap-press.com

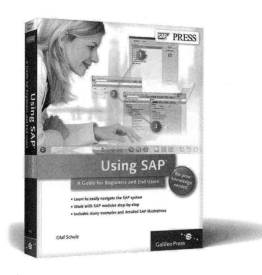

- Learn to easily navigate the SAP system
- Work with SAP modules step-by-step
- Includes many examples and detailed SAP illustrations

Olaf Schulz

Using SAP:
A Guide for Beginners and End Users

This book helps end users and beginners get started in SAP ERP and provides readers with the basic knowledge they need for their daily work. Readers will get to know the essentials of working with the SAP system, learn about the SAP systems' structures and functions, and discover how SAP connects to critical business processes. Whether this book is used as an exercise book or as a reference book, readers will find what they need to help them become more comfortable with SAP ERP.

388 pp., 2012, 39,95 Euro / US$ 39.95
ISBN 978-1-59229-408-4

www.sap-press.com

Interested in reading more?

Please visit our website for all
new book releases from SAP PRESS.

www.sap-press.com